THE IMPERIAL GRIDIRON

The IMPERIAL GRIDIRON

Manhood, Civilization, and Football at the Carlisle Indian Industrial School

MATTHEW BENTLEY & JOHN BLOOM

University of Nebraska Press

LINCOLN

The University of Nebraska Press is part of a land-grant
institution with campuses and programs on the past, present,
and future homelands of the Pawnee, Ponca, Otoe-Missouria,
Omaha, Dakota, Lakota, Kaw, Cheyenne, and Arapaho
Peoples, as well as those of the relocated Ho-Chunk, Sac and
Fox, and Iowa Peoples.

Library of Congress Control Number: 2022013291

Set in Minion Pro by Mikala R. Kolander.

CONTENTS

ILLUSTRATIONS

PREFACE

This book began as Matthew Bentley's doctoral dissertation in American Studies at the University of East Anglia in Norwich, United Kingdom. Matthew defended this work in June 2012 and had begun revising it for publication as a book. He had a contract with the University of Nebraska Press, where he had received positive reviews with constructive and encouraging suggestions from a number of readers. On May 2, 2018, however, having just returned from an exhausting trip to Germany, Matthew died in his sleep, his death stemming from type 1 diabetes that he had been living with for his entire life. His family and his dissertation advisor, knowing I had served on Matthew's doctoral committee, asked if I would consider revising his dissertation for publication. The following pages are the result of our collaboration.

After earning a bachelor's degree in history at Essex University, Matthew came to the American Studies program at the University of East Anglia (UAE) in 2005 in order to work with Jacqueline Fear-Segal, an eminent scholar who has produced some of the most important work on the history of the Carlisle Indian Industrial School. He studied under her as she prepared for publication her landmark book about that institution, *White Man's Club*. She discovered a student boundlessly dedicated to his studies, someone whom his father, Phil Bentley, remembers from an early age as "an avid compiler of data." Phil recalls that Matthew's childhood fascination with numbers led to his interest in sports.

He would draw up fixture lists for a host of imaginary soccer teams, record the results, prepare league tables after each round of fixtures until his 'season' was complete. Naturally his favourite team always topped the league. This gave him an interest in sport, mathematics and data collection, helping him to have a very promising junior school education, excelling in both academic subjects and sport. . . . Sport was still a large part of his life both playing junior soccer and watching the professional game. He regularly travelled 200 miles to watch Charlton Athletic every home match for 20 years right up to his death.[1]

Matthew's brother, Jonathan, also remembers someone with a passion for sports, a competitive spirit, and a love of history. The two spent hours playing computer games together growing up, but Jonathan recalls about Matthew that "his main passion was learning." He adds, "What this book represents is what he was able to achieve at only thirty-three years old whilst dealing with adversities like type 1 diabetes. It shows his inner strength to succeed and we are all incredibly proud of him."[2]

When Matthew first arrived at UEA, the university could not provide him with funding, but he did not let this stop him. He took a job in the local post office so that he could earn an income while attending school and conducting research. Recalling her former student, Fear-Segal remembers, "Matthew's capacity to work with a wide range of people and to be both flexible and amenable was demonstrated very clearly when he was the technical assistant at an international conference, 'Indigenous Bodies,' organized at UEA in the summer of 2009. He helped scholars from around the world set up their presentations and was sensitive to and also very respectful of many different cultural needs and demands. I witnessed a side of him that I had never seen before, as he confidently interacted and joked with academics from across the globe."

Despite going to graduate school on a part-time basis, he finished his dissertation in only five years (others in his position customarily take seven), and afterward Matthew found a full-time teaching position at Paston Sixth Form College in Norfolk. There he became a treasured history teacher preparing students for university, and in no time had been promoted to the position of head of history. He dedicated himself to his students and to improving the school's small library holdings on United States history. In 2017 he accepted a new teaching position, this time a full-time, permanent history lectureship at the College of West Anglia.

I first met Matthew in March 2008 when he traveled to Carlisle to conduct research for his dissertation. Jackie Fear-Segal had moved to town for the year and had invited the two of us over to her apartment for dinner. We talked about the Los Angeles Galaxy's recent signing of David Beckham, the "March Madness" NCAA basketball tournament that was currently taking place, and, of course, the history of sports at the Carlisle Indian Industrial School. Matthew had read my book on sports at Indian boarding schools, and he had some constructively critical comments to make about it. He said that when I wrote about masculinity and sports at the school, I might have benefited from reading Gail Bederman's *Manliness and Civilization*, which distinguishes between Victorian conceptions of manliness and emerging ideas of elemental masculinity that were in tension among elite white men in the United States at the turn of the twentieth century. He also pointed out that I needed to recognize better the changes that took place at Carlisle over time, particularly the distinctive and dramatic transformations at the school after the 1904 departure of its founder and longtime superintendent Richard Henry Pratt. I appreciated his critique, and after Matthew asked if I would serve on his dissertation committee at UEA, I gladly accepted.

Bentley's original manuscript focused primarily upon the ideological conflicts over gender that defined Carlisle's administrative agenda during its history, and the role that football played in these conflicts. Drawing upon the work of James C. Scott, he focused upon what he saw as Carlisle's "public transcript." In his original draft, Bentley wrote, "Scott's idea of a 'public' transcript is implemented into this study by defining it as the image of the school that Pratt, and later other superintendents, wanted the public to see. The school's public transcript was primarily portrayed through the school newspapers, which were edited by white officials at Carlisle." Bentley contrasted this to the concept of a "hidden transcript," a term that scholars have used to describe the expressions "of the subordinate." To Bentley, a "hidden transcript" is "what happens 'off-stage,' away from the eyes of the dominant. This represents [the subordinate's] true feelings and can be seen in acts of resistance towards the dominant."[3]

By paying attention to campus publications and official sources, Bentley noted how Carlisle's public transcript regarding its football program changed over the course of its history. Initially, Pratt's administration used the game to promote the notion that Carlisle could successfully "civilize" American Indian men. In the terminology of Victorian America that Bederman explores, Pratt believed that a disciplined, self-controlled football team would demonstrate to the world that Carlisle could transform its male students into virtuous, "manly" men. After Pratt's removal as Carlisle superintendent, Bentley saw the school's administration severely curtailing Pratt's vision. Rather than use the football team to showcase the school's "civilizing" mission, administrations exploited the team to win games and generate revenue. Bentley saw Carlisle's administration as highlighting students' masculinity, and removing the notion of manly virtue from its public transcript.

Bentley used Antonio Gramsci's concept of cultural hegemony to understand this struggle over male identity within Carlisle's public transcript. He positioned Pratt as symbolizing the prominence of a hegemony of manliness. Bentley argues that after Pratt had left Carlisle, a masculine public transcript assumed hegemonic dominance among Carlisle's white leadership.[4]

Bentley had done an impressive amount of research on football and manhood at Carlisle, going far beyond campus publications. His work delved into student records, popular press coverage, and a wide array of government documents. In some of his most original and insightful work, he dove deeply into the revealing testimonies given to Congress in 1914 when a special joint committee investigated the school. He had a keen eye for important moments of change in the school's history. He saw the most significant dramas and characters in the stories that he discovered, and knew where to locate these moments in the historical record.

As he was revising his manuscript to adapt it for publication, he also began to revisit his theoretical model. Readers who judged his writing found Gramscian theory to be an inadequate framework for interpreting his rich findings. They suggested that he expand the significance of his research and address how the struggles over manhood that he discovered reflected upon Carlisle's mission as an institution of a settler colonial state. In addition, while Bentley's focus had been upon the Carlisle Indian School's public transcript, readers suggested that he try to complicate his analysis, incorporating Native voices as much as he could.

Sadly, Bentley died before being able to make these revisions, and before gaining access to a new trove of primary documents from the school now available digitally. Among the most important of these are the unredacted records from the 1914 government investigation of Carlisle. These include, among other things, transcripts from depositions to a federal investigator that are only summarized in the published report. At the time of his passing, Bentley knew these materials would soon be available and was looking forward to analyzing them.

As Bentley's coauthor, I have picked up where he left off, but I have also added my own perspectives and diverged somewhat from what he had planned. In the following pages I have reoriented the theoretical framework of his research by addressing the idea of "civilization," so central to Pratt's understanding of manhood and of Carlisle's mission. In fact, readers will note that every time that I use the term "civilization," I place it in quotation marks. I do this to highlight it as a fiction that settler colonialists perpetuated, one that justified conquest as an act of white mercy. Anglo Americans tended to portray the history of northern and western Europeans as representing "civilization's" bedrock. In reality, the first peoples to develop what historians recognize as "civilizations" did so in places like Mesopotamia, North Africa, South Asia, East Asia, South America, and Mesoamerica, centuries and millennia before northern and western Europeans developed agriculture, cities, systems of writing, religious institutions, and other components of complex societies.

Reviewers of the manuscript for the University of Nebraska Press had called upon Bentley to address how Carlisle students engaged with the public transcript that school administrators developed at different moments. Bentley had hoped to discuss gender norms and traditions from specific nations and tribes, and to draw some general conclusions about how students from varying backgrounds might have experienced football at the school. I do not do this in my revisions, in part because Carlisle was an especially diverse school, even among Indian boarding schools in the United States that all integrated a wide range of Indigenous communities. Rather than focus upon a school administration struggling with itself over its public transcript, I have focused more upon the ways that students and administrators used football to struggle over the legitimacy of Carlisle's "civilizing" mission. In this endeavor, in addition to the official records that Bentley uncovered, I have drawn from oral histories, student records, and writing by Indigenous scholars and writers. Additionally, I have engaged the work of recent scholars who have addressed issues of manhood and masculinity in settler colonial societies. Finally, I have also reinterpreted the transcript and records from the 1914 government investigation into Carlisle. During that event, students actively intervened in Carlisle's public transcript in ways that were both effective and problematic, and that centered around issues of "civilization," manliness, and football.

Throughout this manuscript, I have also edited many of the footnotes, added notes and sources of my own, and left many of Matthew's notes as they were. At times Matthew provided personalized commentary on the text that he wrote and referenced. Where he has done so, I have ended his note with his initials, "MB." Similarly, where I have inserted a commentary of my own, I have added my initials, "JB." In recognizing the national and tribal affiliations for Indigenous people whom we reference in this book, Matthew and I have changed some of the terminology from the original Carlisle Indian School records. Student information cards on file at the National Archives and Records Administration use outmoded terms like "Sioux," "Chippewa," and "Pueblo" to indicate student backgrounds. Delving into these same student records, we have been able to change how we identify affiliation more appropriately, accurately, and specifically.

During the process of revising this book, I have thought of myself as in a constant dialogue with Matthew. In fact, often while changing a paragraph or adding new thoughts, I have found myself talking to him in my mind, showing him something that I see in his research that he might have missed, or impressed by the detail that he uncovered about a player or a game. I very much regret that Matthew could not finish this book himself, and I find myself deeply curious to know what he might have done with his final revisions. At the same time, both Matthew and I have an enormous responsibility to those who went to Carlisle and their descendants. Writing about the Carlisle Indian Industrial School is something that one must do very carefully, particularly if one is not Native, and especially when one is, as I am, a white scholar who is a beneficiary of the conquests from which this institution flowered. My sincere hope is that my revisions to this book have appropriately honored our responsibilities to all involved.

John Bloom
Carlisle, Pennsylvania
November 2020

ACKNOWLEDGMENTS

Matthew and I owe a tremendous debt of gratitude to a great many people without whom we could not have finished this book. More than anybody else, we must thank Matthew's father, Phil Bentley. Shortly after Matthew died, Phil decided to seek out somebody who could complete this manuscript for publication. This book is, in a very real sense, a product of his effort to keep alive the memory of a son whom he loves.

We must also acknowledge Matthew's dissertation advisor and my long-time friend, Jacqueline Fear-Segal. In consultation with Phil, Jacqueline sought me out as somebody who might be able to finish this project. I had been on Matthew's dissertation committee, so I had familiarity with his work and his argument, and I very much appreciate that she thought of me to continue what he had begun. Additionally, Matthew Bokovoy at the University of Nebraska Press not only helped to clarify the recommended revisions that came from the book's initial readers, but he also helped guide me through the contract process that allowed me to become its coauthor.

Barbara Landis has been a constant source of expertise, wisdom, and support for everything we have both written about the Carlisle Indian Industrial School. Her work at the Cumberland County Historical Society has allowed countless people to learn about family members who went to Carlisle. She has been a teacher of students and a critical guide for researchers, and she has always shared her immense knowledge with empathy for those who attended the school. Her moral courage and caring approach to her work have made her one of our most important role models. We would also like to express our gratitude to Orietta Cuellar, Gary Gordon, Dovie Thomason, and Louellyn White, all of whom have contributed to Carlisle Journeys, a series of symposiums that took place biannually between 2012 and 2018, events that brought descendants back to Carlisle to witness and reclaim the legacy of the Carlisle Indian Industrial School.

Dickinson College Archivist Jim Gerencser helped me both personally and through his incredible work creating the Carlisle Indian School Digital Resource Center. This project has digitized and made accessible thousands of documents from the Carlisle Indian Industrial School, including student records, school publications, photographs, and government documents. Together with Susan Rose, Barb Landis, and Jackie Fear-Segal, Gerencser has worked to make this a resource for Indigenous communities and families of descendants as well as for scholars. Kate Theimer helped out immensely by producing the index for this book, and Shippensburg Center for Faculty Excellence in Scholarship and Teaching funded her work.

I would never have had the opportunity to finish this book had Shippensburg University's Sabbatical Leave Committee not granted me a paid reprieve from teaching to work on it during the 2020–21 academic year. I especially appreciate their grant since this happened to be probably the most challenging school year any of us has seen in our lifetimes. The fact that I was not teaching in the History and Philosophy Department at Shippensburg meant that my colleagues had to pick up my slack during the COVID-19 crisis. I would like to thank each of them: Douglas Birsch, Karin J. Bohleke, Steve Burg, Betty Dessants, Allen Dieterich-Ward, James Edwards, David Godshalk, Justus Hartzok, Kim Klein, Chandrika Paul, Gretchen K. Pierce, John Quist, Christine Senecal, Jonathan Skaff, Mark Spicka, Allan Tulchin, Brian Ulrich, Heather B. Wadas, and David Weaver. Sharon Harrow generously read this entire manuscript and provided valuable insights and comments. I also want to express my appreciation for the hard work that our Department Secretary Janice Reed did in helping me transition onto sabbatical and back to teaching. Shippensburg Applied History Graduate Assistant Nastassia Foose Gantz contributed valuable analysis of correspondence to this book as well.

If Matthew were still alive, I know he would have wanted to send out a special thank you to his brother, Jonathan Bentley, with whom he shared a love not only of sports and computer gaming but also of Dave (Matthew's pet cat), Brian (Matthew's pet snail), and Raphael (Matthew's pet turtle).

I would like to acknowledge my family members who have been with me as I have worked on this project. Thank you to my mother, Maxine Weisfeldt Bloom for being complimentary about my cooking, and for making sure that I was well fed. I want to send a very special thank you to my wife, Amy Farrell. She has been my loving companion for over thirty-four years at the time I write this, and she has also been a wise colleague and thoughtful reader of this manuscript as I revised my drafts, all while she transitioned to teaching online during the coronavirus crisis (not her preferred classroom experience). I am unbelievably lucky to have shared my life with you, Amy, and I cannot express how much I love and appreciate you. The same is true for my children, Catherine Bloom and Nicholas Bloom, both adults on their own journeys. It was a privilege to quarantine with you both as I delved into my work on this book and as you both created your art and scholarship.

THE IMPERIAL GRIDIRON

FIG. 1. Bruce Goesback (Arapaho) at practice, 1912.
Photograph courtesy of the Robert R. Rowe private collection,
Dickinson College Archives and Special Collections.

Introduction

I n an 1892 speech at the Nineteenth Annual Conference of Charities and Correction, Capt. Richard Henry Pratt, founder and superintendent of the Carlisle Indian Industrial School, uttered his most quoted mission statement. He said that in creating a boarding school aimed at transforming the social and psychological lives of Indigenous Americans, he intended to "kill the Indian in him, and save the man."[1] Carlisle, the first federally operated non-reservation boarding school for Native Americans and exemplar of Pratt's statement, was a central pillar of the nineteenth-century Indian reform movement, which also included allotment of reservation land and American citizenship.[2] Pratt founded the Carlisle Indian Industrial School in 1879 with the goal of "civilizing" Indigenous Americans, ideally achieved through immersion in white society and the rejection of anything Indian.[3] Chroniclers of the Indian boarding school system in the United States have rightly focused upon its violent character, reflected in the first portion of Pratt's comment, but his words also show that his "civilizing" process was a gendered one. Indeed, Carlisle directed enormous energy toward "saving" men by teaching them what Pratt and his like-minded white progressive reformers believed to be the essence of manhood. This study is focused upon how Carlisle's founders welded their mission of racial transformation to ideas surrounding concepts of manhood. From the outset, Carlisle incorporated performances of "civilized" manliness into many layers of student life, but ultimately, the most visible, exciting, and problematic public exhibition of manhood was the sport of football.[4]

From an early stage, Carlisle officials motivated themselves to teach students a model of manhood based upon ideals of Victorian "civilization," which stressed the virtues of self-sufficiency, self-control, and individualism. As Pratt's successors abandoned his idealistic ambitions of cultural conversion, students drew the attention of Congress by presenting the school's administration as failing to uphold "civilized" standards of manliness. Throughout, football served as the school's most important stage for the performance of manliness and masculinity. Richard Henry Pratt hoped to use football to demonstrate that Indian men could become "civilized" men. After his departure, Carlisle's leadership mostly used football to earn revenue and garner intense media attention from reporters who treated players as fascinating objects of brute physical masculinity. Throughout, football allowed Carlisle's administrators an opportunity to exploit Indian bodies for their own agendas and interests. Yet students would also discover in football opportunities for empowerment and agency.

Like many in his position and of his time who took it upon themselves to "save" Indigenous Americans, Pratt found it impossible to connect Indianness and manhood.[5] As the violence of his rhetoric suggests, Pratt's statement called for the destruction of all forms of Indianness, with Carlisle releasing the "man" hidden within. For Pratt, this was a central goal of a Carlisle education: the destruction of the Indian to enable the creation of a "civilized man."[6]

Of course, when Indian boarding schools taught lessons about manhood, their efforts reflected much larger relationships between gender and race that defined their curricula. Scholars such as K. Tsianina Lomawaima, Robert Trennert, and Katrina Paxton have all argued that femininity was central to the teaching of "civilization" in Indian schools.[7] Instruction in domestic skills and child rearing was pivotal to teach both "civilization" and female subordination to the Native students.[8] This study builds upon this foundation and argument: with male power linked to "civilization," the teaching of manhood was also a necessary part of a "civilizing" education.

At Carlisle, Pratt aimed to retrieve Indian manhood by replacing "savagery" with "civilization." With the allotment of reservation land, granting of U.S. citizenship, and a "civilized" education, reformers like Pratt hoped that Indigenous populations would disappear by blending into mainstream American society.[9] As an extension of Ulysses S. Grant's "Peace Policy," which had aimed to end white-Indian warfare in the United States, sponsors of Native American boarding schools expressed a desire to include the Native population, sometimes even as equal partners, in what they called "civilization," an ahistorical and problematic concept that elevated western and northern Europeans at the apex of human culture and history.[10]

At the same time, when political leaders directed federal dollars toward an educational system intended to assimilate Indigenous American children into Anglo-Protestant American norms, many expressed coercive motives beyond Pratt's lofty ideals. White government officials did so because such a system would give the United States leverage over Indigenous nations. Children in boarding schools were, after all, captives of the federal government. In the words of Ezra Ayres Hayt, the commissioner of Indian Affairs in 1880, "With children at school the parent will strive toward a better life, and better hostages for good behavior and personal influence in right doing could not be devised."[11]

Soon after its founding, Carlisle's supporters saw themselves as successful. Off-reservation boarding schools quickly spread across the United States, with Haskell and Chilocco both opening in 1884.[12] By 1902 there were twenty-five federally operated off-reservation boarding schools for Native Americans. All with similar aims, such schools often referred to "civilization" as a combination of Jeffersonian and republican ideals of the yeoman farmer, the protection of property rights, male labor, and democracy.[13] Such ideals were strangely out of touch with social trends of the Gilded Age, but they still held currency among many elite white Americans. This camp of progressive era reformers, cultural imperialists, and missionaries of the "White Man's Burden" expected "civilization" to overwhelm "savagery" easily.[14]

By the time that Pratt opened the Carlisle Indian Industrial School, European Americans had been using the term "Indian" for centuries as a catch-all to describe the diverse societies indigenous to America.[15] The term defined Indigenous Americans as an undifferentiated racial category. As much as they understood Indigenous Americans as inherently different from Europeans, some elite white Americans believed that they could teach Native Americans to assimilate fully into European "civilization." Most prominent during the late nineteenth century were Thomas Jefferson Morgan, commissioner of Indian Affairs in 1889–93, and John Wesley Powell of the Smithsonian's Bureau of Ethnology. Powell held that societies existed on a ranked, evolutionary hierarchy. "Indians," according to his way of thinking, lived at a level of "savagery" that was beneath that of Europeans but not impossibly so. Powell argued that Indigenous Americans could, if properly taught, climb up the ladder of "civilization," and it was the responsibility of the more "civilized" to teach them how to do so. He saw boarding schools as institutions that would be central to achieving this uplift.[16]

On the surface, ideas like Pratt's, Morgan's, and Powell's express a sense of equality and universalism. Yet, as Jacqueline Fear-Segal points out in her work on the Carlisle Indian School, they anchored their beliefs in deeply racialized assumptions. Pratt, for example, did not hesitate to pander to the public's fascination with the bodies and physical features of Native American Indians, publicizing his "civilization" mission by capturing his students' physiology with photographs and plaster casts. In fact, Pratt based his entire project upon a racialization of Indigenous societies and nations, ironing over their significant differences and categorizing a diverse population as a single demographic group. Throughout its history, Carlisle's administration would use strict racial categories and formulas of potential students to select for, and disqualify from, admission to the school.[17]

Ideas like those of Powell, Morgan, and Pratt emerged at a time of transition in the history of settler colonialism in the United States. While not entirely done with its conquests, the federal government, by the last decades of the nineteenth century, decreasingly focused upon expansion and settlement of Indigenous lands, and increasingly turned its attention toward the creation of a more explicitly colonial relationship with Indigenous Americans. Through the construction of railroads and mines, investment in bonanza farms, opening of regions to livestock grazing, and the exploitation of forest resources, the United States federal government had assumed rule over an inland empire. By the end of the century, the nation's imperial domain stretched into all of the world's hemispheres. As Fear-Segal points out, drawing from the work of Ashis Nandy, global powers throughout the world accompanied this second generation of colonization with "peaceful" missions to "colonize minds as well as bodies."[18] While Richard Henry Pratt may have been the creator of the Carlisle Indian School, his ideas and actions emerged out of, and in concert with, trends across a late nineteenth-century global imperial landscape.

Along with these economic and political changes, elite white men in the United States during the late nineteenth century were changing ideas about who they were, devaluing Victorian notions of manliness, and embracing a more physical, pugnacious norm that became widely known as "masculinity." In part, they did so as a reaction to the rise of women's rights and the increasing number of southern and eastern European immigrants.[19] Lynne Segal argues that masculinity "exists in the various forms of power men ideally possess: the power to assert control over women, over other men, over their own bodies, over machines and technology."[20] This demonstration of male dominance through the outward show of power was the central concept of this newfound masculinity.[21]

In our analysis of manhood, masculinity, and football at the Carlisle Indian Industrial School, our book is greatly indebted to, and draws significantly from, Gail Bederman's writing about concepts of masculinity, race, and "civilization" in the United States during the late nineteenth century to the beginning of World War I. Bederman illustrates the close relationships between changes in gender ideals for men, on one hand, and racial ideologies that emerged during an era that involved both the end of post–Civil War Reconstruction and rise of U.S. imperialism, on the other.[22] As Bederman writes, in the United States, "Male dominance and white supremacy have a strong historical connection."[23]

Elite white men embraced sports with a remarkable fervor during this same era. Only decades earlier, respectable elite men tended to shun sporting competition. The most prominent and educated men in the country associated sports either with a dangerously uncouth underclass of ruffians or with a corrupt and decadent stratum of young patricians. Both these groups defined the sporting culture of the early nineteenth century by patronizing the bare knuckle boxing ring, the rat pit, the cock fight arena, the horse racetrack, and other vulgar pastimes involving blood and vice.[24]

By the last decades of the century, however, men from the very classes whose parents had rejected sports began to play and enjoy them. Among these were the children of elites attending colleges and universities who created the physically violent game of American football. Intellectuals like G. Stanley Hall, the founder and president of Clark University and a pioneer of psychology and pedagogical theory, argued that play and sports like football could train young white men to maintain their vitality by bringing out their inner "savage." He called football a form of "mental and moral training" that young elites could draw from as they struggled to dominate African Americans and colonized Indigenous populations, both of whom he saw as existing at an "uncivilized" rung of an evolutionary ladder, but as also, increasingly, coming into competition with white men around the world.[25]

Of course, the last thing that Richard Henry Pratt would have wanted was to have drawn out any perceived inner "savage" that a boarding school student might have harbored. Pratt, Hall, Morgan, and Powell would all have seen Indigenous men at boarding schools as too masculine, in need of tempering their masculinity with exercises in manly refinement. Bederman has interpreted "civilized" ideals of gender as espousing the rhetoric of separate spheres; women remained in the home while men earned an income in the workplace. Such roles supposedly produced a gendered "set of truths" which instructed men and women how to behave. This separation of spheres connected white men to the progression of "civilization," with the assumption that male dominance in society was due to "civilization" and vice-versa.[26] "Savage" society, by comparison, did not match this desired gendered hierarchy. White men, for example, believed Indigenous societies oppressed women by forcing them to labor in the fields while the "civilized" alternative promoted the ideals of domesticity and homeliness.[27] By learning and becoming "civilized," Carlisle expected students to move between these two opposite gender roles. Thus the Carlisle students were to further "civilization" by being assimilated into white gender expectations: men worked in the public sphere while women were restricted to domestic affairs.

For Pratt, football served a unique function. Rather than allow an outlet for repressed masculinity, he hoped to use it as a propaganda tool. If a team made up of young Indigenous men, playing a violent game like football, could perform with gentlemanly decorum, he could dramatically demonstrate the worth of his "civilizing" mission. If the college boys whom Carlisle played desired to express their masculinity, Carlisle's leaders hoped to demonstrate their students' Victorian manliness.

Sport seemed to offer Carlisle students the ideal opportunity to demonstrate both manliness and masculinity while remaining within the wider construct of "civilization." Carlisle introduced games against external collegiate opposition in the early 1890s.[28] While Carlisle also played baseball, had successful track teams, and in later years competed in lacrosse, this study examines the construction of an athletic manhood based primarily on football.[29] Carlisle's football team featured more prominently than any other sport, and early on, school administrators used it effectively to exhibit students behaving as gentlemen, and to draw large crowds and raise money. Curious audiences of white fans who attended or read about games often treated Carlisle's football matchups as a re-enactment of the frontier, one where the final score was more symbolic than threatening.[30] Players could be masculine by overpowering the opposition and manly by avoiding excessive violence and displaying good sportsmanship. Carlisle's construction of an athletic manhood also spoke to larger debates over the prominence of masculinity, the use of sport as a tool of "civilization," and its ability to influence public debate. In this respect, the

.y of the athletes' manhood at Carlisle contributes to increas-
ᵹ discussion of the importance and power of sport and its cen-
ral nature in American conceptions of manhood.

After Pratt left Carlisle in 1904, the federal government had
begun to abandon its most ambitious uplift agendas for boarding
school students. Under the Roosevelt administration, the Bureau
of Indian Affairs' policies treated Indigenous Americans as a racial
group incapable of ever climbing to what they saw as the more
advanced level of "civilization" occupied by white Americans.
Estelle Reel, the supervisor of Indian schools between 1898 and
1910, argued that students be introduced into "civilization" over
several generations under a policy of "gradualism."[31] She reasoned
that Indian education should focus more on vocational training,
with the Indigenous students entering at the lower ends of society instead of obtaining equal "civilization."[32] She subsequently
dismissed all academic subjects deemed unnecessary for entry
into manual vocations.[33] At Carlisle, this changed the character
of football as well. No longer a showcase for uplift, school officials recognized the value of the game as a source of revenue and
crass publicity. These were some of Carlisle's most successful years
on the gridiron, but the team also drew media coverage that portrayed players as brute specimens of physicality. Players lived a
life separated from, and at a much higher level of material comfort than, other students, hardly existing as students at all. Rather
than exploiting football for ideological reasons, Carlisle exploited
players for financial gain and glory. Eventually, Carlisle's football
players became stigmatized symbols of a corruption that had, in
fact, come to define scholastic athletics more generally.

Those who organized boarding schools had strong opinions
about gender and masculinity, even if they themselves were often
confused about these definitions. It is important to understand
that tensions over masculinity and manhood said little about how
Indigenous students at Carlisle would have experienced life there.
However, a new generation of scholars, many of whom identify as
Indigenous, have critically examined Indigenous masculinities in
settler colonial societies. Like Bederman, their work recognizes

that during the late nineteenth and early twentieth centuries, white men felt it necessary to reformulate their identities as men, and in the process, gender became a central component of cultural imperialism in settler colonial societies. They recognize sports as a key cultural institution that enforced rigid gender binaries, and one that Indigenous men sometimes have also transformed for their own purposes.

Authors in Robert Alexander Innes's and Kim Anderson's edited volume on Indigenous men and masculinities discuss the central importance of gender socialization to settler colonialism. They often turn a critical eye toward the key role that sports have played in this regard. For contributors to this book, gender ideologies that have followed European colonization have done great harm to Indigenous communities globally. Anderson, Innis, and John Swift identify colonial institutions like boarding schools as contributing to a "vicious cycle of toxic Indigenous masculinity" that continues to the present day.[34]

In his anthropological work on resistance to settler colonialism in Hawaii, Ty P. Kawika Tengan also addresses how processes of colonial conquest, like the European invasion of the Americas or the British conquest of the Hawaiian archipelago, involved a set of overtly forced and more subtly coerced changes in gender identities. His work addresses how contemporary Hawaiian men have developed rituals of cultural revitalization that reimagine and reincorporate traditional Indigenous male identities in the present. It also helps us to understand football as a ritual centrally important to the way that the Carlisle Indian School's leaders attempted to teach manhood to their students.[35]

At times, students seemed to learn these lessons all too well. In 1914 Carlisle students brought complaints about their school to Congress, and their efforts resulted in a joint congressional inquiry. Criticism of football was at the center of their critique, but they also drew upon arguments about "civilization" that had been used to justify their boarding school educations, and denigrate their Indigenous cultures. Brendan Hokowhitu helps us understand this contradiction. He has written extensively about Maori history in New Zealand, masculinity, and sports, particularly rugby. He argues that when Indigenous populations adopt colonial sports, they risk reproducing colonial models of gender norms.[36]

Yet it would be a mistake to believe that football's powerful hegemonic influence over Indigenous masculine identities was total or complete. Despite the manipulative character of football at Carlisle, the team's success became an important resource for pride among Indigenous communities. In his study of Hopi long-distance running and the Indian boarding school system, Matthew Sakiestewa Gilbert writes about how Hopi runners like Carlisle's Louis Tewanema saw their victories on the track as victories for his Indigenous people.[37] It is difficult to discern the multiple and diverse ways that Carlisle students thought about football and gender. Yet this book includes a variety of Native voices, from oral histories to the writings of scholars and artists, to show that students have not allowed the ideas that they confronted at Indian boarding schools like Carlisle to go uncontested.

Along with Gilbert's work, other recent examples of excellent scholarship have inspired us and serve as models for future scholars who might want to explore specific tribal experiences with Carlisle football. Linda Peavy and Ursula Smith have crafted an engaging narrative history of women's basketball at the Fort Shaw Indian School in Montana in their book, *Full Court Quest*. They show how female players brought to that school important women's sports traditions from their native Dakota, Assiniboine, Piegan Blackfeet, and other national backgrounds. Wade Davies also writes about basketball in his book *Native Hoops*. While he does not dive into an exploration of a singular nation or tribe, he, like Peavy and Smith, understands the game as resonating with specific tribal traditions, and he addresses how particular Indigenous societies have adapted basketball for their own purposes. In her recent dissertation on sports at the Haskell Indian Boarding School in Lawrence, Kansas, Beth Eby also makes important connections between gender, race, and empire that resonate very much with the orientation of this book.[38]

Our study of manhood at Carlisle is separated into three sections. The first section, chapter one, examines ideals of gender and "civilization" at the Carlisle Indian School during the period in which Pratt influenced it the most, between 1879 and 1904. Like many prominent citizens of his class and background, Pratt linked the concept of manhood to what he would have understood to have been "civilization." Pratt's ideas contrasted with the growing movement among other elite white men of his time who embraced masculinity in order to protect "civilized" womanhood and "civilized" manhood. Even though Carlisle's earliest champions expressed a desire to uplift those whom they considered to be "savage," the actual curricula only perpetuated white dominance as students were taught skills more suited to a working-class status. Eventually, school officials would all but abandon this "civilizing" mission as a primary goal, but this transition did not occur overnight. The second section, chapters two and three, examines the rise of athletic manhood, particularly during the post-Pratt era. As school administrators retreated from Pratt's idealistic, uplift agenda, they also largely abandoned using football to showcase the ability of Indigenous men to achieve Victorian standards of manhood. Instead, they allowed football to become a rogue institution of the school, its budget, schedule, and operations under the control of the team's charismatic coach, Glenn Scobey "Pop" Warner. Media portrayed Carlisle players not as refined men, but as masculine savages who achieved athletic success only because of their raw physical talent, thereby reaffirming an idea of Indian inferiority as men. The final section examines the 1914 congressional investigation of Carlisle. The hearings allowed the students to voice a remarkably harsh and public collective criticism of the school. Students, initially brought to Carlisle as "savages" to be "civilized," now accused school administrators of being "uncivilized," unmanly, and incompetent. Yet their "civilization" discourse proved to be treacherous. Their testimonies reflect anti-Semitic sentiments, disparage women's suffrage, and express condescending and racist stereotypes about Carlisle's African American population. Moreover, a disproportionate amount of the inquiry and report focused upon the football team, which, ironically, deflected attention away from those who operated the school and toward a student body that media had no problem characterizing as morally corrupt and out of control. By the time Carlisle closed in 1918, the football team, once a symbol of Victorian manhood, had become an allegory for the school's decline into chaos.

Our profile of manhood at the Carlisle Indian Industrial School provides an important foreshadowing of what people of color would experience in the worlds of major league and big time college sports in the United States decades later in the twentieth century. When Branch Rickey told Jackie Robinson to decline from responding to racist taunts from fans, he echoed Pratt's desire for students to exhibit manly self-control on the playing field. When late twentieth-century American universities, and high profile white coaches, began generating hundreds of millions in revenue from the athletic labor provided by people of color, they echoed the sports marketing model pioneered by the Carlisle Indian School Boosters and their team coach, "Pop" Warner. When contemporary sports commentators address players of color as physical specimens, successful because of innate talent rather than because of a work ethic, or when they patronize these same athletes as "articulate," "a class act," or "a real credit," they echo the spectrum of coverage that white print journalists extended to Carlisle football players. Our look at manhood at the Carlisle Indian School unlocks the conflicting messages that accompanied the school's "civilizing" mission and provides a window into the connections between racial ideologies, American colonial power, gender, and sports that are still relevant to this day.

1

Manhood at Carlisle, 1879–1903

In 1899 an article in the *Indian Helper* sought to answer common questions directed at the Carlisle Indian School. When discussing the ideal outcome for departing students, the unnamed author praised Dr. Carlos Montezuma: "Dr. Montezuma, the educated Apache physician of Chicago is a physician amongst educated PHYSICIANS. He is a full Indian and yet is NOT an Indian. He is a MAN. That is the great object for which the Carlisle School is striving. She hopes to turn out MEN and WOMEN, not Indians"[1] (capitals in original). As a child, Montezuma was purchased for thirty dollars from three Pima men by Italian immigrant Carlos Gentile. Gentile subsequently placed Montezuma in a local school and progressed through the American education system until he eventually earned his MD from Chicago Medical College.[2] Montezuma overcame what white elite Americans believed were the deficiencies of Indian-ness by becoming "civilized." Such "civilized" behavior, according to the author, made him a "man." The author considered Montezuma's education a sign of manhood. His education had allowed him to overcome his natural and supposedly inferior Indian-ness. This was a primary message of Carlisle: education overcame the characteristics associated with race. As a "physician amongst educated physicians," Montezuma had his manhood defined through his education and success in white society. In terms of manhood, the author considered Montezuma ideal for emulation by the male students. This, however, raises a pertinent question: what was the process by which Montezuma was judged to have been transformed from an Indian to a "man"?

During the time that he supervised the school, from 1879 to

1904, Capt. Richard Henry Pratt intended to "civilize" Native children by immersing them in white society.[3] Montezuma himself had undergone a similar experience: "In the year 1871 I was taken from the most warlike tribe in America and placed in the midst of 'civilization' in Chicago."[4] Surrounded by "civilized" society, Montezuma had succeeded and become a respected "man."

Pratt most often framed Carlisle as a school designed to uplift Indian students, and he imagined that gender would be at the center of the process. He believed that Indigenous men were too masculine, and Indigenous women were not feminine enough. It is no wonder that the author of the *Indian Helper* article referred to Carlisle using a female pronoun. As in popular fiction depicting the Wild West, Carlisle's founders convinced themselves that masculine men needed to be "civilized," and women needed to be their "civilizing" influence.[5] Carlisle's faculty, most of whom were women, would guide the school's students toward "civilization" by teaching Indigenous women to be women, and Indigenous men to be men.[6]

Montezuma both represented and spoke out forcefully for the transitional experience that Pratt introduced at Carlisle. Richard Pratt, the founder of the Carlisle school, was born in Rushford, New York, in 1840. When Pratt was a child, his father was murdered by his business partner after striking gold in California. Shortly after, Pratt left school and found work to support his mother and family. He was hired as a rail splitter and eventually managed to hold a stable job as a tinsmith.[7] Pratt's mother, Mary Herrick Pratt, a "singing Methodist," heavily influenced his Protestant youth.[8] Methodism, along with other evangelical forms of Protestantism, had flourished since the beginning of the nineteenth century. While the Second Great Awakening focused on individual salvation, such middle-class religious fervor also resulted in a desire for social reform.[9] Issues such as slavery, alcohol, prostitution, and gambling became the central focus of such reform movements. Reformers, alongside such endeavors, also aimed for the introduction of an American common school system. Their work emphasized ideas of republican liberty and virtue, individualism and social mobility, hard work, female domesticity, individual char-

FIG. 2. Carlisle Indian Industrial School founder, Brig. Gen. Richard Henry Pratt. Photograph courtesy of the Dickinson College Archives and Special Collections.

acter, respect for private property, equality of opportunity, Protestant superiority, American exceptionalism, and assimilation.[10] Pratt's personal doctrine lined up well with these values, and with those of the Indian reform movement more generally. His Methodism was a prominent influence upon Carlisle.

After the American Civil War commenced, Pratt decided to join the fight for the Union. He joined the Ninth Indiana Volunteers before being transferred to the Eleventh Indiana Cavalry. Following the culmination of the conflict, Pratt moved home and attempted to settle down as a tinsmith. However, army life still appealed to Pratt and he quickly re-enlisted. Pratt was placed in command of a cavalry regiment of formerly enslaved army fighters known as Buffalo Soldiers, along with Native scouts from several tribes. These Indigenous lookouts included groups of Cherokee, Caddoe, Wichitas, and Tonkawas. Following the 1874 Red River War, in which the United States Army aggressively and violently removed Comanche, Kiowa, Southern Cheyenne, and Arapahoe from the Southern Plains, Pratt followed orders to transport a selection of Native prisoners, the vast majority of whom were men, east to Fort Marion, Florida. The prisoners came from a variety of backgrounds: Kiowas, Comanches, Cheyenne, and Arapahoe formed the basis of Pratt's detail. The journey east was fraught with difficulties. Grey Beard, a Southern Cheyenne medicine man and leader in the Red River War, unsuccessfully attempted suicide by hanging. Later, in northern Florida, he escaped out of a train car window. Soldiers guarding the prisoners pursued him, found him, and killed him with their guns, their deadly shots audible to his fellow prisoners aboard the train.[11] Pratt, wanting to make the ordeal as easy as possible, asked the government for permission to bring the prisoners' families east too. The government, believing that the Indians were responsible for the war, denied the request.[12] The prisoners subsequently remained alone at Fort Marion until April 1878.

The education of the prisoners that Pratt designated at Fort Marion was the foundation for the later construction of manhood at Carlisle. Pratt decided to make the prisoners' incarceration an educational experience. He first moved to remove the prisoners' shackles and allow them to roam the complex freely. Pratt then replaced the white guards after discovering that they were often drunk on duty. He selected the new guards from among the prisoners, resulting in no further incidents of drunkenness. Pratt then ordered the removal of the prisoners' clothes and replaced them with army uniforms. Pratt also decided to teach the prisoners English and a marketable skill. For the former, he used high-society women on holiday from the northern states, such as famed abolitionist Harriet Beecher Stowe. For the latter, the prisoners polished sea-shells. The trade quickly earned the prisoners approximately two thousand dollars. The prisoners later progressed onto other trades, with a few working for local industries while others provided tours of the surrounding areas for northern tourists. Pratt believed that his teaching worked, that the prisoners were learning self-sufficiency through their employment, and he took this even further, arguing that the Indigenous men under his power could become "civilized." Due to such successes, members of Congress and elite white women began to support Pratt, raising his national profile. After the prisoners' release from Fort Marion in 1878, a few decided to remain in the east instead of returning home. The "success" of Pratt's endeavor persuaded him to continue his experiment on a larger scale.[13] Thus the Fort Marion experience provided Pratt with valuable lessons in the teaching of "civilized manhood" to Indians.

Pratt would further develop his ideas about the teaching of manhood during his time at the Hampton Institute. Following the success at Fort Marion, Pratt managed to enroll some of the ex-prisoners at General Samuel Armstrong's Hampton. The school provided a vocational education for the formerly enslaved and their children.[14] Hampton segregated African American and Native students from one another, each having their own buildings and classrooms. Armstrong introduced to Pratt key measures that he used for self-promotion, like the "before-and-after" photograph. The pictures compared the students' initial appearance with another photograph taken several months later. Inevitably, the first picture portrayed an Indian with stereotypical "savage" clothing. The second depicted a "civilized" student dressed in military uniform who had magically become whiter.[15] Pratt would use such pictures at Carlisle to promote the school's success and create a source of income.[16] Yet, Pratt became increasingly concerned that associating with African Americans would only inhibit his students from advancing toward "civilization," even though he professed to believe that all could achieve equality. Pratt began to look for a new location for an Indian only school. The West was too close to recent warfare for many students, so he decided to seek a potential campus on the east coast.

Pratt managed to secure the Carlisle barracks for such an endeavor. In October 1879 Pratt arrived at Gettysburg Junction in Carlisle, Pennsylvania, with eighty-two students. Although they arrived at midnight, a group of eager locals and journalists were present to see the "savages." Such a spectacle must have been terrifying for the children. Transported by train, the students were taken halfway across the country, only to be welcomed by gawking locals. Wanting to make a good impression, Pratt quickly returned to reservations and located an additional sixty-five students. He recruited them from the nations of the Great Plains with eighty-four Lakotas, fifty-two Cheyennes, Kiowas, and Pawnees, and eleven Apaches arriving at Carlisle. Of the 147 students, only 38 were female. Their ages ranged from six to twenty-five.[17]

Luther Standing Bear (Lakota) remembers the long walk from the train station to the gates of their new campus. In his memoir, *My People, the Sioux*, he writes that they arrived to find the barracks gates locked. Finally, after being directed to a building where they were to spend the night, they ran to their new home,

> expecting to find nice little beds like those the white people had. We were so tired and worn out from the long trip that we wanted a good long sleep. . . . But the first room we entered was empty. A cast-iron stove stood in the middle of the room, on which was placed a coal-oil lamp. There was no fire in the stove. We ran through all the rooms, but they were all the same—no fire, no beds. This was a two-story building, but we were all herded into two rooms on the upper floor. Well, we had to make the best of the situation, so we took off our leggins and rolled them

Manhood at Carlisle

up for a pillow. All the covering we had was the blanket which each had brought. We went to sleep on the hard floor, and it was so cold! We had been used to sleeping on the ground, but the floor was so much colder.[18]

The building was originally an old fort for Hessian soldiers during the Revolutionary War, and the majority of the first year was spent fixing the barracks up to a livable standard. By the time Pratt's tenure finished in 1904, almost four and a half thousand Native students had passed through its gates.

Despite their stunning lack of preparation for the first students who arrived at Carlisle, the school's founders saw themselves as imparting "civilization" and competence. The Native students at Carlisle received an education largely based upon assumptions of white superiority. Pratt understood "civilization" to be the prize received at the end of a successful education. According to him, the Carlisle students first had to learn and then had to prove their "civilization." Consistent with Gail Bederman's observations about the connections between nineteenth-century elite concepts of "civ-ilization" and Victorian manhood, this meant that male students had to learn to internalize separate, strictly binary gender roles, and learn to respect individual property, in order to be accepted as men. Some students, for example, could base their manhood on ideals of Protestant morality. Others could prove manhood by becoming self-sufficient. The moral education that the students received mirrored that which Protestant organizations and churches espoused.[19] Pratt and his white support network under-stood manliness primarily as an ability to live within the terms of what they believed to be "civilization."[20] This is what we might define as the Carlisle Indian Industrial School's public transcript, or the overt ways that it, as a dominant institution, defined its relationship to Indigenous Americans. Self-sufficiency and indi-vidualism were taught through a desire for property, male domi-nance was learned through separate gender roles, and democracy taught students the connection between power and "civilization." Other components, including Protestantism, also contributed to the association between "civilization" and manhood at Carlisle. Regardless of which individual variation the students espoused, the school defined the manhood in terms of "civilization."

Gail Bederman has observed that from the late decades of the nineteenth century through the first decade of the twentieth, the time period of Carlisle's existence, elite white men developed conflicting ideas about their identities. They continued to maintain assumptions of white superiority consistent with Victorian ideas of "civilization." At the same time, many leading intellectuals and prominent men became increasingly open to discovering their masculinity. Prominent men like G. Stanley Hall and Theodore Roosevelt saw their gender identities in explicitly racial terms. White American men of privilege believed that they needed to cultivate their physical strength and toughness lest they be overtaken by the "savage" races whom they had conquered and over whom they now ruled.[21]

These thinkers used scientific anthropology, particularly the theories of Charles Darwin, to portray this racial hierarchy as the product of nature, not of human action.[22] Lewis Henry Morgan supplied a fully worked out theory on the link between race and "civilization." Morgan, in his 1877 tour de force *Ancient Society, or Researches in the Lines of Human Progress from Savagery through Barbarism to Civilization*, argued that all races could be placed on a scale of social evolution. Starting with "lower savagery," all societies progressed, he argued, through three levels of savagery and three stages of "barbarism" before reaching "civilization." Assuming Anglo-Saxon society as the superior standard of "civilizations," Morgan classified Indigenous Americans between "upper savagery" and "middle barbarism."[23]

Elite white men also saw the need to masculinize themselves in order to maintain an advantage over the working classes, people whom they identified as occupying a lower stratum of "civilization." A significant number of workers during the late nineteenth century were immigrants from places like eastern and southern Europe, and, until banned from the United States, from Asia. Elites blamed these immigrants who crowded into the tenements of cities for being the primary source of violent crime, prostitution, and alcohol.[24]

If elite white men had begun to prioritize masculinity in the decades following the Civil War, those seeking to reform American Indians had the opposite agenda. Only by becoming middle-class in both behavior and profession, only by demonstrating sober restraint and a tempered masculinity, could the Native student claim to be fully "civilized." For Pratt, "civilizing" the Indian did not necessarily require thousands of years. In an 1892 speech, Pratt outlined the Indians' potential:

> It is a great mistake to think that the Indian is born an inevitable savage. He is born a blank, like all the rest of us. Left in the surroundings of savagery, he grows to possess a savage language, superstition and life. We, left in the surroundings of civilization, grow to possess a civilized language, life, and purpose. Transfer the infant white to the savage surroundings, he will grow to possess a savage language, superstition, and habit. Transfer the savage-born infant to the surroundings of civilization, and he will grow to possess a civilized language and habit.[25]

Pratt and his fellow reformers rejected the natural progression of a society toward "civilization" that people like Hall and Roosevelt espoused. Pratt's plan for Indian education was based upon the idea of environmentalism. If only raised in accordance with the norms of elite, American white society, according to Pratt, anyone, regardless of race, could ideally advance up Morgan's ladder of "civilization."[26] The social evolution of Indian society could ideally be accomplished within a few generations. According to Pratt, Indians' supposed inferiority could be overcome by immersing the younger generation in "civilization."

Pratt drew from his experiences of military service to form his opinions about Indigenous transformation through immersion in a strict, Anglo-Protestant education. During the Red River War, he had met Cherokee soldiers who had received an education in the English language from their tribal government. Using racialized imagery to describe them, he writes, "They had manly bearing and fine physiques. Their intelligence, civilization, and common sense was [sic] a revelation, because I had concluded that as an army officer I was there to deal with atrocious aborigines."[27] After dismissing his original interpretation of Indians as inherently "savage," he recognized the humanity of his prisoners. The Native soldiers were "civilized" and intelligent, and therefore in the eyes of Pratt, those who were male were, in fact, men. Indeed, the Cherokees had adopted lifestyles similar to those of white society, taking up farming, creating a written language, and writing a constitution.[28] Although they were not white, many considered the Cherokees one of the "Five Civilized Tribes." In Pratt's opinion they had adopted "civilized" manhood. However, despite his laudatory claims, Pratt did not consider an education on the reservation sufficient.[29] Carlisle could completely eliminate the Indian-ness and "savagery" within such soldiers. With a "civilized" education, completely detached from the reservation, Carlisle could offer a model of manhood acceptable to both Pratt and white society.

The first step toward "civilized" manhood was overcoming the language barrier. During Carlisle's early existence, only a few students could speak English, but Pratt believed that proficiency in English was a make-or-break lesson for the students, one that he connected directly to "civilization."[30] While teaching English, Carlisle would systematically eliminate students' Indigenous languages. To ensure that students spoke only English, the school banned students from speaking their Native languages at all times.[31] Teachers used *First Lessons for the Deaf and Dumb* to teach English.[32] Its title suggests that the students' Native language was a disability, a hindrance to their progression into "civilization." Teachers used only English in all of their lessons, including arithmetic. As stated in the school's first *Annual Report*, "the mastery of the English language is held to be not less important than the mastery of the lesson."[33]

Evidently, students refused to abandon their languages easily, as in 1882 when authorities offered a reward to anyone who spoke nothing but English for a week. Students received an increased reward if they continued for the following month.[34] Pratt reported that almost the entire school earned both rewards, but the school still needed to introduce it, suggesting that students used their Native languages without detection.[35] Despite this, for the majority of the Pratt era, the use of English was the initial stage of learning "civilized" manhood.

Pratt also believed that American Indian students needed to believe in individual property rights to become "civilized" men. The school's media promoted the desire for property as a sign of individualism and "civilization." For example, in 1888 the school published a piece promoting land ownership, ostensibly from a "Stockbridge Indian" to his cousin at Hampton Institute, in the school publication, the *Indian Helper*. The author wrote: "If I have a piece of land and want to sell it, I could do so, that is if I can find a buyer, and it is nobody's business. But if I lived with the tribe I could not sell my land and go somewhere else, if I liked it ever so well somewhere else. I would have to stay on my land let it be ever so poor or so good. It is just like being in prison."[36]

The author described property in terms of freedom and individuality. By describing the reservation as a "prison," the author invokes the image of a cramped cell. He portrays Indians as lacking independence and being reliant upon others, just as an inmate is reliant upon prison authorities for both food and clothing. According to this author, only by securing land and metaphorically escaping their own prisons could Indians overturn the savagery of the reservation. This argument inspired the Dawes Act of 1887, which divided reservation land into smaller allotments that enrolled members would own individually.[37] By separating Native land into such parcels, the occupants would be forced to become individual land owners and thus demonstrate their potential for "civilization."[38] Providing Indigenous peoples with a distinct plot of land meant they could become "civilized."

Morgan equated subsistence farming with savagery, and in accordance with this thinking, Indian schools taught students to produce for a market.[39] This ideal reinforced the implementation of the Dawes Act. By dividing community land into smaller allotments, supporters of Dawes hoped Natives would grow crops as individual farmers for a profit. A significant number of students, however, were uneducated in this kind of farming. Ideally, students would thrive after graduating from Carlisle having learned not only to grow crops but to compete against one another and against other farmers.[40]

Agricultural education was one of the main lessons for male students at Carlisle. Every male student who attended Carlisle received instruction in agriculture. One of Pratt's first orders after opening Carlisle was the purchase of a farm.[41] The original farm was replaced in 1886 by one closer to campus, and a supplemental farm was acquired in 1901 with funds donated to the school.[42] Students used these farms when not engaged in industrial training, and a significant number learned agricultural skills within the confines of the Carlisle campus.[43]

The farms also had another vital role as the number of students at Carlisle grew. The school needed food, and Congress's miserly appropriations were not enough to feed the students.[44] The farms supplied nearly all the food eaten at Carlisle, allowing the school to become self-sufficient.[45] School leaders believed that this independence provided an advantage. Through Carlisle's self-sufficiency, they could teach students to become independent adults.

The teaching of farming at Carlisle reaffirmed the Jeffersonian republican ideal that valorized the yeoman farmer. Jefferson saw an independent citizenry of producers as key to reproducing the nation's democratic "civilization." He perceived this citizenry to be exclusively white and male but saw an opening for American Indians. While willing to engage in racial warfare, he believed that the federal government could avoid bloodshed as it expanded west by introducing Indigenous populations to Christianity and white agrarianism. Pratt followed this lead, making agricultural training central to the Carlisle curriculum.[46]

Male students also learned to farm during their "outing," a vital component of a Carlisle education that Pratt considered the most important part of the "civilizing" process. During a student outing, Carlisle placed students on local white farms. Pratt believed that this program would expose students to the positive influence of Anglo-American society. Most commonly, male students worked on farms, while female students worked as domestic servants in households. The outing served two purposes: to teach a vocational skill while also teaching "civilized" behavior and conduct.

Pratt wrote that during the outing, "the Indian boy is for this period no longer an Indian, but a man working for wages."[47] During Jefferson's time, many actually associated wage labor with servility and unmanliness.[48] Yet in Pratt's mind, wages introduced Indian students to money and potential independence both from reservation life and from the government. Thus working on a farm during the outing prepared students for the supposed independence inherent in "civilized" society.

Along with income, Pratt associated budgeting, restraint, and careful saving with manliness. In an 1884 *Annual Report* he wrote, "An Indian boy who has earned and saved $25 or $50 is, in every way, more manly and more to be relied upon than one who has nothing."[49] The manly student saved his earnings in order to afford more expensive items, such as a "civilized" home. He controlled his spending habits so as to accumulate wealth and thus become part of American capitalism. The male student's accumulation of wealth allowed him to purchase "civilized" goods, such as a table and chairs. Carlisle's public transcript used such evidence to state that manhood could be partly demonstrated through the "civilized" traits of self-sufficiency and the accumulation of wealth.

Pratt saw his mission as promoting self-sufficiency, and he saw himself as failing at his mission when students "returned to the blanket."[50] The term itself suggests dependency on others and degradation—the student had succumbed to his previous savagery. Pratt clearly believed that if male students were to become men, they had to become independent individuals, no longer tied to a reservation. As he put it in an 1890 annual report, "to fail in self-support destroys manhood." Even if they did go back to their reservations, they would do so as farmers trained in "self-support among civilized people."[51]

Pratt used the story of a Carlisle student who ran away to demonstrate the benefits of agricultural training. A student named Grasshopper (San Carlos Apache), left Carlisle in July 1885 after his privileges were removed. Pratt described Grasshopper as "one of the most incorrigible young fellows in the party." After he ran away, Grasshopper worked on a farm in central Missouri.[52] According to the local farmer, Grasshopper worked well and eventually asked

Pratt if he could return to Carlisle. This example was printed in Pratt's annual report as an amazing success, not only for Carlisle but for the outing process. Grasshopper, by working on a local farm surrounded by white society, had become "civilized" to the extent that he understood the need for an education. Pratt presented Grasshopper's story as an allegory of a prodigal son who had accepted the gospel of "civilization" and progressed toward manhood.

Ultimately, through agricultural or vocational education, a student would earn citizenship. Before 1924 Indigenous Americans were not born United States citizens. Philanthropists fervently hoped that Congress would grant citizenship by statute.[53] The General Allotment Act of 1887 granted citizenship, but only to those who owned allotted land.[54] With more land divided in the sequential years, Carlisle students were more likely to become citizens. It therefore became vital that students were educated to become citizens. By earning such a reward, students would be protected under United States law and, ultimately, would participate in the democratic system. In his 1899 annual report Pratt emphasized the importance of such lessons. Carlisle aimed "to produce, not an abnormal being, but an all-around wide awake American citizen, serving God and the country."[55] Pratt believed citizenship was the ultimate reward of "civilization," the province of someone no longer Indian, but an "American." Such progression included patriotism, loyalty to the United States rather than an Indigenous nation.

Brenda Child reminds us how important it is to understand boarding school education within this larger context of settler colonialism. She notes that boarding schools have become, for many, a "usable past that links tribal people of diverse backgrounds today to a devastating common history, one that must be evoked, many argue, to understand our present conditions and social problems." As important as they are to our understanding of the collective trauma that Indigenous populations have faced, they were only one part of a bigger picture that included broken and violated treaty rights, lost languages, and tragic incidents of violence, starvation, and disease. While Pratt and white progressive reformers saw the General Allotment Act as a pathway toward Indian

26   Manhood at Carlisle

emancipation through citizenship, in practice it more often devastated Indigenous communities like the White Earth Ojibwa, a band that lost huge land tracts to land swindlers who opportunistically exploited the law.[56]

The Carlisle education invariably connected citizenship to manhood. Speaking at the 1898 commencement exercises, Dr. J. A. Lippincott, professor of mathematics and astronomy at Dickinson College, commented on the future citizenship of the Carlisle graduates: "The Indian is DEAD in you. Some one says that the only good Indian is a DEAD Indian and it is true. Be MEN and women, but not Indians! Let all that is Indian within you die! Then you will be men and women, freemen, American citizens"[57] (capitals in original, note only for men). For Lippincott, only by adopting a "civilized" model of manhood could the male graduate hope to be a worthwhile citizen. Like Pratt, Lippincott portrayed Indian-ness as the binary opposite of "civilization," manhood, womanhood, and citizenship. By eliminating Indian-ness and becoming "civilized" men, students were ready for citizenship.

Pratt attempted to teach citizenship by promoting obedience to white authority and law. He set up a student court to try any student who had broken the rules to a serious extent. It mostly mirrored American judicial proceedings, featuring a prosecution and defense, witnesses, and jurors. The court determined the punishment. The jurors were selected from the officer contingent of the school.[58] To avoid bias, the court considered the tribal affiliation of jurors. A junior member of the court kept a full record of proceedings and passed them on to Pratt for "approval or disapproval of its findings."[59] While the courts appeared student-run, Pratt still held the final decision over the outcome, thereby making students obedient to white authority. Although Pratt did not interfere with the majority of the court's rulings, his surveillance could have influenced the court's decisions. Such control ensured that the court mirrored Pratt's beliefs in crime and punishment. Although the courts were portrayed as providing student agency, final authority remained in white hands.

Pratt's autobiography gives an example of the court rewarding student adherence. Spotted Tail's youngest son, an officer at Carlisle, was placed in the lock-up after he stabbed a fellow student in the leg. His punishment was a week in the guardhouse, a sentence astonishingly lenient considering the violence of the crime.[60] More than likely, Spotted Tail's son would also have been stripped of his rank as captain. Before this occurred, however, all of Spotted Tail's children had been removed from Carlisle, albeit for unrelated reasons.[61] The court punished Spotted Tail's son for lacking "civilized" self-control. The court also stripped the student of his agency as the defendant had no power over his immediate future. Repeated misdemeanors could mean that the school would expel the student. In theory, this would mean that the school would effectively deny the student entrance into "civilization" and manhood.[62] Such cases expressed a very clear message that white dominated society was "civilized," superior, and more powerful than the Indigenous society. "Civilized" manhood was partly affirmed through authority, which was taught by entrusting the court jurors with power over students accused of "uncivilized" behavior.

Pratt and the Carlisle Indian School further connected "civilization" to power and manhood by organizing the student body into regiments and companies. The influence of the military on Carlisle was clear: students were dressed in military style uniforms, organized into regiments, and marched on a daily basis.[63] An officer oversaw each regiment and promoted from the rank and file. The criteria for becoming an officer were relatively vague. Any student who adhered to the ideals of "civilization" was eligible for promotion. The *Indian Helper* in 1893 expressed the connections between military discipline and manliness: "The gentlemanly officers put on a great deal of admirable dignity as they passed through the girls quarters Sunday morning."[64] It is apparent that such students were promoted to the officer class because of their "civilized" and gentlemanly behavior. With the promotion to officer came more responsibility: the officer oversaw an entire company.[65]

Once the student had learned the finer aspects of obedience, power, and "civilization," he was to become an American citizen. The school newspaper depicted citizenship as a general reward. A

1901 article from the *Red Man* opined that "the practical men and women" who operated at Carlisle had succeeded in "finding the manhood in the Indian" and "shaping it for citizenship."[66] For the author of this piece, only male students who adhered to a "civilized" model of manhood should earn citizenship. Only an education of the kind that Carlisle offered could reveal the "civilized" man buried deep within the Indian. Anthropological analysis of this same era, steeped in scientific racism, suggested that the savage man could only gradually achieve "civilization" over many generations.[67] In contrast, Pratt separated race from culture, arguing that "civilization" lay within all Indians and would become apparent once they were detached from their savage culture. Yet Pratt also assumed that students could only eliminate their Indian-ness with help from whites.[68] The notion that students had to earn citizenship positioned Carlisle's version of "civilization" as inferior to that of white Americans.

If Carlisle had truly worked to promote Indigenous Americans to become members of a "civilized" elite, it would have trained its male students to become professionals, business leaders, or members of an expanding managerial class. During the years of Carlisle's operations, the second industrial revolution in the United States had shifted the demographics of the middle class. Toward the mid-nineteenth century the middle class increasingly moved toward jobs in management, business retail, or a learned profession, such as medicine or law.[69] Men in these jobs did not need physical strength to do their work. Masculine strength was difficult to demonstrate while confined to an office. While men increasingly undertook sports to prove their masculine prowess during this time, they also linked their manhood to the exercise of rational knowledge.[70] Educational prowess served to differentiate higher status men and their world from the tedious, back-breaking physicality of the working class.[71]

Despite wanting students to reject physicality and embrace middle-class ideals, Carlisle primarily instructed students in working-class occupations. As a result, the school days were split into two. The first half was spent learning English and other disciplines, such as mathematics. For the rest of the day, male students received instruction in a vocational trade.[72] Lessons ranged from shoe-making and blacksmithing to wagon-making.[73] Ironically, given the school's Victorian ideology of "civilization" and manhood, young men at Carlisle learned trades dependent upon physical strength as well as an individual skill. They learned to become blacksmiths and build wagon wheels.[74]

Some students who attended Carlisle did enter the middle-class. For example, Frank Hudson (Laguna) became a bank teller and Luther Standing Bear became an author and teacher on his reservation. [75] Despite this, the school media admitted that Carlisle was largely unable to aid students in becoming part of the middle class. The author of a 1900 article in *Red Man* wrote:

> If the Indian boy or girl is to earn a living by manual labor, let him not therefore be denied the inspiration of a glimpse into the world of beauty—the realm of soul! There is no true calling in which a man does not need his wits, and no one should be compelled to lead a life of joyless and mindless drudgery. On the other hand if a young Indian aspires—as many of them do aspire—to use his brains and his heart in a struggle of minds rather than muscle . . . who would refuse him the chance? . . . Indian lawyers, doctors, teachers, brain-workers of every sort are needed now. . . . The government schools do not and cannot educate them for this task.[76]

This article acknowledges that Carlisle was not preparing the vast majority of its students to rise above even the most menial tasks and compete in a "struggle of minds." The working-class education provided by Carlisle only allowed the students to "glimpse" at the "civilized" world so as to avoid "joyless and mindless drudgery." So, while Pratt and Carlisle officials often preached about "civilizing" the students according to Anglo-American standards, the reality, as this author acknowledged, did not match these aspirations.[77] With the students' manhood inseparable from "civilization," Carlisle's working-class training ensured that both were inferior.

Not only did Carlisle's trades education conflict with Pratt's goal to uplift male students into "civilized" manhood, but it was also poor training for the industrial workplace of the late nineteenth century. Carlisle aimed to create an Indian society based on a rapidly disappearing America. Students received an education for an idealized version of American "civilization" based on a romanticized vision of life in the early republic, and upon Pratt's own personal experiences.[78] By the end of the century the trades that students learned at Carlisle were slowly dying out. Some students entered the "civilized" world actually hindered by their education, and many students returned home to find that their trade was not required.[79] Although educated as a tinsmith at Carlisle, Luther Standing Bear remarked that he never used the trade after leaving the school, which should surprise nobody.[80] In the Fells Point district of nearby Baltimore, by 1880, tin manufacturers had already begun to use machines that could outproduce scores of tradesmen.[81] Carlisle's working-class training firmly positioned the "civilized" Native in the American past.

Along with the wider Indian reform movement in the United States, Pratt placed religion at the center of his "civilizing" mission, promoting Protestant Christianity.[82] The connection between Indian reform and evangelical Protestantism was apparent from its early stages. Protestants dominated the majority of Indian reform groups, such as the Indian Rights Association and "Friends of the Indian."[83] Just as dominant American institutions of the late nineteenth century associated Catholicism with "uncivilized" Irish, German, and Italian immigrants, Pratt marginalized Catholic teaching at the Indian school.[84] Pratt's Methodism may also have played a part in the school's strongly Protestant flavor. Although Catholic students attended Carlisle, it had no campus priest.[85] The school's Protestant foundations were also affirmed through the anti-Catholic sentiment in the *Red Man*.[86] Protestant theology helped Pratt transform his ideology of uplift and individual responsibility into gospel.

The Indian reform movement promoted not only conversion to Protestantism but also the condemnation of Native religions and spiritual practices. Carlisle's framers would have agreed with Morgan when he wrote that "all primitive religions are grotesque and to some extent unintelligible."[87] Despite flouting his ignorance of

Indigenous spirituality, Morgan stubbornly presented any spiritual belief system that existed in the western hemisphere before European contact as inferior to Christianity. Likewise, Carlisle's promoters believed that Native societies needed to experience conversion to Protestant Christianity. A popular theory, parroted by Carlisle physician O. G. Given, argued that Indians lacked morality: "The opinion generally prevails that the Indians as a race are physically strong. In regard to this I would say that where so much immorality and lewdness exists as does among the Indians there must of necessity be a great deal of venereal disease . . . their filthy habits and ignorance of remedial agents, gives the disease the best possible chance to ravage the system and impair the vital powers."[88]

Given argues that Indigenous Americans lack a moral foundation necessary for "civilized" behavior. Importantly, he uses sexual imagery to make his point. When he writes that "Indians as a race are physically strong," that they engage in "lewdness," and that they spread "venereal disease," he does not present factual evidence. Instead, in the most sensational of terms, he presents an image of overly masculine, "uncivilized" Natives that he clearly expected would be revolting to his audience. He implies that any person who does not practice the Protestant Christian code of morals and was naked must naturally be consumed by sexual desire.

In response to stereotypes of Indian sexuality, Protestant teaching aimed to inculcate morality and self-control into the male students. Even as the school promoted "civilization," it taught students how to avoid "civilization's" vices, such as drinking and smoking.[89] Self-control was a central pillar of evangelical Protestantism and manhood.[90] An 1889 story in the *Indian Helper* by a mysterious author known as "The Man in the Bandstand" (in reality, newspaper editor Marianna Burgess) demonstrates how Carlisle used school media to promote its evangelical message. Two students, Phil and Tom, were discussing their recent outing experiences. While on his placement, Tom accepted cigars and chewing tobacco from one of the hired workers. This caused his work to deteriorate, Tom commenting that he no longer "cared for anything."[91] His lack of self-control quickly spread to all areas of his work and damaged his reputation with the outing patron, who ended up returning Tom to Carlisle in disgrace. The article presents Tom behaving in an infantilized manner. He could not control his actions because of his childlike addiction to smoking. Through such an admission, Tom had openly declared his lack of manliness. However, if allowed another chance, Tom declared that "civilization will NOT ruin me."[92]

It might seem strange that an institution dedicated to uplifting into "civilization" those it considered savage would publish a story that portrayed "civilization" as a source of ruin. It makes sense, however, when one sees the centrality of manliness to the story. Without manly self-restraint and a Protestant work ethic, according to this allegory, an individual easily falls prey to hedonistic vices of self-indulgence like drinking and gambling.[93] Upon hearing Tom's declaration, the Man in the Bandstand concludes, "Tom has taken a new start, and will make a man of himself yet."[94]

"Civilized" manhood demanded the constant demonstration of self-control. A poem in an 1889 edition of the *Indian Helper* outlined its importance:

> He is a hero, true and brave,
> Who fights an unseen foe,
> And puts at last beneath his feet
> His passions base and low;
> And stands erect in manhood's might,
> Undaunted, undismayed—
> The bravest man who drew a sword
> In foray or in raid.
> All honor, then, to that brave heart,
> Though poor or rich he be.
> Who struggles with his baser part,
> Who conquers and is free.
> He may not wear a hero's crown
> Or fill a hero's grave,
> But truth will place his name among
> The bravest of the brave.[95]

The male student controls his "baser part," achieving manhood comparable to that of the heroic soldier. Although he might not win any medals or receive vocal support from others, the controlled man is just as heroic. In an attempt to embrace the heroic nature of self-control, the entire poem is underpinned with a masculine vocabulary—although the man "conquers" his base desires, he still "stands erect in manhood's might" in a "battle" against his "baser part."[96] Intriguingly, the poem's author repeatedly uses the term "brave," evoking an image of an Indian warrior, perhaps suggesting that the author sought to spark a sense of racial pride in the reader.[97] Centrally important, however, the poem establishes that a true man needs no public adulation as a reward for the practice of self-discipline. A "civilized" man proves himself through his control over his sexual savagery.

Carlisle established its own branch of the Young Men's Christian Association (YMCA) to teach self-control, morality, and Christianity. The wider YMCA was founded in England in 1844. George Williams and his friends founded the group in London to promote Protestantism and counter the vice and un-Christian behavior that he perceived emerging in the industrialized city. The idea spread to the United States during the 1850s when the YMCA was introduced in American cities.[98] The YMCA became a central part of evangelical Protestantism and aimed for individual and social salvation. The group attracted white-collar workers within urban areas who hoped first to resist and then to reverse the supposed degeneracy of urban life. YMCAs often established entry fees outside the range of the average urban worker, effectively maintaining class boundaries.[99] The organization aimed to improve middle-class manhood through the "fourfold program," which promoted a collection of spiritual, mental, social, and physical qualities as a manly ideal.

Not until the 1880s did the YMCA fully embrace the concept of Muscular Christianity, equating masculine prowess with moral character. By constructing gymnasiums, which originally served to attract young men uninterested in religion, the YMCA connected the ideals of evangelical Protestantism to the physical upkeep of the body. Although not embraced by the European version, athletics became a central feature of the United States' YMCA program.[100] In short, a strong body came to represent a strong mind. By the end of the century, the YMCA focused on spiritual, mental, and physical salvation.

Carlisle's YMCA grew quickly after its introduction, although the precise date of its founding is unclear. In his 1891 annual report Pratt wrote that students led in its creation "several years ago."[101] The YMCA subsequently became a popular institution on campus. In 1894 Pratt reported that over one hundred students were members.[102] In 1897 the YMCA was provided with a meeting place.[103] It frequently sent delegates to the association's State Convention, providing an opportunity to mingle with its white members.[104] By the end of the nineteenth century the YMCA was an important feature of the Carlisle campus.

The school YMCA used the Bible to guide the students toward a Protestant version of manhood, something also promoted in school media. For instance, an 1896 piece in the *Indian Helper* instructed male students to consult the Bible for instructions on manhood.[105] Above anything else, the Bible offered teachings in becoming the "Ideal Man." The report proposed that the study of biblical "people" could be used to demonstrate incorrect and unmanly behavior while promoting the benefits of proper conduct. Later in the same report, the author posited Jesus Christ as the character most worthy of emulation. By listening to the teachings of Jesus and mimicking his behavior, a male student could become an "Ideal Man."

In school media the YMCA depicted a muscular Jesus consistent with the students' vocational education.[106] In a lecture on labor published in the *Indian Helper*, Reverend J. H. Leiper espoused Jesus' profession. "To be recognized as honorable, Jesus said: 'My father worketh hitherto and I work.' Jesus was a carpenter. He drew the saw, pushed the plane and turned the auger."[107] For Leiper, a vocational student at Carlisle would have a great deal in common with Jesus. If a young man at the school received poor job training for industrial society, he received a powerful ideological indoctrination into the principles of Protestant manhood.

At Carlisle the YMCA encouraged its members to participate in non-violent sports. In this respect, football, an inherently violent game gaining popularity among American college students during the last decade of the nineteenth century, presented a problem to the organization. In 1895 Delos Lone Wolf (Kiowa) defended himself as a member of both the YMCA and the school football team. In the *Indian Helper* he promoted football as Christian: "I play foot-ball because I like it; because it has taught me how to control myself as I never could before. It has strengthened me physically and so helped me in my work for God. We do not put off our Christianity when we go to the foot-ball field. We play not only for the good benefits of the game to us as individuals, but for the advancement and glory of our school."[108]

Lone Wolf expresses precisely the most preferred ideological function of football at Carlisle from the point of view of someone like Pratt. Because of the game's inherent violence, it offered a challenge for students, an opportunity to demonstrate the self-control so central to Victorian ideals of Protestant manliness. Lone Wolf writes that through sport, in this case a violent sport, he actually learned qualities of Christian self-control rather than "savagery" and vice. In fact, at the very same time that Lone Wolf made this argument, college men around the United States took to this sport for largely the opposite reason. They sought to exhibit their masculinity, to release their inner "savagery." As an institution, Carlisle would have trouble managing this tension, and as we will see, some Carlisle students would later portray their school's foray into college football as antithetical to Christian virtue.

The YMCA engaged in more than sports, contributing to the wider curriculum at Carlisle. In his annual reports, Pratt frequently praised the work of the YMCA. In 1899 he commented that the YMCA was as "much a part of the life of the School as the work of the class room."[109] Still, the YMCA and Pratt had divergent goals in one important respect. In the *Indian Helper* in 1891, the YMCA stated that it aimed "to train for personal Christian work."[110] Although not explicitly stated, this involved spreading Protestantism through missionary work, meaning that the association hoped students would return to their reservations.[111] Despite this apparent disagreement, Pratt never publicly criticized the YMCA. Rather, he saw it as beneficial in teaching a "civilized" model of manhood. [112]

Indian reformers like Pratt believed that Indian men could only remain "civilized" if in the company of "civilized" women trained to rear the next generation of Indian children. According to this line of thinking, women would pass on "civilization" to their children, who would in turn pass it onto theirs. As such, women would be responsible for the continuation of "civilization" among the Indian population. While Carlisle's framers envisioned Indigenous men as overly masculine, they believed that Indigenous women to be insufficiently feminine. Carlisle's female students experienced an education in "civilized" white femininity, something that reformers believed controlled the savagery of men, white as well as Indian.[113]

Carlisle taught its female students piety, purity, submissiveness, and domesticity, four characteristics of the "Cult of True Womanhood."[114] While female students could reject a solely domestic life in favor of teaching, and the newspaper regularly promoted equal suffrage and espoused the "new woman," in the main, they received an education in "civilized" femininity. After arrival at Carlisle, the female students were taught domestic skills. They received instruction in housekeeping, laundry, sewing, and other homemaking tasks.[115] Pratt envisioned that Carlisle would transform the female students into "Republican Mothers," taught to provide a "civilized" home and education for their children.[116] During their outings female students worked as domestics, cleaning and cooking for their white patrons.[117] Male and female students at Carlisle learned that "civilized" gender norms depended upon strictly separate spheres for women and men.

In many respects Carlisle's curriculum for female and male students parallels that which Indigenous youths experienced in other settler colonial societies of the late nineteenth century. Brendan Hokowhitu, for example, writes of British colonizers creating boarding schools in what would become New Zealand, training Maori young women in domestic labor and Maori young men in manual trades. These also enforced a strictly binary set of gender expectations for males and females, ones very different from the Indigenous gender norms of the Maori. Drawing upon the work of Homi Bhabha, Hokowhitu argues that colonizers have long portrayed those whom they conquer, and over whom they rule, as "degenerate," particularly with regard to gender. Reforming sexual norms and identities, in this respect, justifies colonial administration, making colonial expansion seem like a process of human salvation.[118]

Even under Pratt, however, some female students pushed back against their education in domesticity. In 1890 Jemima Wheelock (Oneida), a fifteen-year-old student in her sixth and final year at Carlisle, wrote an article calling for gender equality. Wheelock demanded equal pay, college-level education, and consistent opportunities for women.[119] Still, Wheelock's article demonstrates that women could only move into the public sphere either when it benefited their domestic abilities or when they were forced to do so. When speaking of equality in the workplace, Wheelock writes, "women who have no homes must work for their living, and this is where I wish to say a word or two for them." Wheelock implies that women should only work if the first option, domesticity, is unavailable. Wheelock praised a woman who only worked as a farmer because her husband was paralyzed. Wheelock even based her argument for equality of education upon a domestic foundation. "There are people who still think it is useless to educate women," she writes, "but I think when they are educated it makes the home pleasanter and the children better."

Pratt and Carlisle educators did, however, encourage female students to enter the public sphere to become teachers in the Indian Service. Carlisle introduced teacher training in 1897.[120] By 1903 the Indian school system employed 101 ex-Carlisle students. Sixteen were teachers, seven assistant teachers, and nine assistant matrons.[121] Pratt, however, admitted that many of these were not educated by Carlisle's teacher training program, reporting in 1898 that only ten students had enrolled in it.[122] In other cases Carlisle graduates earned teaching degrees at state normal schools elsewhere in Pennsylvania.[123] In both the Indian and common school

Manhood at Carlisle

system, increasing numbers of women had entered the teaching profession by the turn of the twentieth century, so it is likely that many teachers from Carlisle were female. By 1880 women occupied over 60 percent of the teaching workforce.[124] School administrators viewed female teachers as agents of "civilization," taming the savage within the wild boy.[125] From early on at Fort Marion, Pratt regularly employed a significant number of upper-class women who believed that their ideal model of "civilized" femininity and could eliminate savagery.[126] Pratt envisioned that Indigenous women, educated in "civilized" femininity at Carlisle, could become ideal teachers.

Even as administrators framed teaching as an appropriate profession for women, female students also received messages that it could serve as a gateway toward emancipation from the constraints of gendered expectations. For example, school publications portrayed Indian teachers as "new women," a late-nineteenth-century construct in which popular media encouraged middle- and upper-class females to explore interests in health and personal pleasure and to challenge male dominance in the public sphere.[127] In 1895 the *Red Man* printed an article linking Indian school teachers to the "new woman." The author argued that Indian school teachers could provide their own home, demonstrate equal intelligence to men, and become breadwinners in their own right.[128] Of course, the article largely contradicted the limited female education provided by Carlisle, and perhaps not surprisingly, only a few female students took up the option of teaching.

Carlisle officials connected female domesticity to piety. While the boys attended church in Carlisle town center, the girls received Sunday service on the school grounds from visiting Protestant preachers who provided conservative sermons regarding femininity.[129] In an article reprinted in school media from *Harper's Bazaar*, Reverend Henry van Dyke (Presbyterian) spoke on the subject of the "Strenuous Life." He claimed, "A woman's power avails most when it is asserted least . . . A woman's special and inestimable value in the world lies just in the qualities which make her womanhood. And these are things which strenuosity must disturb, if not destroy."[130] For Van Dyke, womanhood should be a life of minimal exertion in which men held control of the public arena. For the female students who had become Christian, their domestic position was ordained by God. To break into the public sphere was to challenge biblical teaching and face possible damnation.

Nevertheless, even under Pratt, female students at Carlisle at times asserted a desire for independence. Josephine Langley (Piegan) learned the new sport of basketball at Carlisle, and brought her knowledge of the game to Fort Shaw Indian School in Montana, where in 1904 the team would become crowned world champions at the St. Louis World's Fair.[131] In 1903 the female students organized a Young Women's Christian Association (YWCA).[132] Although Van Dyke had spoken out against women practicing the "Strenuous Life," the YWCA embraced athletics. Like the YMCA, the wider YWCA invoked the athleticism of sport and the moral lessons of the Bible.[133] The school YWCA promoted female health with the girls organizing several basketball teams.[134] It is difficult to ascertain the long-term impact of the YWCA. Its only report during Pratt's tenure stated that the school chapter had forty active members and fifteen associate members.[135] Considering that Carlisle had 551 female students in August 1903, the membership of the YWCA was relatively limited during the Pratt era.[136]

The introduction of the YWCA may have been a reaction to wider issues concerning women in the United States. Pratt strictly forbade the kinds of rebellion associated with the "new woman," but this does not mean that he could suppress the desire of female students for freedom. The YWCA allowed an outlet for such students, albeit one that was extremely limited.[137] Still, female students at Carlisle knew the limits to their freedom, particularly when it came to their sexuality. Carlisle officials strictly protected students' "purity," which they directly connected to sexuality and virginity. For Carlisle's administrators, a "civilized" woman stayed a virgin until marriage.[138] Indian reformers portrayed Indigenous women as sexually uninhibited.[139] As a result, they vigorously policed gender boundaries between students. They divided dormitories by sex and meetings between male and female students occurred only once a week.[140] They recorded female student menstrual cycles, even advising outing patrons to check the female students' beds for blood. The outing agents monitored the behavior of female students, reporting if they met local boys.[141] Pratt acknowledged only one student during his tenure to have become pregnant. He expelled her.[142]

Even the *Red Man* article that promoted the "new woman" did so in a way that portrayed Indigenous men as true oppressors, and Native women needing the liberating hand of a new colonial patriarch. The article said of Carlisle's female students, "She will not be a Ruth and live upon the gleanings that the sickle and rake of a man have left. She will have her own field, her own sickle, and the full yield of her effort."[143] Referencing the biblical story of Ruth, such women differed from the Indian, whom the article portrayed as working in the field while her husband lazed. This "new woman" was independent and proud of it. Yet a Carlisle education restricted farming to the male students. School media might have promoted gender equality, but the female students actually received an education firmly centered on domesticity and reliance.

The liberal rhetoric of the school media may have been due to its editor, Marianna Burgess. Historian Genevieve Bell has speculated that she and Annie Ely, the supervisor of the outing program, were lovers. If so, they would have lived more in accordance with the independent "new woman" than in submissive femininity. While they lived and vacationed together, there is no specific evidence that Burgess and Ely were lesbian partners, but Burgess's work with the *Red Man* certainly suggests that, at times, students may have received a range of messages about gender beyond what they learned in the classroom or experienced from the disciplinarian.[144]

As the school elevated female domesticity and subordination, it paid particular attention to the students' conception of family. Burgess might have celebrated the "new woman," but the school newspaper disparaged Indigenous customs in marriage. In an 1896 article, it reported on a "strange Indian custom," where the groom would actively avoid his father-in-law.[145] The article states,

"It seems that among these Indians, the act of marriage—I should perhaps have said 'the imaginary act,'—places between the bridegroom on the one side, and the parent of the bride on the other, an impassable barrier."[146] According to the teaching that students received at Carlisle, only those joined by Christian doctrine were "really" married. Only a Christian wedding based on "civilized" ideals ensured a proper family.

Pratt's vision of racial progress, in a very real sense, depended upon the family. The school newspaper warned male students about marrying a woman incapable of providing a "civilizing" influence upon them or their children. An 1892 article in the *Indian Helper* placed this in explicitly racial terms, demanding that male students avoid the lure of "the dusky maids of his tribe."[147] According to this piece, the allure of the tribal woman was appealing for the "uncivilized" Indian, but Carlisle-educated men should select an educated partner.[148] He would prove his self-control by choosing a woman educated in femininity and domesticity and denying himself the sexual freedom that students learned to associate with Indigenous women not exposed to a proper education.

If men learned to choose domestically virtuous women, female students were taught to select a responsible man who could provide for a family. An 1892 article in the *Indian Helper* included a sad bulletin about a recently deceased former student who "married a husband who was not able to support her and becoming ill was obliged to end her days in the county poor-house."[149] The short piece suggests that the woman had chosen poorly and died because of it. Only by demonstrating the ability to support a family could a male student hope to marry a "civilized" woman.

To conflate self-support and manhood with earning power, Carlisle introduced a pay scale based on gender. On their first outing, students earned very little: one dollar per month for the girls and two for the boys. In these cases, the patron paid for board and transport. As the students became more experienced, their pay increased. The highest wage for a male student was seventeen dollars per month. By comparison, only one female student earned the maximum twelve dollars and fifty cents a month.[150] The pay discrepancy has little to do with the value of their labor. Both field work and household work are essential on a farm. Instead, by paying male students more, the outing program sent a clear message that only men should be family providers. With this expectation, the outing program established clear roles within a patriarchal family with the male, working in the public sphere, responsible for money and the woman completely reliant upon her husband for survival.[151]

Pratt firmly believed that Protestant "civilization" also inspired good health. In 1888 he reported on a group of Apache students who arrived at Carlisle, writing that they were at "a very low ebb physically."[152] To Pratt, Apache society, which he considered savage, gave them a "naturally weak constitution."[153] In fact, away from Apache and other Indigenous societies, both tuberculosis and trachoma ravaged the student populations at Carlisle due to unsanitary living conditions and close quarters.[154] Today one can find 186 headstones in the cemetery next to what was the Carlisle Indian School campus along Claremont Road. Many memorialize people who died from tuberculosis. Researcher Preston McBride has concluded that the actual number of students who died at Carlisle was about five hundred, most having been sent home when they became ill in order to reduce the toll attributed to school administration.[155]

Nevertheless, Pratt believed that he could improve student health through military exercises. He had students march on a daily basis, arguing that it provided, "a means of physical training and giving habits of prompt, unquestioning obedience."[156] Not only did marching improve student health, but it also taught subservience to authority figures. Soon after Carlisle opened, Pratt also had a gymnasium constructed on campus.[157] Aside from the competitive sports played by the school athletes, the gymnasium allowed students to participate in gymnastics and other non-competitive activities. Such an approach allowed non-athletic students to maintain their fitness, although such indoor exercise also undoubtedly helped to spread disease. As much as promoting health, gymnastic exercises taught control over the body. Pratt believed that physical education steered students away from laziness and sexual immorality. He wrote, "Busy people are generally long lived. Active exercise of brain and muscle, provided it not be excessive, is the life of life."[158]

Carlisle promoted the "civilized" manly ideal for its Indigenous students, but like G. Stanley Hall, Pratt also believed that elite white men should not reject their masculine traits entirely. In 1902 Reverend Dr. Moss gave a speech to the student body on the "square man." In describing the ideals of manhood, Moss laid out a square of four distinct qualities: courtesy, thoroughness, reverence, and manliness, consistent with the Protestant ideal of manly self-control.[159] In response, Pratt stated that "a man must be more than a square." Using an example of an Irish worker who struck his employer, Pratt argued that violence could be used to maintain order. The employer, "struck the Irishman a blow that knocked him down, and then he dragged him to the head of the stairs to throw him down, but was hindered by others interfering."[160]

Pratt might not have endorsed excessive violence, but he certainly believed that the employer had a right to self-defense. The Irish worker had challenged the social order by attacking his socially superior employer. Perhaps the employer should not have come so close to murdering his worker, but to Pratt, he needed to react violently in order to maintain power. When the power of the employer's "civilized" manliness was compromised, it became necessary for him to demonstrate superiority over the Irishman.[161] Pratt portrayed the working-class immigrant in his story very much as he might an Indian on the frontier: violent, overly masculine, and in need of discipline.[162] Conversely, the employer needed to use his masculinity to defend "civilization" and his manhood.

When Pratt accepted retaliatory masculinity, he reflected changes in the definition of white "civilization" and manhood. In a letter to the recently inaugurated President Roosevelt, Pratt included a note stating, "I believe in your Strenuous Life."[163] Toward the end of his tenure, Pratt became increasingly concerned about the manhood of some students. Pratt's statement that a man needed to be "more than a square" suggests that he had grown to believe in the need for masculinity to guarantee manhood.[164] Yet Pratt also

Manhood at Carlisle

understood the problems of implementing masculinity: Indian students could not be violent without being accused of savagery.

In a plea for subscribers in 1896, an anonymous author in the *Indian Helper* wrote: "Millions of people think of the Indian as a wild, paint-besmeared, feather-bedecked savage. The Carlisle Indian is rising into manhood and womanhood, and we want everyone to KNOW it. Help us to exterminate the scalping, howling, paint debaubed [*sic*] buffalo bill Indian from the minds of the people and to spread the information that the native American is a man" (capitals in original).[165] According to this piece, the "buffalo bill" Indian was not a man. Carlisle placed manhood in a simplified equation: "civilization" resulted in manhood, savagery did not. It did not matter what particular aspect of "civilization" the Carlisle man adopted. As long as Pratt was in charge, the Protestant student, a member of the YMCA, deserved to be treated as a man, and a Carlisle education established the student's manhood.

In 1904 Pratt resigned from his position as superintendent at Carlisle. In many respects, the institution's ideological focus blurred after his departure. As K. Tsianina Lomawaima has argued, it is also important not to exaggerate his influence upon the federal Indian boarding school system, or upon federal policy for Indigenous Americans. Pratt arrogantly believed that American Indians existed at a plane of "civilization" below that of European Americans, and as a school superintendent, he was rigid and authoritarian. The federal government did develop a system of twenty-five federally operated Indian boarding schools that generally followed Carlisle's model. Yet Pratt constantly battled with the federal Indian service. Not everyone in the government even entertained the possibility that a federally funded educational institution had the capability to uplift Indigenous Americans to a higher level of "civilization." In fact, the Office of Indian Affairs for much of Pratt's tenure at Carlisle focused mostly upon making sure that Indians obeyed the federal government.

A strong believer in the Fourteenth Amendment to the United States Constitution, he saw the school's function as that of preparing its students for citizenship and the political equality that it would engender. Pratt never questioned that the United States, as a settler colonial nation, had the right to seize Indigenous peoples' lands, but unlike the Office of Indian Affairs, he envisioned a future in which Indians could be equal citizens. Particularly during his last years at Carlisle, this is not a position that many in the federal government shared.[166] Yet as much as Pratt rejected biological racial doctrines of his era, theories that ran counter to his uplift agenda, he based his ideas about "civilization" upon fundamentally racist assumptions of European cultural superiority.

One can easily find examples of students who appreciated Pratt's missionary zeal, but they did not speak as one. The histories of Indian boarding schools brim with stories of student rebellion and resistance to their cultural annihilation. Indian boarding school students spoke their Native languages, committed arson, and engaged in collective uprisings.[167] In many cases this was a form of survival. Students found that non-fatal resistance made their passage through boarding schools slightly less traumatic. Although the students at Carlisle challenged authority in many different ways, one of the more noticeable involved running away. In her study of the Carlisle school, Genevieve Bell used student records to obtain an accurate portrayal of the runaways. She discovered that the vast majority of runners were male, with only a handful of female students deciding to flee.[168] In 1901, Pratt reported as well that boys made up the majority of those who tended to run away.[169]

Pratt considered running away as an affront to the "civilizing" attempts of Carlisle.[170] He recommended strict punishment for runners and their families: the withdrawal of rations from family members until the errant student returned. The runner would also be enrolled in a semi-reformatory school situated on an isolated island.[171] Such extreme proposals revealed the extent of this problem at Carlisle: Pratt excluded such students from "civilization." He blamed the reservation schools for Carlisle's runaway problem. According to him, the reservation school did not sufficiently punish runners.[172] He interpreted their actions as a demonstration of the runners' reverence for savagery. Pratt did not even consider the idea that Carlisle was an awful place for students who missed their family. Instead, he interpreted their actions as evidence of weakness in the face of "civilization," and as being, by extension, unmanly.

In his 1901 annual report he described runaways as following "a nice little lark."[173] Pratt represented their behavior as childish, something only to fill their free time. Through infantilization, Pratt denied the runners any form of manhood. By implication, the runners were not "men" but children, too immature to internalize manly "civilization."[174] The act of running away also demonstrated a lack of self-control over savagery. Pratt argued that a "civilized" student remained at Carlisle, completed his immersion, and emerged with an education and manhood. Pratt's own autobiography recalled an incident involving a pair of male runaways that demonstrates how students might have had their own interpretations for their actions. The two had been arrested by a chief of police and returned to Carlisle. On their arrival, Pratt questioned them as to the cause of their disappearance. The first, James, replied that a lack of food caused him to flee. The second, John, gave a more forthright answer: "I just wanted to let you know I wasn't stuck on your durned old school!"[175] Through such a reply, John claimed agency over his future. While "stuck" at Carlisle, John was forced to acquiesce to white authority. By running away, he attempted to demonstrate his power over his own life.

The Carlisle Indian school aimed to indoctrinate the male students with a version of "civilized" manhood drawn from American society during the Victorian era. Students could affirm their manhood in several different ways: through their self-control, their acceptance of Protestant morality, dominance over femininity, or their ability to earn a living. They learned that becoming "civilized" meant conforming to such gender roles. As long as students were "civilized" in some fashion, they could claim manhood. Yet Carlisle also taught its male students to accept life on level of society below that of their white counterparts, their education limited to the working-class trades, and their citizenship granted only after white oversight and surveillance. While Pratt expressed an evangelical belief that any Indigenous American could become the next Carlos Montezuma, he provided an education that ensured most students would spend their lives as struggling workers. Meanwhile, male students like Delos Lone Wolf walked a tightrope between Christian manly responsibility and masculine toughness, joining organizations like the school's chapter of the YMCA, while also playing football, a violent and immensely popular sport among college students across the United States. His story provides an appropriate introduction to the relationships between gender, race, and "civilization" that were so important to the story of the Carlisle Indian Industrial School's football team.

2

Playing White Men, 1893–1903

D uring an 1897 debate on the Indian appropriations bill, Congressman Nathan Oakes Murphy (R-AZ) protested against Congress continuing to fund the Carlisle Indian School, claiming that the institution's assimilationist goals were a foolish waste of government revenue. "Every Apache who was educated in the East and who returned to his reservation is wearing a breechclout today," he said. Congressman Charles Henry Grosvenor (R-OH) responded by commenting on Carlisle's football team. "Have not the Indians developed great powers in football?" he said. "And is not football considered in our modern colleges the highest level of culture and civilization?"[1] According to reports, the entire chamber laughed in support. The laughter of the United States House of Representatives notwithstanding, Rep. Grosvenor very adeptly demonstrated the serious role of sports, and of football in particular, within the Carlisle Indian School. Richard Henry Pratt would find no more powerful symbol of the school's success (and, ultimately, the school's critics would find no more sensationally treacherous exhibit of its corruption) than its celebrated football team. Pratt used football to earn revenue for the school. He used football to gain publicity for the school. But most important, he used football to demonstrate to the world that the Carlisle Indian Industrial School was accomplishing what Genevieve Bell has argued was its most central mission, to give "the American public a new kind of Indian."[2] Pratt used football to exhibit potently what he believed to be his successful metamorphosing of Indigenous males into what elite whites considered to be men.

Football ended up becoming the most recognized feature of

the Carlisle Indian School. As Barbara Landis has written of Carlisle's most famous players, "They are the names that bring a kind of magic to Carlisle, because they were larger than life, performing legendary feats."[3] Yet, considering the impact of football at Carlisle, the school's leaders often struggled to control what football meant to the school and to its assimilationist project. In fact, Pratt exhibited a deep reluctance to allow his students an opportunity even to play the game. According to his memoirs, he did so only as a concession to students who demanded it, and under strict conditions that he hoped would frame the sport in a productive way.

In his autobiography, *Battlefield and Classroom*, Pratt tells the story of how he ended up allowing students to form an interscholastic football squad. He writes that in 1892, Stacy Matlock (Pawnee) suffered a broken leg in a football match against the local Dickinson College. Pratt accompanied Matlock to the local hospital and helped set the leg.[4] In a similar instance the same year, Paul Shattuck/Zauitzela (Laguna) shattered his collarbone in a "fiendish football game."[5] Pratt writes that both instances persuaded him success in football required an unacceptable level of brutality and aggression. He subsequently outlawed all external matches, but he soon changed his mind, citing an extraordinary instance in which he bent to the will of his students, particularly considering his own authoritarian style of leadership. Pratt remembers that forty male students, who evidently enjoyed football despite possible injury, came to him, upset by his decision. They engaged the school's champion orator to persuade Pratt to reinstate the football team. Listening silently, Pratt was convinced by the "genius" of this forensic master's argument. He relented to the students' demand on two conditions:

First, that you will never, under any circumstances, slug. That you will play fair straight through, and if the other fellows slug you will in no case return it. Can't you see that if you slug, people who are looking on will say, "There, that's the Indian of it. Just see them. They are savages and you can't get it out of them." . . . My other condition is this. That, in the course of two, three, or four years you will develop your strength and ability to such a degree that you will whip the biggest football team in the country.[6]

The students considered his conditions and agreed to both. This promise of fair play and victory over white colleges was the foundation for football's reintroduction and continuation at Carlisle.

Pratt's first demand reinforced a strict level of manly self-control, idealized through the rejection of "slugging." Pratt clearly saw that football's violent character actually presented him with a remarkable opportunity. If students could behave in a controlled and gentlemanly fashion on the field during a physically brutal football game, he could demonstrate that Indigenous people could become "civilized" men. If they could actually beat the most elite of white men on the gridiron, American Indian students could prove that they were indeed equal to their white counterparts.[7] Young white college men attending Ivy League universities had turned football into a popular sensation by performing their own masculine "savagery" and, in their minds, racial superiority.[8] Pratt needed his players to strike a completely opposite stance, something that would prove to be very difficult to balance. Although Pratt demanded a clashing combination of sportsmanship, self-control, and gamesmanship, he saw the athletes' masculinity as secondary to their manliness.[9] This left Carlisle players vulnerable to violence from opposing players without any recourse.[10]

As Gail Bederman illustrates, middle-class and elite white men who embraced masculinity in the late nineteenth century directly tied their new ideas about gender to race. Thinkers like G. Stanley Hall and Teddy Roosevelt deeply believed that white men needed to elevate their physical fitness in order to dominate races whom they considered to be "primitive."[11] It should come as no surprise that only thirteen African American students played college football before 1900, and only twenty-seven between 1900 and 1914.[12] When white college men played football in the late nineteenth century, they most often downplayed their "civilized" manhood and performed their most "savage" masculinity, often in order to feel emboldened as white men. As articulated by W. Cameron Forbes, Harvard's coach in 1898 and 1899, football embodied "the expression of strength of the Anglo-Saxon. It is the dominant spirit of a dominant race, and to this it owes its popularity and its hope of permanence."[13] Or, as Yale's Professor Eugene Richards wrote in 1895 in the *Yale Medical Journal*, "For a virile race, like the Anglo-Saxon, the dangerous sports have always had the greatest fascination, because they call for just those qualities which make that race the dominant race of the world. Foot-ball is one of these sports."[14] The men who saw football as a way of preparing their elite white brethren for racial dominance represented some of the most powerful institutions of their time. Walter Camp, the "father" of American football, quoted Richards in his writing. Reading their thoughts about the game, one can clearly understand that when Carlisle played Harvard or Yale or any other college team of white players, they had to play under a different set of rules than their white counterparts.[15] As long as Carlisle played under Pratt, they were expected to prove their manliness and status as equals by behaving like gentlemen, while Ivy League opponents sought to prove their masculinity and their racial dominance by behaving like "savages."

Not only did elite thinkers like Hall and Richards identify football with ideas of masculinity and manhood, but as Michael Oriard has observed, journalists and coaches of the late nineteenth century also infused their discussions of the sport with gender, race, and narratives of "civilization's" competition with savagery.[16] Some, like Camp, emphasized the tactical aspects of the sport and framed football manhood as managerial. As a running back for Yale between 1876 and 1882, and its unofficial coach for the following thirty years, Camp developed the rules that became the universal standard for college football. He saw the sport as preparation for a future career in American industry, and believed football equipped the athletes with a "manly personality," which primed the players, especially the captain and coach, to process tactical situations quickly, dispense orders, and acquire loyalty. He saw football as preparing college men for careers as managers in the burgeoning American industrial complex. As Carlisle players began to win games, he attributed their success to the scientific training of their white coach.[17]

Journalist and writer Caspar Whitney, who named the first All-American football team for *Harper's* magazine, believed that the American ruling class had become too feminized. Like Hall, he believed that "civilization" served as a metric of elite white supremacy, yet he also feared that it made men soft. To counteract such anxiety, Whitney openly approved of football's violence by asking the reader to contemplate "a race of Americans fearful of bagging its trousers or of sustaining a few bruises."[18] Writing in *Harper's* and in *Outing*, Whitney infrequently wrote about Carlisle, and when he did, he struck a patronizing and dismissive tone. When Carlisle narrowly lost to Princeton in 1899, Whitney attributed the outcome to "a question of race." He wrote, "The Indian has not an alert mind, the white man has, and whenever the two are otherwise evenly matched, the latter is sure to win. It is destiny." For Whitney and his loyal readers a game against Carlisle was a test of racial supremacy with profound implications.[19]

Some of football's pioneers, like University of Chicago coach Amos Alonzo Stagg, downplayed the sport's violence, and instead celebrated it for the same reasons that Pratt embraced the game: its emphasis on discipline, hierarchy, and adherence to rules. Some, like the University of Minnesota's coach, Henry Williams, aligned their football philosophy with the burgeoning "Muscular Christianity" movement.[20] Evangelical proponents of football, like Williams, considered football's violence a necessary evil to regenerate manly character and repeatedly emphasized the game's combination of physical manliness and retaliatory morality. As such, Christian writers differentiated between compulsory roughness, which was inescapable within football, and unnecessary brutality.[21] The manly athlete demonstrated his morality and self-control by understanding this distinction.

Carlisle authorities chose to mirror the Christian narrative of manhood. The Christian narrative conflated on-field behavior with Protestant ideals and manhood, and Pratt further connected the actions of Carlisle football players to a broader definition of "civilization." By mimicking the wider narrative of Christian manliness, the players' model of manhood emphasized the demonstration of "civilization" through morality, self-control, and victory. Yet adherence to the morality of muscular Christianity did not necessarily offer Carlisle's players the respect that Pratt desired. As Brian Ingrassia has shown, football commentators of the game's formative era overtly associated Christian grace and fair play with whiteness.[22]

Despite commentators' laudatory claims of manliness, football was still a brutal sport, particularly among the major Eastern colleges. Only a year after football was reintroduced at Carlisle, an 1894 game between Harvard and Yale was notoriously brutal and was later called "the Bloody Battle of Hampden Field." Yale's Frank Butterworth had his eye gouged, while Frank Hinkey used his knee to shatter Edgar Wrightington's collarbone.[23] The much-sensationalized "flying wedge," where the entire team would build a triangle around the ball carrier, became representative of football's brutality. By the 1890s football games had begun to result in on-field deaths or serious injuries. Between 1893 and 1902, three deaths occurred on the gridiron, which rose to ten in 1909 alone, while 2 percent of players were seriously injured.[24] Football had begun to resemble war. For Pratt, a victory on the field might represent a successful battle, but ultimate victory would only come if he could persuade spectators that the Carlisle athletes were "civilized" men.

The school media promoted Pratt's demand for clean play and manly behavior after football's reintroduction at Carlisle. In 1895, just after Carlisle had begun to play a schedule against outside schools, the *Red Man* reprinted blurbs from articles in local newspapers about the football team's performances. A number of them described Carlisle's victory over the Duquesne County and Athletic Club. The *Pittsburg [sic] Dispatch* wrote, "Those Indian football kickers from Carlisle scalped the chaps of the Duquesne Country and Athletic Club Yesterday," but went on to say, "The Indians are particularly clean and fair players."[25] A blurb reprinted from the *Pittsburgh Post* hit the same tone, the writer saying that the Duquesne team "struck a tribe of the tamest wild men that ever drew a scalping knife or took to the warpath. There were no guttural sounds or lowering glances to be heard or seen. The Indians played good, clean ball, and had the spectators with them almost from the start."[26] Another piece from the *Bulletin* asserted, "The Indian has been, locally, subject to elevation by the doings of full-blooded Indians on the football field. These young men, descended from the dusky race of crafty, scalp raising, indolent tribes that are fast disappearing, have put up as clean a game of football as was ever witnessed. The entire absence of 'toughness' in the play, the manly and courteous qualities of the young men from the Indian School at Carlisle have set an example well worthy the following by American youth."[27] The *Red Man*'s own report stated, "The game was one of the cleanest ever played. . . . The [Carlisle] boys won many friends by their gentlemanly playing and their good plays received most generous applause from the crowd."

The editors reprinted excerpts from several other articles about the Carlisle team, focusing as much on behavior as on performance, and using blatantly racist language that mocks the Carlisle players. Excerpted articles described a 36–0 loss to the University of Pennsylvania in remarkably positive terms, writing that Carlisle played impressive defense but also "acted courteously throughout," that they played a game "free from objectionable features," and that their tackles "were all fair." These articles described Carlisle's players in racial terms that undercut any idea of readers looking at them as men fully equal to their white opponents. Even when complimentary, one sportswriter excerpted in the *Red Man* attributed Carlisle's success to inherited traits rather than hard work and preparation, writing, "If all Indians can play foot-ball like the boys from Carlisle Training School, foot-ball is bred in the Red Man."[28]

Carlisle's clean play and sportsmanship were most famously challenged in an 1896 game at Manhattan Field in New York against Yale. During the game Jacob Jamison (Seneca) had broken through the Yale line, dodged an opposing player, run for the end zone, and scored a touchdown. As Jamison struggled through the line of scrimmage, however, the referee blew his whistle, declaring that

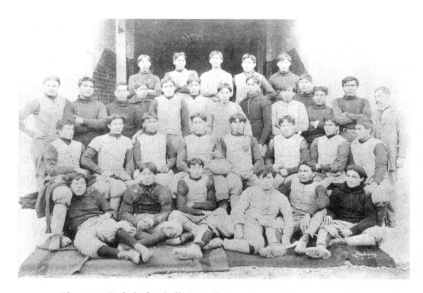

FIG. 3. The 1896 Carlisle football team. Sportswriters who witnessed this team's loss to Yale believed that they had been robbed by a poor call from the official, Carlisle's own coach William Hickock. These same writers praised this team for its manly sportsmanship in response to the unjust ruling on the field. Photograph courtesy of the Cumberland County Historical Society, Carlisle, Pennsylvania.

Yale had stopped Jamison's forward progress. During this era it was common for each team's coach to participate in the game as a referee, yet the umpire who negated Jamison's touchdown was not Yale's coach but Carlisle's William O. Hickok, who also happened to be a former player for Yale. To reporters at the game, it appeared that Hickok himself almost immediately realized that the decision was incorrect, but Yale's players convinced the umpire Josh Hartwell to call the play back because the whistle had blown the play dead. Unsurprisingly, the Carlisle players and the crowd, who were chanting for Carlisle, were outraged at the judgment. The score finished 12–6 in favor of Yale, Carlisle losing by exactly one touchdown.[29] Such was the outrage over the incident that the *New York Sun* compared Hickok's betrayal of his own team to a corrupt reservation agent and proclaimed that "they had a right to trust him just as many a time the Indians at an agency have

Playing White Men

believed they could trust the Government agent in whose charge they lived. And just as many an agent has proved false to his trust so this referee was to his."[30]

Prior to the game, a writer for the *New York World* described Yale's team as "the perfection of modern athletics and intellectually the culture and refinement of the best modern American life" and described the typical Carlisle player as "the real son of the forest and plain."[31] Ultimately, reporters seemed convinced that it was Carlisle that demonstrated true manly comportment. In his memoirs, Pratt takes credit in the narrative of events that he constructs. According to his version, the players were adamant about leaving the field following Hickok's decision. Sensing the situation was spiraling out of control, Pratt claims that he ran down to the field and persuaded the athletes to play on. Pratt writes that despite his entreaties, Jamison refused to return to the field and argued that it "was as fair a touchdown as was ever made, and it belongs to us." Pratt, realizing Jamison's intransigence, called on the athlete's school spirit and manhood. "Go back and do your best and wait for tomorrow morning's papers," Pratt remembers saying, "and you will find that you are a bigger man because the touchdown was denied than you would be if it had been allowed. Now go and help the boys keep Carlisle at the top."[32] Pratt reports that he convinced Jamison, who then returned to the gridiron.

Pratt tells a compelling story, but it does not exactly match what the *New York Times* reported the day after this incident. In their report, Hickok, after realizing his mistake, told the umpire and opposing coach that Carlisle would leave the field if the touchdown were not allowed. After he lost his appeal, it was Hickok who had to return to his players and convince them to continue with their play. There is no mention of Pratt running onto the field, successfully calling on his players to continue.[33]

Regardless of whether Pratt's version of this story is true, it shows that he worried about the possible damage to the school's public image if the players left the field. He wanted to show that he had successfully elevated his students into "civilized" manliness, that he was elevating his young Indians to a higher moral plane. Pratt surely cared less about the actual players than he did about the incident's negative impact upon Carlisle's reputation. If the players' had left the field, their rebellion against white authority would surely have dominated media reports, which had already questioned their "civilization" and manhood. Pratt clearly saw it as more important to display the success of Carlisle's "civilizing" mission than to demonstrate that his players could beat Yale. According to Pratt, Jamison was a "bigger man" for continuing with the game. Ultimately, Pratt presents himself as the true hero of the story, for he saved the day by descending upon the Carlisle bench with his inspirational pep talk. As such, Pratt's narrative revealed his belief that the players' sportsmanship, "civilization," and manhood were only maintained via white oversight.

The Yale game illustrated how hard it would be for Carlisle's players to fulfill the second of Pratt's conditions for the football team: victory over the best white colleges. When Vance McCormick, an ex-Yale player, arrived to coach the team in 1894, he discovered a group of enthusiastic but inexperienced athletes. Pratt writes that at one point while trying to teach players how to fall properly on a loose football, McCormick, without removing his hat or coat, threw himself into the mud of a rain-drenched field to demonstrate proper technique. A significant amount of training was evidently needed if Carlisle was to defeat any of the Big Four (Harvard, Pennsylvania, Princeton, and Yale) within Pratt's self-imposed timeframe.[34]

Yet the Yale game was not the only time that Carlisle would come close. On November 6, 1897, Carlisle took a 10–8 lead into halftime against a Pennsylvania team that ended the season with fifteen wins and no losses or ties. Carlisle ultimately lost by a score of 20–10, but the close call against another of the top football universities merited the attention of the *Indian Helper*'s "Man in the Bandstand," an anonymous regular column that, as Jacqueline Fear-Segal has pointed out, was actually written by Marianna Burgess, the supervisor of school publications.[35] Burgess states forthrightly that as a fierce and violent game, football offered Carlisle a potent tool with which it could propagandize its mission. She writes,

There has been with many an uneasy kind of feeling that in these fierce contests Indian savagery might burst out and make things unpleasant in more ways than one for their opponents. But the Carlisle team has been thoroughly tested, and no such tendency has appeared. It plays the game for all it is worth, but it never loses its head, and is invariably as safe and dependable as any college team that could be named. Incidentally, this is a high tribute to the institution from which it comes; it shows that Carlisle has succeeded in civilizing these wards of the nation in other ways than book-learning.[36]

Nevertheless, while Pratt might have prioritized player behavior over performance, he needed his team to win in order to demonstrate progress. In a 1902 speech following a victory over Cornell, Pratt celebrated the event by conflating victory and "civilization," saying, "When we began playing universities, they said, 'The Indians can't beat us. They haven't got the head.' But you see the heads of the Cornell team did not keep them from losing yesterday. They have more respect for us now than they had yesterday." Pratt obviously enjoyed the event and interpreted Carlisle's victory as verification of his ideas on assimilation. He took the analysis a step further, saying, "Pennsylvania is more anxious now than Cornell was, and I shouldn't wonder if even Harvard is beginning to meditate seriously. The lesson of it all is that now after long practice and struggle we are admitted into the upper-tendom of football."[37]

During the early years of Carlisle football, school publications first developed narratives that reconciled gentlemanly "civilization" with competitive ambitions. Following a victory over Duquesne Athletic Club in 1895, the school newspaper, the *Indian Helper*, featured a cartoon and commentary that shrewdly contained a desire for victory on the football battlefield within a larger story of "civilization." The cartoon, entitled "Revenge!" features a smiling Carlisle player in uniform holding a ball in one hand while waving a banner in the other displaying the score, "Carlisle 16 Duq. Club 4." His foot rests upon the stomach of a frowning Duquesne player who raises his left hand up as if to ask for mercy. Above the Duquesne player's head is the contemporary year, "1895." On each side of the Carlisle player are images in round bubbles. To the upper left is a frontiersman in leather stocking attire and coon skin cap pointing the barrel of a rifle at a dark skinned Indian wearing a loincloth and two feathers on his head, kneeling on one knee, begging for his life. To the lower right is a victorious Carlisle player being carried off the field by adoring white fans. The commentary below the cartoon states that Duquesne player Charles Payne drew the image and sent it to Carlisle player David McFarland (Nez Pierce) the day after Carlisle's win. The author deftly turns an image of Indigenous reprisal into a message of assimilation.

> A hundred years have passed and the Indian comes out on top. If he can do it at foot-ball, he can do it in the arts and sciences. All he needs is a fair chance, and Carlisle is fast opening the way. He will always be at the mercy of the whites (as shown in the view in the left circle) as long as he is penned in on reservations or in any way encouraged to cling together in ignorant masses. The whites know that. . . . Carlisle has shown repeatedly and for a thousand times has proclaimed the truth that all the Indians want is a chance to lift THEMSELVES up, and then like the boy in the right circle the multitudes will carry them along. 'Revenge,' is written below the illustration, but it is a cheerful if determined revenge.[38]

Even though one might justifiably interpret this cartoon as celebrating Indigenous retribution for the violence of settler conquest, the commentary portrays it very differently. According to the *Indian Helper*, Carlisle actually defeated white domination by showing that its students could win at a white sport. By winning a football game, Carlisle students successfully embraced "civilization."

According to the *Indian Helper* report, Charles Payne included a note accompanying his cartoon, stating, "From one of the many friends you boys have made here by your gentlemanly playing." While Pratt, the popular press, and school publications might have celebrated Carlisle's gentlemanly restraint, it is much less clear that this is what students most fondly remembered about football and sports at Carlisle. As we will see, after 1904, when Pratt was forced to step down as superintendent, the team became much less concerned with performing "civilized" behavior and much more focused upon winning. Former students interviewed as part of oral history projects conducted decades after Carlisle closed often mention the football team's glory years of the teens, and their star players who received international fame, like Jim Thorpe. Charlie "Hobo" Atsye (Laguna), who arrived at Carlisle in 1913, remembers playing football on the second team, called the "Hot Shots," with Jim Thorpe. "The Indians were real good," he remembers. "Always beating the whites."[39] A woman identified as Mrs. George Serracino remembers of her parents, "The reason why we think they liked Carlisle so much is because there were many students attending Carlisle who made a name for themselves in sports. They are proud to have known and have gone to the same school where such great names as Jim Thorpe, Gus Welch, and Frank Hudson went to school."[40] Asked about the Carlisle football team, John Alonzo (Laguna) said he still had a photograph of the players and could name every one. He proudly stated, "I know practically all of the football players that played on that squad."[41] None of these students proudly recalled the gentlemanly comportment with which Carlisle's football team conducted itself. The football team that they remember won, and they liked that.[42]

On the other hand, David McFarland, the Carlisle football player who received the "Revenge" cartoon in the mail, and played left half-back during the infamous 1896 loss to Yale, lived a life that Pratt might have celebrated as one of exemplary virtuous manhood. His student file reveals that he was one of the few who actually graduated, matriculating after seven years at the age of twenty-one. After he left, however, he returned to his reservation in Idaho, something that Pratt would not have condoned. Yet he faithfully returned surveys that Carlisle sent out to former students, and in these, he indicated his struggles, his successes, and his feelings toward his old school. In one letter, for example, after discussing his new job training to be an assistant cashier at Fort Lapwai State Bank, he finished by writing, "I got to be honest and true and wish to be remembered by my friends all that knew me at Carlisle, as one of the old member of the foot player." In a letter to the superintendent in 1910, he articulated the manly values that Pratt would have wanted him to internalize as a football player. He wrote, "If I done nothing good towards the school I have done this much, I live up the school discipline and all what I've learned. I have many failures but I'll try to be true, trustful, in all my duties whatever I do. . . . If I done anything wrong towards this school or when I was as a student, I regret. At present I am clerking one of our stores in our reservation." In the last survey that he filled out, he reported that he had married, briefly attended the University of Idaho, had worked as a real estate agent, and owned about $800 worth of property—including two framed houses, eight work horses, five cows, two hundred and forty acres of land, and $400 in savings. He also reported that he volunteered as a Sunday school teacher. In answer to the final survey question asking him to report additional news of interest, MacFarland wrote, "Most interesting in my life that I been living against the liquor and live the rulings of institution discipline Carlisle Indian School."[43]

While MacFarland certainly seemed to embrace Pratt's image of virtuous manhood, he never experienced his team beating any of the top universities that Pratt dreamed Carlisle might defeat. Until the very end of the late nineteenth century, Carlisle had only beaten second tier universities, small colleges, and athletic clubs. Football writers like Caspar Whitney doubted whether Carlisle could ever achieve victory over Harvard, Princeton, Yale, or any other team of their caliber. As Michael Oriard has observed, Whitney saw Carlisle as capable physically, but lacking in the intelligence required to defeat teams in college football's elite.[44] He wrote, "It is easy to see how they [Carlisle] can stand the knocks and bruises of the play, but if Walter Camp has diagnosed football properly, it is the sport of all sports in which muscle cannot win over brains." He portrayed Carlisle as over-reliant on bodily strength, concluding that white teams could use their cunning to defeat the Indians easily. "Criss-crosses, round-the-end plays, fake kicks and all the other tactical maneuvres [sic] of a University eleven," he wrote,

Playing White Men

"cannot be foreseen and prevented by men who have only physical strength at their command."[45] Influenced by white assumptions of Indian inferiority, Whitney acknowledged that the Carlisle players possessed the necessary masculinity for victory but doubted whether the team had the intellectual capacity to defeat the Big Four. When Pratt attributed Carlisle's victory over Cornell to their "head," he pointedly defended his mission at Carlisle, one that saw victory as a demonstration of intelligence and "civilization."

Whitney believed that trick plays were another measurement of "civilization" that Carlisle could not match. The "University elevens," predominantly all-white, all performed trick plays, which Whitney described demonstrating intelligence and white "civilization." Whitney doubted that Carlisle could outwit an opponent using misdirection and sleights of hand. When describing the success of Carlisle's 1899 football season, he wrote, "If the present Carlisle team, which is composed of veterans of long experience, had the strategy and the capacity for quickly meeting emergencies, it would challenge the very leaders of the season. But it is a question of race."[46] Basing his assessment on the idea of a structured and unchanging racial hierarchy and the strict racial segregation of college football, Whitney's statement indicated a belief that Indians were naturally incapable of intelligent play. In Whitney's mind, the Indian player did not have power over his mind as he was unable to outwit the white opponent quickly. Whitney argued that white players, by comparison, possessed superior history and "civilization," and were intelligent enough to overwhelm Carlisle's inferior minds easily. For Whitney, Indian football players were "destined" to lose.

In his writing Whitney not only disseminated the views of "scientific racism" that predominated in public life in the late nineteenth century, but he also attacked the assumptions upon which Pratt had founded the Carlisle Indian Industrial School. Pratt based his entire enterprise upon a public declaration that Indigenous Americans were as intellectually capable as whites. As Jacqueline Fear-Segal has demonstrated, Pratt, ironically, paid no respect toward the immense diversity of nations, languages, and cultures that comprised Indigenous America, and therefore dealt with Native American populations on purely racial terms.[47] Yet Whitney's writings demonstrate that whenever Carlisle took the field against a white opponent (as it did pretty much every week), more was at stake for Pratt than just a football game. Every victory potentially validated Pratt's mission.

If intelligence on the football field was measured in trick plays, the appointment of Glenn "Pop" Warner as coach was a step in the right direction. The previous coaches, McCormick, Hickok, William T. Bull, and John A. Hall, had all employed "straight football." This involved hitting the opposition's defensive line in the center or at the ends without the use of misdirection and trick plays. This choice of straight football was hardly surprising as all these coaches had played in this style for Yale during a period when mass plays were the standard.[48] Some commentators praised Carlisle for this style of play. After her column about Carlisle's 1897 loss to Pennsylvania, Burgess includes a newspaper blurb that states, "The Indians played straight, old-fashioned football most of the time. That is to say, they did not parley with fancy and new-fangled tricks."[49] Such a statement invokes the masculinity and violence of straight football while also feminizing trick-plays as the last resort of the weak and feeble "man." Yet this approach also reaffirmed the wider conception of Indian physicality over intelligence, which thereby undermined Carlisle's main reason for playing football. If the players did not perform the simplest of trick plays like their white opponents, there was little chance of commentators admitting that Carlisle players were intellectual enough to compete at football.

After his 1899 appointment as athletic director, Warner introduced a collection of intelligent trick plays to Carlisle's tactics, thus allowing the athletes to argue that their intelligence, and consequently their "civilization," was equal to that of whites. Although Warner demonstrated an array of misdirection and tricks throughout his coaching career, one incident during his Carlisle tenure is worthy of recollection.[50] During a game against Harvard in 1903 the Native players employed the "hidden ball" trick. Harvard started the second half by kicking to the Carlisle quarterback, Jimmie Johnson (Stockbridge), who was then quickly surrounded by the entire team. Suddenly, the players broke in every different direction, each clutching his stomach. Assuming he was the ball-carrier, the Harvard players all attempted to tackle Johnson. Little did they know that the ball had been placed in the back of Charles Dillon's (Dakota) jersey. The maneuver completely outwitted the Harvard players' intellect. No one on the Crimson side realized what had happened until Dillon scored a touchdown. Even though Harvard won 12–11, the media reports were full of praise for Carlisle's ingenious trick. The report of the game in the *Boston Sunday-Post*, reprinted in the next week's edition of the *Red Man and Helper*, noted that Harvard players were physically larger than Carlisle's. "Outweighed by fully fifteen pounds to the man," the article states, "Carlisle put up a game that surprised everybody." It credits Carlisle with "lightning exchanges" on offense, and "peculiar formations" on defense, that "completely baffled Harvard." Of the hidden ball trick, the Boston scribe writes, "The cleverness of the play was never questioned, and even Harvard's most ardent supporters were loud in their applause." Nevertheless, throughout the piece, the author describes the Carlisle players in disparagingly racist terms, calling them "the swarthy red men."[51] While the report credits the intellect of the Indian players in performing the play, it also expresses disappointment with Harvard's "weak defense," complaining that "Harvard played anything but encouraging football."[52] No doubt Caspar Whitney would have found this game to have been a humiliation, perhaps even a call for white men to reassert their sporting and masculine dominance so as to overturn this racial emasculation, and again bring forth the comparison between football and the frontier.

In 1899 Carlisle was victorious over one of the Big Four, although not within Pratt's four-year timeframe. Early in the season Carlisle defeated the University of Pennsylvania by a score of 16–5. Caspar Whitney blamed the white team for allowing Carlisle to win. He wrote, "Pennsylvania's defeat was due directly to the weakness of her ends and tackles, and poor, practically no interference. Yet the Indians won on the merit of their game, and played football as one seldom sees at this time of the season." Whitney, desperately trying to find a reason behind Carlisle's undermining of the racial hierarchy, argued that Penn were defeated by experience, writing, "That Carlisle is largely a veteran team is partially answerable for this early form, but individual excellence and sharp team work are equally responsible. . . . With such important places as ends and tackles being filled by comparatively new men, and no especial punting ability revealed, Pennsylvania could hardly expect to defend her goal against a hard-playing veteran team of Carlisle's class."[53] Despite Whitney admitting that Carlisle outplayed the University of Pennsylvania, he argued that this was mainly due to Penn's poor play and inexperience rather than the Indians' skill and excellent performance. Whitney ignored that Carlisle had previously pushed all of the Big Four to close scores, blaming Pennsylvania's loss on the early date of the contest. Carlisle did not defeat any other Big Four team while Pratt served as superintendent, but they did defeat Pennsylvania two more times before he left the school.[54]

When Carlisle players used trick plays and strategy to achieve victories on the football field, the school media gave credit to Warner for the team's success. During the 1902 football banquet, which celebrated sporting successes over the previous year, team captain, Charles Williams (Caddo), spoke to the assembled supporters and staff, saying, "I also thank Mr. Warner very much. It is to him that all the glory is due."[55] In crediting his white coach for Carlisle's success, Williams foreshadows a pattern that would emerge later in the twentieth century when, in an era after integration, media would represent white coaches as saviors who not only coached but provided stern discipline, mentorship, and moral leadership to their Black and Brown athletes. He also echoes Camp, who credited Carlisle's white coaches even before Warner arrived.[56] Players might not actually have believed that Warner deserved "all the glory," but perhaps they felt a need to perform as if they believed the idea that they were incapable of mounting a championship team without oversight from this particular white leader.

Williams's praise for Warner further implied that the players were unable to design their own intelligent tactics and relied on mimicking Warner's directions to secure victory.[57]

Like Warner, Pratt became more focused on victory during his later years at Carlisle. Although he initially emphasized sportsmanship and "civilization" as the primary focus of football, Pratt eventually started to recruit players. Such a change in attitude might have been because of Pratt's declining influence over the national discourse in Indian affairs, which paralleled transformations in the character of United States settler colonialism and its relationship to the Indian boarding school system. As Genevieve Bell points out in her influential dissertation on the history of the Carlisle Indian School, by the late nineteenth century, the growing industrialization of the American economy threw Carlisle into a legitimacy crisis. Pratt created a curriculum designed to demonstrate his ability to "civilize" Indigenous Americans through education. For men, this meant learning to become independent yeomen farmers and craftsmen. By the turn of the century, both farming and manufacturing were rapidly becoming industrialized, rendering this curriculum obsolete. In this context, lawmakers no longer identified assimilation of Indians as an imperative, so a football team that only behaved well, and did not win, certainly would have had diminished value.[58] Pratt understood football's use as a spectacle, but in this new landscape of Indian affairs, Carlisle needed to remain relevant to survive, and winning made the school relevant.

Pratt's aggressive "civilization" agenda actually conflicted with the team's ability to win. Because "civilizing" Indian men meant curtailing expressions of masculinity, Carlisle's players lacked the size and strength of their toughest opponents. Such physical imbalance between Carlisle and the white collegians encouraged Warner to rely on trick plays to outwit rather than overpower the opposition. When Warner first met the Carlisle players in 1899, he encountered a group of underweight and tired athletes and complained they "ought to be trying for beds in a hospital rather than places on the football team."[59] Pratt explained that the players had spent the entire summer on local farms as part of their outing.[60] The football program was supposed to have demonstrated how programs like the outing successfully elevated Indians into respectable men. Now the outing program had just become a barrier to the football team's success.[61]

As Pratt became more focused on winning games, he allowed for the athletes to have diminished workloads to support their sporting success. Instead of working on a farm, like the majority of male students did, he began to justify the opportunity to meet white "civilized" collegians as an alternative form of the outing.[62] Visits to Harvard, Yale, Princeton, and other colleges, brought the athletes into contact with the finest intellectual minds created by the model of "civilization" that he wanted his students to respect and follow. Perhaps Pratt really believed this, but it also provided him with a convenient rationalization for creating an increasingly professionalized football team.

In the entire time of its existence, forty years, only about 758 students, roughly 10 percent of the total number who attended, actually graduated from the Carlisle Indian Industrial School.[63] Often students, including football players, did not stay at the school very long. Some players, like David MacFarland did graduate. Ed Rogers (Ojibwe, White Earth), captain of the football team in 1900 and later coach in 1904, graduated from Carlisle to study law at the University of Minnesota. While there, he played football and was named to the All-Western team for three consecutive years.[64] Other times, however, students simply left. Some were expelled, many deserted, and others just never completed the curriculum. Supporters of the team constantly complained at the start of every football season about the players' lack of experience. Before the beginning of the 1900 schedule, the *Red Man and Helper* commented, "As there are only five of last season's regular football players and only three substitutes left in school from last year's team, it can easily be seen that most of the candidates this season start in without any previous football experience."[65]

So, if it were not enough that Carlisle players had to prove their "civilized" manhood while on the playing field, they also lacked

Playing White Men

experience. As we have already seen, even when they proved themselves as gentlemen who could play, and sometimes win, sports reporters still filed stories that reflected the most deeply seeded racial assumptions of Indian-ness. In a report republished in *The Red Man* from the *New York Journal*, the commentator positioned the match within an exciting frontier narrative, writing, "How old Geronimo would have enjoyed it! . . . Here is an opportunity. The white men line up in their pride. If sacrifices of bone and sinew can square the thing, let us sacrifice, and perhaps the smoke of our wigwam camp fire will blow softly against the dangling scalps of our enemies."[66] It is mystifying why the school (presumably Marianna Burgess) would openly print these racist tracts in the school newspaper. However, when one reads accounts of Carlisle games that appeared in the popular press, it is almost impossible not to find these kinds of caricatures. For students to have read such words on weekly basis must have been deeply demoralizing.

One report, printed in the *New York Journal* following Carlisle's 1896 defeat by Harvard, particularly promoted the degradation and eroticization of the Indian players.[67] Five naked or partially naked pictures of Carlisle players accompanied the article. Two of the pictures feature "action" sequences while the remainder are of players standing still. The photographer's use of light and dark immediately draws the reader's gaze to the Indians' musculature. The newspaper pornographically presents the players as specimens at a zoo, devoid of humanity and reason, to be examined closely by scientists for biological study and brought out for the entertainment of spectators. The photographs represent Indian sexuality vis-à-vis their nakedness. As Michael Oriard has observed, it is impossible to imagine a mainstream American newspaper publishing a comparable photo spread of Harvard players. Without clothing, the newspaper reduces these people to their most primitive, masculine selves, literally stripped of any connection to human society. The display of the players' bodily strength is perhaps most striking because of its dissonance with reality. As stated earlier, Carlisle players tended to be smaller and less physically strong than their opponents. While the newspaper attempts to portray them as specimens of physical masculinity, they actually won games because of their ability to overcome the physical deficiencies in size, training, and even nutrition that they faced in contrast to their opponents. Through such pictures of supposed Indian savagery, the national media reminded readers that no matter how well-mannered Carlisle students were on the field, white audiences would always see them as an undifferentiated race who would forever lack "civilization" and who could never truly live as equal men. It is hard to imagine why Pratt would have allowed his students to participate in a photo spread that ran so directly counter to the stated mission of his lifetime project.

Yet despite Pratt's mission to uplift the Indians, this photo spread was not entirely out of step with the way that the Carlisle Indian School officials addressed students in racial terms. The 1902 end of season banquet for the football team serves as a glaring example. That season, Carlisle had won eight games and only lost three, defeating Pennsylvania, one of the Big Four, along the way. One of the high points of the academic year, it broke the school's conventions as players were allowed to invite a female date to a dinner featuring ice cream and oysters. Despite these trappings of "civilization," the school decorated individual tables with a scalp.[68] While seemingly done in jest, one might interpret this strange choice of table settings in several different ways. Perhaps school authorities considered the athletes so reformed that they could now "play" Indian in a way that only white men could, and subsequently return to "normality."[69] The "playing" of Indian also served to remind the athletes that they were "civilized"—their "mask" of playing Indian resulted in a critical self-assessment of their individual progress toward "civilization." Perhaps administrators also believed that the scalps reminded students of what they had left behind.

The 1897 football banquet, following a six-win and four-loss record that represented their second winning season in a row, went beyond the symbolic in reminding the players of their racial identities. In addition to the creamed oyster dinner, dignitaries were called on to give speeches to the attendees. Proclaiming the successes of Carlisle football, the school's assistant superintendent,

Alfred Standing, remarked, "the Indians are making a record that is very creditable to them. For our own team, I am glad of the record they have made, but they still need a white man to coach, and to manage their finances, and are much indebted to both the officials who have been engaged during the past season."[70] Standing managed to praise and insult the Carlisle players simultaneously, at once applauding the students' progress while also asserting their dependence upon white leadership, a strange comment, considering that Pratt portrayed Carlisle as an institution that would emancipate Indians from dependence upon whites. His comments suggest that he doubted his players could truly handle real-life situations which might give the power over white men, such as controlling finances.

Students did not let comments like Standing's go unanswered. A year later, football captain Bemus Pierce presented a very different opinion at the banquet. He said, "Now, I am glad to say we have a white man for a coach, but we have no white men on the team when we are on the gridiron. Therefore, I say if the Indian can do this, why can he not as well handle the team, and handle the financial part? If he can do so well in this game, I believe in time he can do most anything."[71] While Standing promoted racial inferiority, Pierce argued that the Indigenous players on the team deserved as much credit as the coach and that they were as capable as anybody.[72] Pierce cleverly embraced Pratt's "civilization" mission to point out the hypocrisy in attitudes of a school administrator like Standing.[73] As it turned out, Pierce and Ed Rogers, both on the 1897 team, were examples of Native achievement. One of Pratt's last directives was to hire Rogers as coach in 1904, with Pierce taking over in 1906.[74] Both led Carlisle to successful seasons with records of 9–2.[75]

During the 1902 football banquet, Pratt spoke about the use of football in the "civilizing" process and revealed the professions of the school's ex-players, striking a very different tone from Standing.[76] It is easy to imagine the attendees squirming with discomfort when Pratt told students they would never escape his gaze. Pratt stated that of the sixty ex-players, only five should be ashamed of their conduct. Although Pratt did not go into detail, this included any "Indian" behavior, what he and others called "returning to the blanket."[77] Two ex-players had died. The school did not know what had happened to four others. School officials had marked the remaining forty-nine ex-players as "o.k." Pratt related the various success stories with several ex-players working in banking, many studying at university, while two were school superintendents.[78] Pratt's inclusion of these details connected football and these players to successful, "civilized" manhood. Pratt argued that by adapting the various lessons learned on the gridiron, the students were more likely to enter the middle-class definition of "civilization." When Pratt hired Rogers, he did more than appoint a new football coach, he sent a message to his administrators and his successor that he still believed in his "civilizing" mission.

Pratt also argued that non-athletic students were less likely to be men. In a letter to Abram R. Vail in December 1897, Pratt made this connection clear: "My boys who play foot-ball are among the gentlest and best behaved in the school, and they have been made strong and exceedingly quick and active, and able to cope with difficulties; whereas those who take no part in foot-ball, who stand around with their hands in their pockets, become effeminate, and give no promise of aroused energy to meet the issues of life."[79]

In Pratt's opinion, while football required players to demonstrate their physical masculinity actively, it also demanded that they exhibit manliness and behavioral self-control. By comparison, the non-athletic students were effeminate—their unenergetic approach was emblematic of a lack of manhood. He portrays the effeminate student who does not play football as lazy and unable to meet the challenges or expectations of "civilized" manhood. For Pratt the players' tempered masculinity demonstrated self-control and the "gentlest" behavior.

Throughout his tenure, Pratt consistently conflated football, manhood, and "civilization." He positioned the active demonstration of "civilization" as the central focus of the players' education and manhood at Carlisle, both on and off the field. This was necessary to convince the public that Indian "civilization" was possible

Playing White Men

and that Carlisle was the only logical choice for such an education. However, the public, media, and even school employees also constantly reminded the players of their second-class status as Indians. The media assumption of Indian savagery undermined the players' and Pratt's claim to "civilization" and challenged their manhood.

In June 1904 the War Department forced Pratt to resign as superintendent at Carlisle. He had provoked his dismissal with bitter criticism of the Bureau of Indian Affairs.[80] Pratt had firmly believed in the superiority of white, Anglo-Protestant society, and he thoroughly disparaged Indigenous cultures, languages, and spiritual beliefs. Yet he also asserted that Indigenous Americans were human beings, fully equal and as capable as anyone from Europe. A new generation of policymakers in Washington disagreed, ascribing differences between European society and Indigenous American societies to a pseudo-scientific theory of race. More than just being in conflict with the policies of a new presidential administration, however, Pratt also found himself representing a movement of the past. When it came to relations with Indians, most federal policymakers had turned their attention away from conquest and settlement and more toward exploitation of resources on reservations, like coal, oil, timber, ranching, agriculture, and transportation routes. As Oriard has observed, Carlisle had become famous "for their exemplary sportsmanship, an affront to the brutality of the gentleman's sons at Princeton and Harvard."[81] As the appeal of assimilation faded, so did the novelty of Indian sportsmanship and the relevance of the Carlisle Indian School itself. In this light, a new generation of administrators saw the spectacle of football as a lifeline for the school, but one that could only be effective if the team won games. Winning games, however, sometimes meant putting "exemplary sportsmanship" to the side.

3

The Rise of Athletic Masculinity at Carlisle, 1904–1913

In 1904 the Bureau of Indian Affairs had forced Richard Henry Pratt from his position as superintendent—from the school that he had founded, the school through which he had hoped to transform the diaspora of Indigenous Americans into white citizens in a single generation. The Carlisle Indian Industrial School faced a crisis. The very government that had sanctioned the school no longer believed in it. As Jacqueline Fear-Segal has pointed out, Pratt's mission had two components: the first being the total assimilation of Native American Indians into Anglo-Protestant American society, and the second being "to demonstrate to white Americans that this transformation was both possible and desirable."[1] Pratt had clearly failed on both counts.

The football team, by 1904, had become probably his most potent tool for demonstrating to the general public the second of these two goals. Now the federal government, upon whose largesse the school had relied, no longer believed that training for "civilization" was either possible or desirable. Unmoored from Pratt's grandiose vision, the football program would take on a life of its own, one where winning games became more important than demonstrating sportsmanship. In the process, Carlisle's football program began to highlight and celebrate masculinity more than "civilized" manly restraint. The consequences of this transformation were important but also complex. White sports media continued to portray Carlisle players in stereotypical fashion, as purely physical, primitive beings who needed white paternal guidance. Yet victories also provided a sense of pride for Indians and students, even if victories on the gridiron were, ultimately, just symbolic.

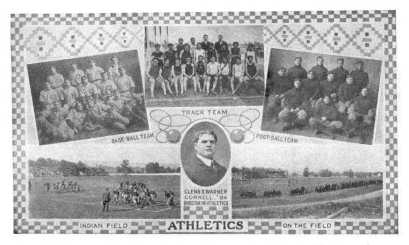

FIG. 4. Photo spread celebrating Carlisle Indian School Athletics, with Athletic Director Glenn S. "Pop" Warner in the center, printed in the school publication, the *Red Man*. Image courtesy of the Dickinson College Archives and Special Collections.

The football team emerged from 1904 as an institution in its own right rather than a public relations vehicle for the school, and in many respects, the school became a prop for the team.

Following the 1912 football season, Carlisle printed a celebratory edition of their newspaper, the *Carlisle Arrow*.[2] The year had seen only a single defeat at the University of Pennsylvania as Carlisle finished third in the national standings. The effort of athletes, such as Jim Thorpe (Sac and Fox), Gus Welch (Ojibwe), and Joe Guyon (Ojibwe, White Earth), ensured Carlisle emerged victorious over powerhouses such as the Army and Georgetown. The *Arrow* reprinted a report from the *Buffalo Commercial*:

> It is nothing new for the redskins to do the remarkable. It is a yearly matter for them to play a harder schedule than any of the college elevens. For one thing, the aboriginal charges of the United States government take very kindly to the game. They have all that is required in the way of fleetness, they put the fighting spirit into their contests and they exercise in the heat of actual battle all the craft credited to their fathers in the days

Athletic Masculinity

when the domain of this hemisphere belonged exclusively to the red races.[3]

The author of this blurb directly connects the athletes' success to their inherent Indian masculinity: their "fighting spirit," an Indian trait developed from a supposedly natural predilection for battle, resulting in Carlisle's success on the gridiron.[4] This article broke no new ground by evoking these stereotypical images. Yet it is striking that, eight years after Pratt's removal, a school publication reprinted media coverage that no longer emphasized "civilized" manliness but instead celebrated masculinity.

Pratt's dismissal in 1904 introduced a new direction for both Carlisle and the athletes' model of manhood. The presidential administration of Theodore Roosevelt, and specifically the policies of Estelle Reel, the new superintendent of Indian Education, had marginalized Pratt's ideals of education. Like General Samuel Chapman Armstrong of Hampton Institute in Virginia, Reel established new policies built upon belief in the principle that Indigenous Americans were inherently racially inferior to whites. In 1901 she issued a new *Course of Study* for the Indian boarding school system in which she made clear the new government policy, that Indians could only become "civilized" over several generations.[5] She argued that teaching Indians was akin to educating the blind and deaf, that Indigenous Americans were, literally, racially disabled.

After Pratt's departure, Carlisle increasingly focused on vocational education. Reel insisted that Indian students did not benefit from education in the liberal arts and mathematics. In a stark reversal from Carlisle's foundational mission, the school's new administration introduced Indian crafts, such as basketry, into the curriculum.[6] In fact, revenue from the athletic fund helped to finance the construction of the Francis Leupp art building where students would practice these skills.[7] The federal government began to turn its attention from residential boarding schools and toward reservation schools which officials saw as the future of the government's educational efforts. While Carlisle still represented, along with other off-reservation schools, the pinnacle of Indian educa-

FIG. 5. Superintendent Capt. William Mercer. Photograph courtesy of the Cumberland County Historical Society, Carlisle, Pennsylvania.

tion, federal officials began to doubt the utility of sending students to a boarding school in the East. Haskell, Riverside, and Chilocco, all located on the plains, challenged Carlisle's position as the premier residential institution for Indians.[8]

Unlike Pratt, his successor as Carlisle superintendent, Capt. William Mercer, loyally followed government guidelines. Serving from 1904 to 1908, Mercer was, like Pratt, a military officer, one who had served as an agent on both the Omaha and Winnebago reservations. Mercer subsequently brought Carlisle into line with Reel's *Course of Study*.[9] With his administration came a new cohort of students, many of whom were recruited specifically for football and other sports.[10]

Mercer's replacement, Moses Friedman, drew his experience from civilian work within Indian education both at Phoenix Indian School and at Haskell. The first Carlisle superintendent not to have been a career military officer, he still continued Mercer's changes to the curriculum but with an increased focus on mechanical training.[11] Neither Mercer nor Friedman shared Pratt's vision for the school, and it was under both that athletics became Carlisle's identity.

FIG. 6. Superintendent Moses Friedman. Photograph courtesy of the Cumberland County Historical Society, Carlisle, Pennsylvania.

From close range, this transformation in the school's character appears to be a bureaucratic conflict between two school administrators, but it fits into a larger global pattern that reflects upon the relationships between colonizers and Indigenous populations. Brendan Hokowhitu's work on masculinity among Indigenous communities in New Zealand (the Tene/Maori) observed a very similar development with their education. As with Carlisle, government agents criticized schools that provided education in sub-

Athletic Masculinity

jects like science and literature, and between the 1860s and 1940s pushed for Indigenous youths to learn manual trades like "agriculture, market gardening, stock farming, poultry keeping and bacon curing." Hokowhitu argues that as in the United States, colonizers in New Zealand have long portrayed the Tene/Maori as primitive and "degenerate," in need of their colonizers' education and administration. The British who occupied New Zealand "believed that only the white man possessed the mental fortitude to tackle such a burden; he was free to exercise his own will, virtuous, secular, liberated in thought, and autonomous. Conversely, the Other—the savage man—was represented as unencumbered by his inability to evolve, ruled by his passions, physical, immoral, and sinful." And, just as Indian students took to football at Carlisle, sports like rugby became popular among the Tene/Maori. In both cases, sports provided Indigenous men an avenue for advancement and recognition in mainstream society in ways that did not contradict their representation as overly masculine, violent, and physical. The reason for these patterns lies less in some magical bond between the Tene/Maori and the diverse Indigenous peoples of North America, and more in the fact that both shared in common a similar relationship to Anglo-Protestant settlers.[12]

So, for Indigenous Americans, Carlisle's winning football team generated pride but also reproduced damaging racial stereotypes. After Pratt left, Carlisle's administrators only compounded associations between masculine football prowess and racial inferiority by hiring white coaches like Warner, suggesting that in order to win, Indians needed white guidance. Importantly, however, Carlisle players had already proven this assumption false.

Until the end of his tenure as superintendent, Pratt had always hired white men to lead the team. Yet, as we saw in the last chapter, one of Pratt's final decisions, made as Carlisle had begun to achieve modest success on the field, had actually been to appoint an Indian as coach, choosing ex-Carlisle star Ed Rogers, and hiring another former Carlisle player, Bemus Pierce (Seneca), as his assistant. Pratt had hoped to show the extent of Indian progress by demonstrating that immediate white oversight was not required to construct a successful football team. Rogers had played for seven years at Carlisle, then three more at the University of Minnesota, where he had also earned a law degree. The school newspaper lauded this as the ultimate sign of "civilization"—the first Native coach in college football.[13] Rogers subsequently had a successful season in 1904 with a record of nine victories and two defeats.

Despite Rogers's accomplishments, he did not return in 1905, and instead the school hired a white "Advisory Coach," George Woodruff, who had played for Yale and coached at the University of Pennsylvania. Bemus Pierce stayed, however, joined by another ex-Carlisle player, Frank Hudson.[14] Woodruff did not last long and departed Carlisle after the Army game in November 1905, nine games into a fifteen-game season.[15] Pierce and Hudson finished as coaches that year and remained to coach for the 1906 season. The pair subsequently led Carlisle to another winning record of 9 wins and 3 defeats, including a 24 to 6 victory over the University of Pennsylvania.

Yet school media diminished the accomplishments of these coaches, lobbying to bring Warner back to Carlisle. Commenting on the 1906 pre-season hopes, the *Arrow* stated, "The Carlisle Indian football management has decided to have its eleven directly coached by full-blooded redskins of intelligence. This was done largely because the Indian will work harder for an Indian coach than for the average college expert trainer. Coach Glenn S. Warner is undoubtedly the only white man who has ever been able to hold fast the attention of the redskinned footballist and teach him better things."[16]

The *Arrow*, while acknowledging the mental capabilities of its Indian coaches, dismisses these. This writer instead attributes any success that an Indigenous American coach might enjoy to his ability to motivate his fellow Indians, not to his ability to develop strategies or to fine-tune tactics. Ironically, during the 1906 season under Pierce, Carlisle pioneered probably the most important tactic in the history of the game, the forward pass. This helped to fundamentally change the sport by taking advantage of a revolutionary set of rule changes just made before that season.[17]

Athletic Masculinity

FIG. 7. Peter Calac (Mission) throwing a forward pass during practice in 1910. Carlisle pioneered the use of the forward pass shortly after it became a legal part of the game in 1906. Photograph courtesy of the Robert R. Rowe private collection, Dickinson College Archives and Special Collections.

By the end of the 1906 season, however, Warner had been approached by Mercer to return as coach. Mercer had already tried to attract University of Michigan coach Fielding "Hurry Up" Yost to take the Carlisle job. [18] He failed to do so, but he was able to lure back Warner, who, by 1906, had grown tired of coaching at his alma mater, Cornell.[19] Despite three overwhelmingly winning seasons under Indian leadership, the *Arrow* asserted that an Indian coach was a "handicap" to the football team's success in the white world of college football.[20] Like Estelle Reel, and consistent with eugenic science of the early twentieth century, the *Arrow* portrayed racial identity for people of color as a disability.[21]

Warner was, undoubtedly, a master tactician on the gridiron. As we saw in the last chapter with his use of the hidden ball trick, he had long used tactics of misdirection and deception on the field. In fact, during the summer of 1906, he attended the Carlisle football training camp to develop plays using the forward pass. After returning to Carlisle, he quickly reestablished his reputation as a coach willing to employ all manner of misdirection. A 1908 report on a game against Syracuse detailed the extent of Warner's tactics. Demonstrating the elevated status of the team, the *Carlisle Arrow* devoted the first page and a half of its October 16 issue to this game, with excerpted quotes from several Buffalo papers. In one the writer praises Warner's gamesmanship, stating, "Coach Warner's lugubrious reports about the crippled condition of his team were taken with a few lumps of salt, but the fans were hardly prepared for such a frisky lot of invalids as cavorted around the lot yesterday."[22] To complete the deception, the Carlisle players arrived in bandages. Such debilitating injuries did not apparently affect the Carlisle team. They secured a 12–0 victory.[23]

Yet he was much more of a significant figure than just a cunning coach willing to employ trickery to his advantage. Because of his success coaching the team to wins, Carlisle's football team became more important than the school itself, and Warner became an extraordinarily powerful figure at the school who ultimately controlled athletics with relatively little oversight. He was a charismatic evangelical minister spreading the gospel of football to the Indians, and who very much relished his reputation as a white savior with an almost magical ability to command his Indigenous players.[24] To anybody lamenting the loss of an Indigenous coach, the *Arrow* reassured its readers that Warner was "as much an Indian as our own 'Bemis.'"[25] Yet such a claim only exposed the supposedly inferior status of Indian manhood at Carlisle, as Warner could perform Indian-ness, but neither Pierce nor Hudson could successfully mimic whiteness. Warner had little problem appropriating Indian identities in response to questions about his suitability as athletic director, while allowing his whiteness to ensure that his authority remained secure throughout his tenure at Carlisle.

Like Carlisle's own newspaper, national media reports on the Carlisle team also promoted the idea of Warner as an Indian trapped inside of the body of a white man. As commentators framed Carlisle games within exciting frontier narratives to attract readers, they also portrayed Warner as a respected figure of authority, someone who could control the potentially savage masculinity of his play-

FIG. 8. A live-action photograph of a Carlisle Indian School football game in 1910. Photograph courtesy of Dickinson College Archives and Special Collections.

ers. Following Carlisle's win over Penn in 1911, the *Carlisle Arrow* reprinted a story from the *Philadelphia Record* that described Carlisle's players as, "big, muscular and quick, possessing all the artfulness and cunning natural to their race, and brimful of the crafty teaching of foxy Glenn Warner, their coach." The reporter also writes of Carlisle's players as "pupils of the Grand Sachem Warner, medicine man of football and holder of all knowledge."[26] Although the report described Sampson Burd (Piegan), the 1911 captain, as a "chief," he was still depicted as reliant on Warner's "knowledge." As with the team itself, the article represents his masculine power as completely reliant on Warner's superior knowledge of football for victory. Describing Warner as a "medicine man" also cast him in a frontier narrative, someone whom white readers would have identified as having supernatural powers.[27] In his position as a "medicine man," readers might have understood Warner as enjoying an Indian identity, while simultaneously maintaining a superior position over the players.

In 1931 Warner published a three-part series of articles in *Collier's Weekly* reminiscing upon his coaching history at Carlisle. Included alongside one of the articles is a photograph of Warner

Glenn S. "Pop" Warner in Indian regalia

FIG. 9. Pop Warner posing for *Colliers* magazine in 1931. Photograph courtesy of the Cumberland County Historical Society, Carlisle, Pennsylvania.

in full Indian regalia.[28] It shows him with a full Indian headdress, a shield, and what appears to be a smoking pipe. The photograph portrayed the fluid nature of Warner's racial categorization—he claimed Indian-ness, but was still distinctly white. The photograph achieved this by appropriating white views of Indian primitive masculinity. Warner was holding a shield, for example, an item that white readers of *Colliers*, by now exposed to Hollywood portrayals of Indigenous Americans for years, would have identified with warfare on the frontier. Yet Warner's headdress also symbolized a position of authority as chief. His "chiefdom" provided authority in Indian culture, but his whiteness also signified his racial superiority.

Warner's "playing Indian" resonated with football's appeal to the racialized anti-modernism and frontier masculinity discussed in chapter 2. Political leaders and leading intellectuals alike lauded football as a replacement for a lost violent masculinity that the over-"civilized" repressed, something necessary for white men to maintain dominance and control as trustees over an imperial landscape. For many, football combined "civilization" and primitiveness by promoting its modernist scientific approach and violent anti-modernism, and Warner responded by appropriating Indian-ness into a conception of manhood inflected with an image of "savage" masculinity. [29]

It is important here to address how little Warner's appropriation of Indigenous identity had to do with the people whom he coached. As Matthew Sakiestewa Gilbert reminds us in his profile of Hopi runners, athletes like Louis Tewanima truly did bring their own identities and understandings of sports to Carlisle, ones derived from deeply rooted traditions and histories. Tewanima was a Hopi runner who competed in the Olympics in London in 1908 and in Stockholm in 1912. At the second of these he won the silver medal in the 10,000-meter run, becoming the first United States athlete to earn a medal in this event, and the only one to do so until Lakota runner Billy Mills won the gold in the 1964 Tokyo games.

Tewanima came of age within the Bear Strap Clan, or the Piqos-ngyam. He arrived at Carlisle as a prisoner of war, his people among a group of Hopis who had refused to send their children to boarding schools. Federal agents arrested these resisters, sending many to Alcatraz Island in San Francisco Bay. Some of their children, like Tewanima, eventually were forcibly sent to Carlisle.[30] Growing up in this matrilineal clan, he learned to run over long distances to bring rain to his people. Running would have been something that he would have associated strongly with a sense of responsibility to a collective group, something quite different from the individualized trophies and prizes awarded to athletic champions in American sports. Yet as Gilbert reports, he was eager to bring his running talents to Carlisle. On one hand, Gilbert writes, "Americans considered Tewanima to be their trophy of colonization. His accomplishments in U.S. marathons reflected the presumed 'success' of American democracy, which allowed him to be a civilized, and therefore colonized, member of U.S. society."[31] At the same time, Gilbert notes that "other Hopi students understood that Tewanima's desire and ability to run stemmed from his culture."[32] At Carlisle he was able to continue to thrive as a runner and present an image of his people that might counter what Gilbert calls the "racist 'ideologies' emphasized in American and European newspapers."[33]

Warner may have promoted himself as a "medicine man," but in reality he won by professionalizing athletics at Carlisle. In fact, the increased professionalism of sport at the school indicated how centrally important winning had become. In his work on the history of college football in the United States, Ronald Smith has documented the rising professionalism of the sport, identifying eight categories that defined a turn away from amateur status in scholastic athletics. These included the awarding of money or non-cash prizes, competing against other professionals, charging an entrance fee, a training table, payment of "athletic tutors" and professional coaches, and the recruitment and payment of players.[34]

Warner did all of these things at Carlisle, but he also had to avoid accusations of professionalism. If Carlisle was professional, the team's supposed amateur status would be compromised. The amateur ideal was very hard to maintain for all but the most affluent classes.[35] Few enjoyed a luxury of time that they could devote to athletic training without pay. Complicating things for Warner, Pratt still had allies, angry at the way that he had been dismissed as superintendent, and they did not let the team's detour into professional status go unnoticed. Only three years after Pratt's departure, the football team became the focus for critics who viewed Carlisle as betraying its "civilizing" mission.

In 1907 Carlos Montezuma wrote an explosive editorial for the *Chicago Tribune*, syndicated in papers across the country, in which he criticized the Carlisle sports program. Earlier, Montezuma had served as the team's doctor and had praised football for the way that it showcased Carlisle as a producer of "civilized" men.[36] In 1907, though, citing his correspondence with a former disciplinarian named W. G. Thompson, he excoriated the football team, writing that it had become a corrupt, professionalized outfit that violated ethics in order to win. He claimed that Carlisle's coach, Glenn S. "Pop" Warner, whom Mercer had recently rehired, kept a "schedule of prices" as rewards for outstanding plays on the field. Montezuma wrote, "There is no reason why the Carlisle students should be proud of the success which in 1907 attended the football efforts of a lot of hired outsiders."[37] According to Montezuma, only a third of the football players actually attended Carlisle, while Warner recruited athletes from other Indian schools such as Haskell.[38] Montezuma's criticisms were actually even less stringent than the original letter from Thompson, which featured several other examples of professionalism that he claimed occurred during Pratt's tenure, alleging, for example, that Warner paid Jonas Metoxen during the 1899 season.[39] Instead, Montezuma focused entirely on Mercer's and Warner's influence upon professionalism at Carlisle.

The school's response, printed in the *Arrow* and authored by the Warner-led athletic committee, dismissed Montezuma's criticisms as "groundless," "misguided," "venomous," and "sensational." The school accepted some of Montezuma's accusations—some of the players did "preliminary" work at Haskell while two of the athletes were employees of the school.[40] Mostly, however, the committee defended his team's record of gentlemanly conduct, writing, "The whole squad in every way reflects credit upon the school, and every institution that has met them upon the gridiron can rest assured that they have met as fine and deserving a body of young men as the Indian race can produce."[41] In a striking attack upon Montezuma, however, the *Arrow* also printed an editorial by Gus Beaulieu, identified in the paper as "the well known Chippewa sportsman and editor of the *Tomahawk*," writing for the *Minneapolis Tribune*. Beaulieu condemned Montezuma for his attack on the Carlisle football team: "We are at a loss when we come to analyze the criticism, coming as it does from an Indian, *or one who claims to be such*. . . . We assume that personal differences with Major Mercer, superintendent of Carlisle, lie at the bottom. We have been informed that Major Mercer did not treat him well at Carlisle upon one occasion"[42] (italics in original).

Beaulieu primarily characterizes Montezuma as petty, unable to forget Mercer's slight, but there is a deeper debate over the nature of his racial identity. He argues that Montezuma's immersion in white society, something that the Indian School had formerly praised, disqualified the doctor to speak as an Indian. This is a remarkable argument for Mercer to have printed in the *Arrow*. As we saw in chapter 1, just eight years earlier, the school paper (at that time the *Indian Helper*) wrote of Montezuma, "He is a full Indian and yet is NOT an Indian. He is a MAN." Montezuma, by rejecting his Indian identity, had become a model of what a new Indian manhood at Carlisle could produce. Now Carlisle had reprinted an entirely opposite opinion, that because he had rejected his Indian-ness, Montezuma's opinion was no longer valid. In this line of thought, Montezuma was betraying the Indian race by challenging the team's legitimacy. In Beaulieu's opinion, Montezuma was now akin to white commentators who criticized the team. Beaulieu continued, "Dr. Montezuma evidently *has none of the feelings of kinship with the Indian*, and perhaps this is not to be wondered at since he has not been much in contact with his red brethren since his childhood, and because the greater part of his life has been passed within the circles of refined 'civilization.'"[43]

Athletic Masculinity

The very characteristics that had made Montezuma a hero and role model less than a decade earlier now made his opinions illegitimate. The disparaging tone of Beaulieu's article makes his disdain of Montezuma's upbringing clear. According to Beaulieu, Montezuma's manhood, which was based upon "refined civilization," was not Indian. Instead, Beaulieu argues that the players' Indianness and masculinity made them superior, as proved through victories on the gridiron.

Mercer printed the rebuke of Montezuma to support the players in their masculine approach to football because masculinity won games, secured income, and increased Carlisle's athletic reputation. In this respect the players were allowed to be masculine for the benefit of the institution. Beaulieu's editorial, however, also represents the perspective of an Indigenous American who embraced the football field as an arena of contestation between white and Indian masculinities.

While Beaulieu, and other Indigenous Americans, might have applauded Carlisle's display of masculinity, popular representations, like Wild West Shows, equated Indian masculinity with savagery. Pratt had detested these, only allowing Carlisle students to play football as long as it served as a showcase for "civilization."[44] Yet, as Carlisle officials embraced winning and accepted athletes' masculinity, they did so during an era when Buffalo Bill's romanticized version of the American frontier after 1890 drew large audiences and generated enormous revenue.[45] During the post-Pratt era, Carlisle's administrators capitalized upon this new public fascination with Indian identities.[46] They did so not only through sports but also through the construction of the Francis Leupp Art Building, which specialized in Indian art.[47] Less than suggesting a newfound respect for Indigenous American cultural expression, the Indian arts program at Carlisle reflected a new market in which elite whites romanticized and appropriated Indigenous arts, idealizing them as primitive alternatives to the modern world.[48] By the early twentieth century the white general public no longer felt as fearful of Indian masculinity as they had decades earlier, and they had no problem paying money to experience the Carlisle football team as a contestant on a romantic reconstruction of the frontier battlefield.

As Mercer and Friedman steered Carlisle away from Pratt's vision, the football team became increasingly disconnected from the school, very closely resembling the professional outfit that Montezuma described in his editorial. Athletes lived separate lives from the rest of the student body. Their quality of life, on the whole, was better than that of the majority of their peers, and they became male role models whom students admired.[49] They received monetary loans, lived in significantly better rooms than the rest of the student body, and were often away from the campus for up to four weeks at a time.[50] The athletes' sleeping quarters also represented the finest Carlisle had to offer, with forty-five spacious rooms. The health of the athletes was a primary concern, with shower baths, wash rooms, and bath rooms provided for their comfort.[51] The athletic building far outshone the rest of the campus in terms of quality. The building only affirmed what had become clear to anybody observing the place: the athletic department ruled over the school.[52]

This would not have made Carlisle unique during the early twentieth century, and would actually have brought it up to speed with the competition. Publicly, colleges subscribed to the code of amateurism. The reality, however, was far different. In 1905 Henry Beach Needham published two articles in *McClure's Magazine* that revealed the prominence of professionalism in college athletics. Included in Needham's articles were accusations of "tramp" students who "enrolled" at several colleges, payments to players, and enticements for potential athletes. At Princeton, Charles Patterson, the college's "oldest living undergraduate," persuaded athletes to enroll there with promises of financial incentives. One athlete played for Pennsylvania State College then mysteriously appeared in the University of Pennsylvania's starting team shortly after.[53] A reason for such professionalism was the sheer advertising power football possessed. The University of Chicago, for example, appointed Amos Alonzo Stagg in 1892 to develop a football team capable of defeating the best colleges. Such victories became a form

Athletic Masculinity

of advertising for Chicago.[54] A successful football team could propel the college into national discourse. Professionalism was thus essential for colleges to create and maintain prominence on the national scene. Yet despite this evidence, the ideal of amateurism still remained part of college football's public image.[55]

Despite Montezuma's suggestion to the contrary, Pratt had allowed the football team to implement a limited form of professionalism during his tenure as superintendent. An entrance fee was a common occurrence at the vast majority of college sports.[56] The gate receipts allowed Pratt and his successors to expand the school, pay for various new buildings, and buy new equipment. After Pratt's departure, Carlisle reaped enormous income from gate receipts. In 1907, for example, Carlisle earned slightly less than eighteen thousand dollars from a game at the University of Chicago, and almost eleven and a half thousand from their game with Harvard.[57] Without the athletic fund, Carlisle certainly would not have expanded to the extent it did. Caspar Whitney, a vocal proponent of amateurism, defended Carlisle on this issue. In response to criticism over Carlisle's money-making trip to play the University of Wisconsin in 1896, Whitney argued that their non-college status exempted them from accusations of professionalism.[58] Carlisle, unlike their white opponents, did not have a sustainable income from student tuition, and instead had to rely upon athletics to supplement governmental appropriations. Yet the Carlisle team earned huge profits from ticket sales.

Also during Pratt's tenure, Carlisle used the athletic fund to pay players. Jonas Metoxen (Oneida) received two hundred dollars for playing in the 1899 season. The following season all Carlisle football players received some form of payment. W. G. Thompson, an employee of the school, remarked that this "was in violation of the ethics of college sport and made the players professionals."[59] Pratt managed to keep this level of professionalism remarkably well hidden, and for good reason. A football team corrupted by professionalism would certainly have capsized the "civilized" image that he had hope to cultivate through the sport. Yet he must have seen it as worth the risk. Payment persuaded the athletes to remain at Carlisle. With the promise of a payday, the players would not leave Carlisle or attempt to run before their education finished.[60] Such an incentive ensured that players stayed at the school and produced a successful team. In all, Pratt's payment of players was a small sacrifice for such a large return from match tickets.

Although the professionalization of the Carlisle football team started during Pratt's tenure, the paying of players and staff increased in the Mercer era. The athletic fund became a private bank for the players. Albert Exendine (Delaware/Oklahoma) received a loan of two hundred dollars, the famed distance runner and Olympic silver medal winner Lewis Tewanima (Hopi) three hundred, and Gus Welch fifty. All "loans" were made with the understanding that repayment was unnecessary. Other players, including Jim Thorpe, were paid ten to fifteen dollars per month out of the athletic fund. The total payment of players took up a significant part of the fund's income. In the 1907 season, for example, the football players received over nine thousand dollars in payment. Warner also benefited from Carlisle's move toward professionalism. By the end of the 1913 season, Warner earned four thousand dollars per year—more than either Mercer or Friedman. This trend of payment continued during Friedman's administration, but to a lesser degree as players received their "pay" in the form of a suit at the end of the season.[61] Whatever the type of payment, by steering toward professionalism, Carlisle placed a premium upon winning. Even Pratt seemed to recognize that football's value to the school could not be limited to good sportsmanship and gentlemanly behavior alone. A viable team won games, performing the masculinity that their white opponents were all too eager to embrace.

Carlisle also began heavily recruiting students specifically for athletics after Pratt had left. Mercer and Friedman actively increased player recruitment during their tenures. Alongside recruitment from reservations, players were also enlisted from Haskell and the Phoenix Indian School.[62] Thompson outlined the extent of these efforts in his letter to Carlos Montezuma. He named six players who had previously played for the Haskell football team.[63] Four of the six, Alfred DuBois (Ojibwe), Scott Porter (Ojibwe,

Athletic Masculinity

White Earth), Chauncey Archiquette (Oneida), and Emil Houser (Cheyenne), played in the 1904 "Indian Championship" match against Carlisle.[64] Despite a resounding 38–4 victory for Carlisle, the match provided the opportunity to scout and attract Haskell's better players. In this respect, Haskell served as a feeder school for Carlisle athletes. While many players arrived at Carlisle with little prior knowledge of football, the Haskell athletes were already well versed in the game. Such players required minimal training to adapt them to Carlisle's tactics as they already knew the rules of football. Carlisle enticed these students to play for the football team rather than receive an education.

Even the architecture of Carlisle's campus began to reflect the school's drift toward athletic professionalism. In 1907 a new building was constructed specifically for the athletes.[65] The building featured living quarters, a reading room, a training table, and even a billiards table. Warner particularly valued the training table. He often complained that Carlisle players were too light to compete physically with white opposition, a sad commentary about the starvation and inadequate nutrition that non-athletes experienced on a daily basis.[66] The table itself had better quality food than the rest of the school with a diet of milk, beef, potatoes, and bread. The athletes sometimes dined on oysters during trips, a delicacy not readily available to their peers back in Carlisle. In fact, non-athletic students even joined the squad in an attempt to acquire better food, something that school authorities ended quickly. The school athletic fund financed the training table, and opened Carlisle up to more criticisms of professionalism. While this may have been true, Carlisle players still enjoyed fewer luxuries than their white counterparts, and it was their labor on the field that did, in fact, fill the athletic fund coffers.

With luxuries and attention afforded to the football team, becoming an athlete was an attractive proposition for students. It should come as no surprise that male students became very eager to join the football team over other choices. Before the rise of football, the officer class at Carlisle had signified the progression of a student into "civilization" and conveyed the greatest honor. Upon joining Carlisle, students were placed in regiments, overseen by a student officer. It was thought that becoming an officer would be a rewarding incentive to act "civilized." A promotion signified that the student was succeeding at Carlisle and possessed the qualities for manhood. Yet by 1913 teachers complained that the students were more interested in becoming athletes than joining the school's officer class.[67]

Not surprisingly, as Carlisle players became increasingly recognized for their racial masculinity, it was Warner who received most of the credit for Carlisle's success. An article from the *Philadelphia Public Ledger*, reprinted in the December 1909 edition of the *Indian Craftsman*, explained the reason behind Carlisle's success. The *Indian Craftsman* was, at this time, a new monthly school publication that purported to be "not only *about* Indians, but mainly *by* Indians." In a sharp deviation from Pratt's ideal, the journal featured and celebrated Native weaving, pottery, and design.[68] Most of its first page is devoted to Warner, whom the author of the piece calls "the principal factor in developing football at Carlisle. . . . It has been due to his instruction that the Indians have proven so adept in the sport and developed such remarkable elevens."[69] The placing of Warner's contribution at the beginning of the article positions him as the most important cause of Carlisle's success. While the author acknowledges that Warner was not responsible for the introduction of football at the school, the writer rarely deviates from the coach's career. For example, addressing when Warner left Carlisle in 1903 to return to Cornell, the author's narrative follows him, and only briefly mentions Rogers, Pierce, and Hudson, ignoring their success entirely. The "Pierce brothers are well remembered as famous players," while "Rogers and Exendine stand out as Carlisle's great ends."[70] There is no discussion of their successful coaching careers. The article implies that although such Indigenous standouts have the necessary masculinity to emerge victorious, they do not possess the manly intelligence to create winning tactics.

Warner benefited greatly from a racial hierarchy that allowed him to direct an athletic program for Indigenous Americans and reap the financial rewards of their success. He had few qualms about exploiting these same racial hierarchies to fuel resentment that might inspire his players. Prior to the 1912 match against the Army, Warner remarked that the grandparents of the Army players were responsible for killing their relatives.[71] Warner offered the players the chance of masculine redemption. Carlisle players may have come from a diverse set of backgrounds, but on the gridiron, they represented all Indians, past and present. Carlisle beat the Army 27–6, but Warner could once again take credit for motivating his team by framing their win as a symbolic victory for Native masculinity.[72]

Very early in the post-Pratt era, school media struck a new tone when covering or reprinting articles about football games. Reports no longer emphasized sportsmanship and gentlemanly virtue. Instead, they unapologetically gloated when the team won, using violent, masculine language to describe contests. In a 1906 game against the Western University of Pennsylvania (later the University of Pittsburgh), the *Arrow* reported, "The weather was fine, the audience large, the enthusiasm immense, the rooting fierce, the opponents heavy, the Indians in form, and the score—it's almost a shame to mention it—22 to 0 in the Indians favor. Now, what do you think of that?"[73]

The entire passage brims with masculinity: "fierce" rooting, heavy opponents, and "immense" enthusiasm. The author's verbs indicated that the game was solely masculine—there was little manly self-control by either the crowd or the team, whose players so thoroughly dominated WUP that even to report the score emasculated a shamed opposition. The Carlisle players affirmed their manhood through triumphant—and masculine—victory on the gridiron.

The *Arrow* gloated even more when the team beat one of the Big Four. When Carlisle defeated the mighty University of Pennsylvania in 1906, the paper wrote, "Carlisle Indian School is not in the habit of running special trains and taking several hundred people down to Philadelphia for a funeral. She took them down to see the Red Men make the University of Pennsylvania team look like a Kindergarten. Did they do it? Well, I guess."[74]

The idea that the Penn players "looked like a Kindergarten" affirmed the manhood of the Carlisle players. Comparing the match to a "funeral," the article mockingly presents Carlisle as slaying its opposition in its 24–6 victory, symbolically reversing the idea of Indian extinction, with the white opposition dying because of Carlisle's superior offense.[75]

The masculine reporting against the Big Four went further in a 1907 article commenting on the Harvard-Carlisle game: "It was not so much that Harvard was merely beaten in the score, but she was outclassed individually and as a team, ripped and torn throughout the line and shown up in pitiable weakness."[76] Once more, the *Arrow*'s words emasculated the vanquished team, referring to Harvard as "she." Instead of lauding Carlisle's sportsmanship, the author immediately affirmed the overwhelming masculinity of the Native players. Such manhood was not measured through the self-control of masculinity, but rather the demonstration of overwhelming power against their white opponents.

Beginning with Mercer, Carlisle football players were now playing under a new set of rules. Rather than having to exhibit sportsmanship in order to achieve respectability in a "civilized" world, Carlisle's football team played to win in order to prepare for success in a savage business world.[77] The following blurb from a 1907 issue of the *Arrow* illustrates this shift: "Far more important than the fun derived from American athletic contests is the foundation built in these wholesome sports for greater and more serious contests in the real business of living. The wholesome athletics of America—football, baseball, rowing, tennis and the like—give to young manhood a training for every day matches against the world which is invaluable."[78]

The article transforms the masculinity gained from victory playing "wholesome athletics" into a moral virtue. Victories on the field of any sport translated into victories in life. Pratt's goal had been for students to achieve self-sufficiency by showing that they could assimilate. Now school publications were striking a new tone. To navigate the avenue toward independence, one had to fight and win. Sport prepared the student for "matches against the world," victory demonstrating how to defeat similar opponents in "the real business of living."

Athletic Masculinity

Throughout the post-Pratt era, school publications printed stories about the status of former athletes. Although undoubtedly edited to improve the school's public image, all such reports projected a positive message of athletic success, economic prosperity, and, subsequently, patriarchal manhood. Articles, such as one from 1912 printed in the *Carlisle Arrow* under the headline "Carlisle's Football Players of the Past Make Good in Real Life," followed a similar pattern: "Johnson, for instance . . . went to Porto Rico [*sic*], and is now one of the leading dentists on that island. . . . Ben Caswell (Ojibwe) . . . is the principal of an Indian school in Minnesota. . . . Jonas Metoxen . . . is now a successful farmer in Wisconsin."[79] Such pieces credited football when former players became self-sufficient and affluent. These articles hail a particular model of manliness, one based upon the ability to earn a living and support a family in the modern world. It is a model that Pratt would have admired. Yet during the post-Pratt era, Carlisle's official media argued that ex-players achieved this level of success in the modern world because of, not in spite of, the masculine aggression they experienced as football players. The message to the male student body was clear: there was a greater chance of future success and public affirmation of manhood if they played football. The gridiron provided an opportunity to prove Indian competitiveness, and football provided the education Carlisle was unable to—the ideal of direct competition with whites on an equal playing field. By prioritizing victory on the gridiron, the school also positioned masculinity as the dominant component of the players' manhood.

Examining the football team reveals how dramatically the Carlisle Indian School changed over time. As school administrators sought to exploit Indigenous Americans' bodies to keep the school open, draw publicity, and accumulate money, athletics became more important than the school's mission. And the school took in a significant amount of money. As one example, their game against Harvard in 1907 earned Carlisle over eleven thousand dollars.[80] Even as early as the 1890s, under Pratt's command, sports had started to dominate the institution's public image.

As much as Carlisle's administrators used sports to spin nar-

FIG. 10. Five Carlisle football players at practice in 1910: Edward Bracklin (Ojibwe), Peter Calac, Joseph Guyon (Ojibwe, White Earth), and Gus Welch (Ojibwe). Photograph courtesy of the Robert R. Rowe private collection, Dickinson College Archives and Special Collections.

ratives of white supremacy, however, athletic students became a remarkably powerful force in their own right, and not only for exhibiting white imaginations of masculinity. Women played some sports, including basketball, which arrived as early as 1895. Josephine Langley, mentioned briefly in chapter 1, thought the game resembled something called double ball that her grandmother had remembered playing as a child. She took to it quickly, and after falling sick and having to return home, brought the sport to the Fort Shaw Indian School in Montana. She helped to build a team at Fort Shaw that, eventually, would win the women's basketball championship at the St. Louis World's Fair in 1904.[81] During an era when male students concentrated their school athletic pursuits upon football, the women at Fort Shaw pioneered a fast-paced basketball game and played an important role in the development of the sport that both women and men play today.[82]

Male athletes who never played football became heroic figures

Athletic Masculinity

independent from their relationships to the school. Perhaps the most famous was Hopi Louis Tewanima, who, as seen earlier in this chapter, earned fame for his 10,000-meter silver medal performance at the 1912 Stockholm Olympics. Tewanima first came to Carlisle as a prisoner of war. The Army had taken him from his family and clan, enforcing federal orders that had sided with Mormon farmers in a land dispute. Tewanima foreshadowed future people of color who competed successfully for the United States on an international stage, sports figures who have brought laurels to a nation that has systematically oppressed them. In fact, in the case of Tewanima during the 1912 Stockholm games, the United States was still twelve years away from granting Native Americans citizenship. Yet Tewanima and other Hopi runners always saw themselves as representing more than just one nation. In the words of historian Matthew Sakiestewa Gilbert, "Americans considered Tewanima to be their trophy of colonization," but his "desire to join Carlisle's track team and his participation in marathons was deeply rooted in who he was as a Hopi runner for the Bear Strap Clan."[83]

On the football gridiron and in the world of track and field, however, no player achieved greater fame and stature than Jim Thorpe.[84] Few athletes anywhere in the world have ever demonstrated Thorpe's versatility. He played and starred for Carlisle between 1907 and 1912, helping to guide the team to twenty-three wins over his final two years, including victories over Harvard and the Army. He won gold medals for the modern pentathlon and decathlon in the 1912 Olympics. He had a twenty-year professional baseball career and was a founding member of the professional football organization that became the National Football League. In various narratives of the football team, Thorpe features most prominently with Warner.[85] Even though his achievements took place during the first decades of the twentieth century, a time before television and electronic mass media, sports fans still selected him as the athlete of the century in an ABC Sports internet poll in 1999.[86]

After arriving at Carlisle in 1906, Thorpe made a name for himself on the track team. According to one legend, one day, shortly after arriving at the school, Thorpe sat next to a field where students were attempting the high jump. Replete in uniform, Thorpe asked if he could try to jump, and proceeded to beat the school record. Warner quickly placed Thorpe on the track team.[87] Whether this legend is true or not, it contributes to a large body of stories about him that focus upon Thorpe as a natural, physical athlete. Most also present him as a tragic figure whose flame once burned bright but who experienced only bitterness and tragedy in his post-athletic life. In the Victorian gender rubric, these stories add up to a narrative of an overly masculine Indian athlete without the character to achieve respectable manhood.

Thorpe's first stint at Carlisle finished in 1909. That summer, instead of attending to a traditional outing program, he opted to play professional baseball in North Carolina, and later traveled home to Oklahoma under the impression he would never return to Carlisle. However, Thorpe was persuaded to return for the 1911 football season, with an eye on the 1912 Olympics.[88] After returning from Stockholm with Tewanima as a national hero, Thorpe stayed at Carlisle for the 1912 football season.[89] In late 1912, however, a reporter from North Carolina recognized Thorpe as a professional baseball player for the Rocky Mount team during his break from Carlisle. The reporter sat on the story for a couple of months, eventually breaking it in early 1913.[90] In response, Warner and Friedman drafted an explanatory letter for Thorpe to sign.[91] The letter fully admitted Thorpe's guilt, but argued that he had copied the professionalism of many white collegians.[92] Thorpe, however, had made a pivotal mistake—unlike some white college players, he did not use a pseudonym. At the time, the fact Thorpe was not expecting a return to track and field, let alone the Olympics, made a pseudonym unnecessary. Despite Thorpe's letter, his two gold medals were confiscated by the Amateur Athletic Union.

Shortly thereafter, Thorpe signed a contract to play for the New York Giants baseball team with a salary of five thousand dollars.[93] He later played professional football for a number of clubs, including the Oorang Indians, a team that he helped to form for the NFL, consisting mostly of ex-Carlisle players.[94] Yet Thorpe died a poor

Athletic Masculinity

man, allegedly with a drinking problem, contributing to narratives about him as a natural athlete with tremendous physical ability but whose life arch ultimately belonged to a tragic fallen hero. Perhaps no accounting of his life expresses this narrative better than the film, *Jim Thorpe: All American* (1951), starring Burt Lancaster as Thorpe, and made while he was still alive. The film presents Warner (Charles Bickford), as a tough but kind-hearted father figure for Thorpe, somebody who stood beside him and inspired him to be the best person that he could be. Toward the end of the film, Warner lectures Thorpe, who according to the film had by then become angry and sulking, embittered by the loss of his Olympic medals and the death of his son. Warner scolds Thorpe, saying, "Somewhere along the line you've gone completely haywire. Picked up the idea the world owes you something. Well, it doesn't owe you a thing. So you've had some tough ones. Been kicked around. They took your medals away from you. So what. All I can say is when the real battle started, the great Jim Thorpe turned out to be a powder puff."[95]

All Hollywood films about history take liberties with the past, but one must really strain oneself to recognize the morally centered, patriarchal Warner projected on screens as the same person who offered a "schedule of prices" to his players for their play on the field. This portrayal of Warner was only one of many fabrications in this biopic, but it did recast a familiar narrative about the coach's influence over Thorpe. Shortly after his victory in Stockholm, a *Carlisle Arrow* commentator remarked, "When you come to look at him he appears to be a normal human being, having developed through normal proportions to abnormal power by careful, persistent, scientific training. He is the supreme example of what can be done with the physical man when brought under control and bent to the processes which create perfect physical manhood."[96]

Like the film, this article from a school publication portrays Thorpe's manhood in mostly physical terms and credited his success not only to his masculine abilities and "abnormal power" but also to his coach's "scientific training." Thorpe might have had the body, but Warner honed it to perfection. Warner's "scientific" train-

FIG. 11. Pop Warner with Jim Thorpe (Sac and Fox) at football practice in 1910. Sportswriters often portrayed Warner as a paternal role model for his players, particularly Thorpe. Photograph courtesy of the Robert R. Rowe private collection, Dickinson College Archives and Special Collections.

ing brought Thorpe "under control," giving the impression that Thorpe was incapable of such transformation on his own. Thorpe's success, according to the author, was primarily due to Warner's ability to "bend" his extraordinary physical capabilities into "perfect physical manhood."

We can see a similar portrait of Thorpe as a man-child in the confessional letter that he signed after the professionalism scandal that resulted in the confiscation of his medals. According to Fred Bruce, a pipe fitter at the school in 1913, Warner actually wrote the following in Thorpe's voice:[97] "I hope I will be partly excused by the fact that I was simply an Indian schoolboy and I did not know all about such things. In fact I did not know I was doing wrong because I was doing what I knew several other college men had done. . . . I have always liked sport and only played or ran races for the fun of the thing and never to earn money."[98]

Thorpe's self-defense, that he was "simply an Indian schoolboy," infantilizes his actions, portraying himself as a naïve child unwit-

Athletic Masculinity

The Three Men Carlisle will Honor
Left to Right: Thorpe, Tewanima, Warner

FIG. 12. Postcard celebrating Jim Thorpe, Louis Tewanima (Hopi), and Pop
Warner after their return from the 1912 Olympics in Stockholm. Thorpe won gold
medals in the Pentathlon and Decathlon, and Tewanima a silver in the
10,000-meter run. Photograph courtesy of Dickinson College
Archives and Special Collections.

tingly caught in the net of professionalism. Unlike the white college "men," the letter portrays Thorpe's "schoolboy" attitude as
having caused the entire scandal.[99]

Despite the tragic narratives of his life, his daughter Grace
remembers him living his life with the kind of style and dignity
that he displayed running through the open field at Carlisle. Speaking to *People* magazine in 1996, she remembers the last time that
she saw him: "I dropped him off at the corner to take a bus to New
York City. . . . He stood underneath the marquee of the theater
there, and right above his head were the words 'Jim Thorpe—All
American.' I remember glancing over there and seeing him with
the marquee and his scarred leather luggage. That was my last
memory of him. He was kind of cool."[100]

As discussed in chapter 2, Carlisle graduates interviewed about
their memories frequently mention Jim Thorpe. While for white
media, he may have represented a specimen of untamed masculinity unable to cope in the modern world, for these students, his
success as an athlete served as an inspiration. Like Grace, they

FIG. 13. Jim Thorpe shaking hands with Moses Friedman after his return from the 1912 Olympics as Lewis Tewanima stands to his left, and Pop Warner stands behind him. After the International Olympic Committee stripped Thorpe of his medals for having played semi-professional baseball during a summer, Warner reportedly wrote an infantilizing letter of apology in Thorpe's voice. National Archives and Records Administration. Reproduced with permission of the Dickinson College Archives and Special Collections.

remember a great athlete who won and, in her words, was "kind of cool."

Without Thorpe, the Carlisle team missed a powerful and game-winning star. Carlisle, however, attempted to distance itself from Thorpe and the professionalism scandal after he had left. During the 1913 football season the school media attempted to belittle Thorpe's contribution. As the *Carlisle Arrow* explained, Thorpe's departure was not a devastating loss:

> Carlisle adherents who bewailed the loss of Jim Thorpe need wail no longer, for he has a worthy successor in a big Chippewa, Guyon by name, who is built like the famous Jim, acts like him and will merit All-Eastern consideration when the season is

Athletic Masculinity

over. Guyon tore through the Dartmouth line like old fury, and there was no stopping him. He carried his 182 pounds of muscle into the green midst with the speed and power of a battering ram and was a big factor in the scoring of every touchdown. Two of them he carried across the line himself.[101]

The *Carlisle Arrow* reassures Carlisle fans that they need not miss Thorpe, for the school had a new star in Joe Guyon. The article's author clearly works hard to present Guyon as Carlisle's next hero of the gridiron. And as had been the case with Thorpe in the past, this coverage describes the new star in physical terms highlighting his masculinity. Guyon's "182 pounds of muscle" and "power of a battering ram" represent him entirely in terms of overwhelming and aggressive male power. As with Thorpe, Guyon's masculinity was the central characteristic of his manhood. Although Thorpe was extremely difficult to replace, the school did, in fact, amazingly accomplish a record of ten wins, one loss, and one tie for 1913, suggesting that as great as Thorpe was, he had a strong crew supporting him.

During their tenures, Mercer and Friedman fundamentally changed the importance of football to the Carlisle Indian Industrial School, and they used the football team very differently from the way Pratt had. Following colleges and universities around the United States at the turn of the twentieth century, they allowed the football team to become the most important public face of their institution. Rather than using the team to advertise the school's "civilizing mission," they simply sought to have the team win games and generate revenue. Rather than downplay what white audiences would have perceived as the overly masculine character of Indigenous American men, they exploited their students' bodies to the fullest extent, and constructed their white football coach to become a core symbol of "civilization" and control.

Despite the obvious exploitation and corruption involved with Carlisle's football team, students often took pride in their victories in a context where they were very rarely allowed to win. Grace Thorpe remembers that her famous father told her once that "his happiest years were spent at Carlisle."

I'm thinking back on why he would say such a thing like that. . . . That's where he first came to fame, . . . in Pennsylvania, at Carlisle. . . . And then that's where he met my mother, and he was very much in love with my mother. . . . So that's where they met, that's where they fell in love, and that's where they married, was at Carlisle. Mother was a student there, too. . . . She was very happy there, too. She liked Carlisle. I never heard one of them say anything against the Indian boarding schools, and both of them grew up in them. I know that there is a lot of talk today, and a lot of writing about how terrible the Indian boarding schools are, but my mother and father never had anything wrong to say about them, and I don't either. I went to them too.[102]

Today, a great many descendants of Carlisle Indian School students would strongly disagree with Grace Thorpe's assessment of Indian boarding school education. Yet her positive understanding should not be dismissed either. In a very real way, the football team was something that students could claim as their own. Perhaps for Jim Thorpe, it was less Mercer and Friedman who made football the public identity of the school, but the players and students who played the game on the field.

Jim Thorpe and the football team play a role in a play that N. Scott Momaday wrote about Carlisle called *The Moon in Two Windows*. Luther Standing Bear, a first generation Carlisle student who famously described arriving at the school in his book, *My People the Sioux*, revisits Pratt after Carlisle's celebrated victory over the Army in 1912. He asks if Pratt has been to the cemetery on campus where students who had died while at Carlisle are buried. "What? The Cemetery?" Pratt asks. Their conversation continues,

Luther: At the school. The graves of the children. Many people go there now. They bring flowers and ribbons—sometimes tobacco and cornmeal, pollen. Have you gone there?

Pratt: You have to understand that the young people who died there were beyond help. They were dying before they left the camps. We must think of the ones who didn't die, the many hundreds who lived. They are healthy, happy human beings. And they produce healthy, happy children of their own. They are well-adjusted Americans. They are . . .

Luther: Civilized.

Pratt: Yes, indeed, civilized.[103]

The play ends with Luther's voice reflecting that "the Indian Industrial School at Carlisle was a kind of laboratory in which our hearts were tested." He continues, "For every one of them, for every single child, it was a passage into darkness. It was a kind of quest, not a quest for glory, but a quest for survival. They were all brave; they did a brave thing." Luther and his son, Stone, walk to Indian Field, the small stadium where Carlisle played their home games, a place still inhabited by the ghosts of those who never made it home.[104]

The students, in large part due to their criticisms of the football team, ultimately brought an end to the Carlisle Indian School. Decades earlier, Richard Henry Pratt might very well have brought them to Carlisle in order to baptize them in "civilization," but this new generation looked around at their institution and saw deeply entrenched corruption. They saw those who were supposed to have been teaching them "civilization" elevating a football team over the interests of the common student. In fact, for many, the Carlisle Indian School had never been an opportunity for any sort of advancement. It much more closely resembled a prison. In their protest against the school, students would cleverly turn the tables upon Carlisle and the federal government. They would stand upon the mantle of "civilization" and accuse their white overseers of savagery. Their criticisms struck a chord and won them an audience with a joint committee of the United States Congress in 1914. The records of the 1914 hearings show students airing their grievances in public to a remarkable degree. Yet the mantle of "civilization" rests upon a very unsteady foundation. Or, to use another metaphor, they chose to play a game according to their colonizers' rules.

4

"Civilization" on Trial

etween the late fall of 1913 and spring of 1914 Carlisle students drafted two petitions to government officials. Montreville Yuda (Oneida), a former student, carried the first, a petition of 276 signatures, to the secretary of the interior, Franklin Lane.[1] The petition featured six complaints against the school's administration, including accusations of lax discipline, unwarranted expulsions, unsanitary conditions, insufficient food, and excessive punishment.[2] The students blamed Superintendent Moses Friedman for the unbearable conditions. As a result of the students' complaints, Indian Service Inspector E. B. Linnen conducted a surprise inspection of the school in January, and largely as a result of his report, on February 6, 1914, a joint committee of U.S. representatives and senators arrived in Carlisle to question students, employees, and members of the public about the state of the school. The panel included Senators Joe Robinson (D-AR) and Harry Lane (D-OR) and Representatives John Stephens (D-TX) and Charles Carter (D-OK).[3] Just before the final day of their inquiry, in March 1914, Gus Welch, a prominent member of the football team, presented to Congressman Arthur Rupley (R-PA) a second petition from school athletes containing over two hundred signatures.[4]

The hearings revealed a school in ruins, a student body on the verge of rebellion, and a widely disliked superintendent. The evidence condemned Friedman's administration. Students testified that school advertising was fraudulent, that farms were used for punishment, and that athletics ruled the campus. The congressio-

FIG. 14. The Carlisle Indian School graduating class of 1913. That fall, Montreville Yuda (Oneida, back row, third from left), a member of this class, initiated a petition to the secretary of the interior to investigate mismanagement of the Carlisle Indian School. The petition led to a congressional investigation. Photograph courtesy of the Cumberland County Historical Society, Carlisle, Pennsylvania.

nal hearings represented the culmination of student and staff disillusionment with Friedman's tenure at Carlisle.

The 1914 congressional hearings into the Carlisle Indian Industrial School represent one of the most effective student rebellions in the history of the federal Indian boarding school system. Scholars who study Indian boarding schools often point out how students rebelled against their schools by running away, burning buildings, or even committing suicide. Carlisle students did all of these things.[5] In 1914, however, they did something else that was different and remarkable. They petitioned the federal government to investigate their school, and then drew the attention of both the Bureau of Indian Affairs and Congress. Their efforts did not close down Carlisle immediately, but they did lead to the dismissal of some of its most important leaders, and ultimately, four years later, led the federal government to abandon its first and most iconic off reservation boarding school. They accomplished this by exposing the school's profoundly hypocritical actions at a place dedicated to uplifting Indigenous Americans. Reading their complaints, the government report, and the congressional hearing testimony, students make one point central and clear: the administrators who operated Carlisle exhibited far less "civilization" than their student body. Far from serving as "civilized" role models, Carlisle's white leadership demonstrated selfishness, laziness, greed, and corruption.

The students who petitioned against Carlisle masterfully turned the tables upon their school. They positioned themselves as the "civilized" ones, and their school's overseers as the barbarians. This tactic closely resembles Gail Bederman's discussion of Ida B. Wells, the fiercely heroic African American journalist who fought against lynching in the late nineteenth and early twentieth centuries. Yet Bederman also points out that Wells encountered an unexpected risk when she portrayed white lynch mobs as "uncivilized." At the very time that she took up the cause of "civilization," many white men were embracing their inner "savage," sometimes in colleges and in sports like football. Some actually desired for white men to detour from manly "civilization" into masculine "savagery" in precisely the ways that Wells described in her writings.[6] Although not exactly the same as the risks that Wells encountered when she adopted the high road of "civilization," those who used a similar argument against Carlisle also took a gamble by accepting uncritically the binary between manly self-control and masculine physicality. In doing so, some students would find it difficult to untangle patriarchal whiteness from the position of "civilization" that they appropriated. Student testimonies woven with expressions of antisemitism, racism, and sexism suggest that some had learned the lessons of "civilization" all too well. Furthermore, they castigated many of their fellow students, often members of the football team, as hedonistic and sexually immoral, making them scapegoats for Carlisle's administrative incompetence.

"Civilization" on Trial

Yet it is critically important to recognize that the most power-ful testimonies during the 1914 hearings dealt with physical abuse, corruption, and incompetence. In their petitions, students directed their criticisms at three principle figures: Friedman, Athletic Direc-tor Warner, and Bandmaster Claude Stauffer. They accused Warner and Stauffer of violent behavior with students, and Warner of also using profane language, gambling on Carlisle's games, and drink-ing to excess. They portrayed Friedman as an impotent superin-tendent, incapable of doing anything to hinder the behavior of the other two. A significant number of male students who testified to the congressional delegation also were members of the campus's YMCA chapter, something that had existed since Pratt's tenure, and that preached Protestant ideals of manly self-control as its prin-cipal virtues. Inspector Linnen devoted the balance of his report to hedonistic behavior, particularly among football players, but in their testimony, students clearly aimed to establish a strong crit-ical voice toward an institution that exploited and abused them.

Aside from their sharp critique of Carlisle's administration, some students who testified to the congressional delegation painted a picture of a student body that had descended into uncontrolled drinking and sexual activity, testimony that was devastating to school authorities who could not allow students to engage in vice without compromising Carlisle's mission of education and "civ-ilization." These accusations stung. Despite the wider rejection of Pratt's ideal of equal and immediate "civilization," Carlisle still aimed to elevate the Indian from what most white Americans per-ceived to be a state of "savagery."[7]

A wide range of students, led by members of the school's YMCA, testified during the hearings. Witnesses John Gibson (Pima) and Peter Eastman (Dakota) were prominent members of the chap-ter, one that had gone into sharp decline in the year before the congressional hearings. The pair subsequently became president and vice-president of the school chapter in March 1914, a decision undoubtedly influenced by their participation in the hearings.[8] Additionally, Hiram Chase (Omaha) was the YMCA reporter for the *Carlisle Arrow* between 1913 and 1914.[9] With the organization

providing three of the seven male witnesses, testimony often circulated around grievances about student morality. At the same
time, several students not associated with the YMCA also testified,
including Edward Bracklin (Ojibwe), a member of the school's
football team and the Invincibles Debating Society, and Henry
Broker (Ojibwe, Middle Earth).[10] Montreville Yuda and Louis Schweigman (Lakota), both ex-Carlisle students, also appeared at
the hearings.[11] It is likely that Gus Welch would have testified too.
However, afraid of what he might say, Friedman and Warner paid
for Welch to see an ill relative prior to the commission's arrival.[12]
Although the YMCA was a foundation for some students who testified, a significant proportion of the campus not affiliated with
the organization also supported the campaign against Friedman.

Students did testify to there being lax discipline and rampant
vice among students. In their testimony before Congress, students
discussed examples of drinking and sex in some detail. Many said
that most students imprisoned in the guardhouse were guilty of
intoxication, and that students who drank had a negative impact
upon the campus atmosphere.[13] Yet, importantly, this was not their
only, nor necessarily their most significant criticism of the school.
In their original petition students also accused Carlisle's administration of providing insufficient food, allowing unsanitary conditions, and engaging in extreme punishment.[14]

More than the students, it appears that the congressional committee took particular interest in sexuality and drinking among
those attending Carlisle. In fact, in their questioning of students,
they sometimes expressed more interest in the potential of sex
among students than they were in some basic aspects of student
health and campus safety. For example, Bracklin testified about a
lack of building safety that he observed in the men's dormitory, but
the congressmen who questioned him seemed more concerned
with students who might escape their dorms in the middle of the
night to meet up with members of the opposite sex. As part of his
testimony in which he expressed concerns over student safety,
Bracklin revealed that girls could not have escaped out of their
windows because the frames were nailed shut.

"Civilization" on Trial

Mr. Bracklin: I don't know whether to speak of the girls' quarters or not. The girls' windows are nailed down. The bottom sash is nailed solid to the top, and the only way they can get any fresh air is to have a little opening on top and they can not open the bottom sash up.

The Chairman: Do you know why that is done?

Mr. Bracklin: No, sir.

The Chairman: I presume that is done to keep them from passing in and out of the rooms through the windows.

Mr. Bracklin: I do not think they could pass down there and jump to the ground.

The Chairman: You do not think it would be necessary to fasten the windows for that purpose?

Mr. Bracklin: No sir.[15]

Bracklin mentioned the windows out of concern for student fire safety and the need for ventilation in the dorm, and the committee chairman, Joe Robinson, would certainly have known that nailing windows shut posed a serious hazard in the event of a fire (the Triangle Shirtwaist Factory Fire had taken place only three years earlier). Moreover, tuberculosis posed one of the most serious infectious disease risks to Carlisle students, and by the time of this testimony, most people would have been well aware of the importance of ventilation in preventing the spread of the disease. Nevertheless, in questioning, the committee chair mentions neither of these topics in relation to the fastened windows. Instead, he was much more interested in girls escaping from their rooms. Considering this, the congressional committee appears to have partly steered students toward an emphasis upon student conduct through its questioning, an interrogation that certainly reflected the attitudes and interest of its members.

Testimony of student drinking effectively portrayed Friedman as incompetent at controlling students, and provided fodder for his enemies. In testimony to Indian Commissioner Cato Sells the previous year, Matthew K. Sniffen, the white head of the Indian Rights

Association and someone who had long disagreed with Friedman's administration, alleged that on June 13, 1913, fifty students returned to campus drunk.[16] Even though this incident allegedly occurred during the summer when the vast majority of students were on their outing, Carlisle residents who testified before the congressional committee seemed to have missed it.[17] Locals all remarked on the good behavior of the students with many stating that they never witnessed student drinking.[18] This is not to say that Carlisle students did not drink, even excessively.[19] Some even alleged that Montreville Yuda, the prominent student who had presented a petition to Franklin Lane, disobeyed student directives by staying out late at night and providing whisky for other students.[20] Others accused athletes Gus Welch and Jim Thorpe of drinking.[21] Yet by detailing alcohol abuse on campus, students who did not like Friedman found a powerful story that they knew would interest the congressional committee.

In addition to the use of alcohol, those who appeared before the committee testified that some students regularly engaged in sex on campus. Once again, they took the high road of "civilization" and condemned their fellow students' behavior. For example, Hiram Chase (Omaha), who had testified against the unjust punishment given to some students, commended Friedman for expelling those who were sexually active. He said in testimony, "The greatest case for expelling these students, those that deserved it, is that the boys and girls have met at various times. And the student body as a whole, they wish to have such students expelled from the school. We do not want to have such students as that."[22] For Chase, students who engaged in sex did not deserve the benefits of a "civilized" education, and should be returned to their previous state on the reservation. Chase also typifies the degree to which Carlisle's administration infantilized its students. While he may have called them "boys" and "girls," many of the students who engaged in sexual activity at Carlisle were well into their twenties, an age when many in their generation, both on and off reservations, were partnered and having children. It is likely that many actually would have been sexually active before even arriving at Carlisle.[23]

"Civilization" on Trial

Art teacher Angel Decora Dietz (Winnebago) emphasized "immoral" behavior among students much more than Chase did. She produced a list of twenty-eight "ruined" female students, or female students presumed to have been permanently tarnished by engaging in sexual activity.[24] Portraying sexually active women as "ruined" is an idea deeply rooted in the history of patriarchy whereby men control women's sexuality. That Carlisle administrators presented no list of "ruined" men further illustrates how the school established a particularly Victorian standard of gender norms. Students testified that their male peers sometimes faced no punishment for engaging in sex. For example, Bertha Canfield, a teacher, said that Carlisle disciplinarians expelled female students without giving them a chance to speak for themselves, while Sampson Burd, a member of the football team, had engaged in sex with a female student without punishment.[25]

Teachers frequently mentioned that male sexual advancements placed female students in vulnerable situations. Lelah Burns, a teacher, testified about a male student named Leo White (Winnebago) who harassed young women on campus. She described him as a "will-o'-the-wisp" who had a habit of leering at his female cohorts.[26] Canfield, a Friedman opponent, testified that during a 1911 trip to Philadelphia, lacking an adequate number of chaperones, members of the opposite sexes had slept in the same rooms. In particular, she remembered a student named Amos Komah (Comanche) spending the night in the room of a female student. This led to both students being expelled. Eventually, when the female student tried to return to campus, she was sent off without even receiving money for the train fare home, leaving her stranded in Harrisburg.[27] Anna Ridenour told Linnen that even male staff had engaged improperly with female students. Chalmers Behney was dismissed from Carlisle after a liaison with Anna La Fernier (Ojibwe), a student. In a letter to La Fernier, Behney called her his "Chippewa squaw," a disparaging term of endearment that La Fernier, according to Behney's own letter, did not like.[28]

Those who testified about a lack of sexual restraint among students tended to blame Friedman for inconsistent punishments and incompetent management. For example, students who spoke before the committee often mentioned those whom Friedman failed to expel for violating the school's behavioral code. The school expelled La Fernier briefly for her relationship with Chalmers Behney, but allowed her to return to Carlisle in September 1914.[29] School officials accused Agnes Jacobs (Onondaga) of engaging in sexual activity during the often criticized trip to Philadelphia. Yet she remained at Carlisle.[30] Carlisle not only failed to expel Leo White, but they hired him as an interpreter in Washington DC to represent the school before government officials.[31] Ultimately, Friedman did pay a price for these student testimonies. Yet students also treaded upon dangerous terrain when they called out their peers as "immoral" or "hedonistic." After the final reports had been filed, it would be easy for the public and for government officials to tarnish all Indian school students as having a low moral posture.

While these cases show that some students did avoid permanent severe punishment, Genevieve Bell, discovered that Friedman actually expelled a significant number of students for sexual misconduct prior to the hearings, a disproportionate number of whom were female.[32] In fact, this is something that female teachers discussed in their testimony as an injustice. Adelaide Reichel testified about Irvin Sherman (Dakota), a male student. Sherman was confined to his room after meeting a group of female students. Yet he was quickly released and danced with two other girls the following evening. The original female students were also restricted to their rooms, and they were not allowed to attend the school dance.[33] The committee asked Reichel to comment on why she believed Sherman received a lighter punishment than the female students involved.

> Miss Reichel: The boys are not being punished as severely as the girls are punished, or even more severely.
>
> Senator Lane: Whose fault is that?
>
> Miss Reichel: I do not know.
>
> Representative Stephens: What remedy would you suggest?

"Civilization" on Trial

Miss Reichel: Punish the boys the same as the girls are punished, or even more severely.

Representative Stephens: Who is guilty of that discrimination against the girls?

Miss Reichel: I do not know. I think the girls are being punished as hard as they should be.[34]

Committee members pressed Reichel to blame Friedman for the discrimination that she observed, but she refused to do so, criticizing disciplinarians instead. For his part, despite his reputation for lax enforcement of school rules, Friedman did inflict harsh punishments by having students whom he perceived to be troublemakers from untrustworthy backgrounds adjudicated off campus. In September 1913, he had Edward McKean charge Paul Jones (Cayuse) and Ethel Williams with fornication.[35] Friedman believed that both had engaged in criminal behavior before arriving at Carlisle, so sent them to a local court. They both were sentenced to sixty days in jail. Jones, however, remained in jail for seventy days, while Williams served her punishment working for the sheriff's wife. In his report on Carlisle, Inspector Linnen mentioned this incident as an example of injustice and incompetence under Friedman's management. Linnen pointed out that Pennsylvania law actually considered fornication a misdemeanor punishable by a fine, not a term in jail.[36]

In testimony, Friedman claimed not to support overly harsh punishments for students, saying that he did not support corporal punishments, although, as we will see, these did take place while he was superintendent. Students seemed to perceive him as lacking in masculine attributes, so much so that he became a particular target for student violence. Once, for example, when Friedman came to inspect the dormitories at night, the students threw shoes at him.[37] During his testimony Friedman stated: "I am not an active man, nor a prizefighter, and any blackguard can come into my office and say anything he pleases."[38] The placid image of student disciplinary life contrasted sharply with some student testimonies. A student identified in the published hearing transcripts as Lewis Braun (most likely Lewis Brown [Dakota]), testified that his peers often mocked and showed disrespect for Wallace Denny (Oneida), the school disciplinarian, a former student who had stayed to work at Carlisle. According to Braun/Brown, Denny often responded violently, hitting a small boy with his fists, and attacking others with a baseball bat, sending one to the hospital. Braun/ Brown reported that Denny pushed James Kallowat (Kootenai) down a flight of stairs for dropping a rag on the floor.[39] Undoubtedly Denny's violence influenced student willingness to engage in similar behavior and was a source of their discontent with the school, a sentiment evidenced in the petitions that brought the federal inspection to Carlisle in the first place.

In their testimony the school staff often connected drinking, sex, and violence to a lack of "civilization" that they perceived some students had brought to the school. They portrayed troublesome female students as unfeminine, and misbehaving male students as overly masculine. For example, when Friedman justified having Williams and Jones prosecuted off campus, he said during testimony that "the girl . . . lived on a reservation up in New York, and their influences were extremely bad." About Jones, he said, "The boy came from one of the Western States," and "had been sentenced for horse stealing." Wallace Denny also conflated uncontrolled drinking with the reservation:

> The Chairman: What is the drinking attributable to? Is there much drunkenness?
>
> Mr. Denny: No. Those pupils that are drunkards before they came here are the ones that are carrying on that.[40]

Denny directly connected unmanly behavior, hedonism, and reservation life. According to Denny, reservations promoted vice among the male students. As a student during the Pratt era, Denny was taught to despise the reservation and Indian culture. By working at Carlisle, alongside his wife Nellie Robertson Denny (Sioux), he disconnected himself from Native society and culture while connecting reservation life to vice.[41]

"Civilization" on Trial

School staff also portrayed student sexual activity as a product their Indigenous lives. Of course, students arrived at Carlisle from a variety of societies with their own rituals and traditions regarding childhood, adulthood, and sexuality. Most who worked at Carlisle, however, classified all Indigenous life as "savagery." Facing questions about student "immorality," school physician Dr. A. R. Allen remarked, "You take the Indian boy and girl that come from the reservation, not thoroughly covered over with the veneer of 'civilization,' with nothing to restrain their passions, and bring them under the environment of 'civilization,' and you are going to have those things occur."[42] In these comments Allen not only portrayed students as sexually uncontrolled, but he even diminished model students by stating that they exhibited only the "veneer of civilization."

Yet members of the school YMCA chapter embraced "civilization" zealously. They distinguished themselves from students who drank and engaged in sex by portraying themselves as restrained, self-controlled, and sober. In 1914 they expressed tremendous concern over the fact that, in late 1913, the school's YMCA chapter had collapsed. Friedman initiated this when he dismissed Dr. James Walker, resident secretary of the school's YMCA. The organization's members clearly liked Walker. Peter Eastman stated that some students cried when Walker departed in early 1913.[43] Friedman replaced Walker with increasingly ineffective and disliked leaders, like Roy Mann, the mathematics teacher.[44] Eastman declared that Mann was "no example to the boys at all," alleging that he regularly smoked and told inappropriate jokes.[45] Mann's unpopularity resulted in the student body abandoning the YMCA. Membership declined from 206 prior to Walker's dismissal to only twenty-eight by the time Linnen investigated Carlisle.[46] Despite this, the YMCA provided a position of "civilized" authority from which the three male members who testified could condemn the savagery of the Carlisle Indian School itself.

Testimony connected the disintegration of the YMCA with the rise of student protest on campus. One of the male YMCA members, Peter Eastman, specifically connected Walker's dismissal with student resistance:

The Chairman: You say the insubordination practically began with the dismissal of Mr. Walker, the Y.M.C.A. man?

Mr. Eastman: Some of it did.

The Chairman: The students were attached to Mr. Walker, were they?

Mr. Eastman: Yes, sir. He had the interest of the boys at heart.[47]

In their solidarity in support of Walker, the students did more than express admiration for their old mentor, and more than communicate their attachment to the YMCA. Profoundly, they positioned themselves as manly and "civilized." In part, this meant that they became a faction in the school that reported on and ostracized students who drank or engaged in sex. When these students testified, they offered the YMCA as the "civilized" solution to the rampant hedonism that they argued existed among the male students. Eastman, a prominent member of the school chapter, presented such an answer in his testimony:

The Chairman: You have no organization within the student body that is designed to protect the good name of the school from that kind of reputation?

Mr. Eastman: No, sir; the only step that was taken was that [*sic*] Y.M.C.A.

The Chairman: You say the Y.M.C.A. did that?

Mr. Eastman: The only thing that had any influence at all. Dr. Walker had an office over in the large boys' quarters—he did not stay there all the time—and in the evening he had reading and entertained the boys there himself.[48]

The members of the YMCA would have lent an air of legitimacy to the student protest against Carlisle staff and administration, something that would have been more likely to have drawn the attention of Congress than throwing shoes at the superintendent. Significantly, by claiming a "civilized" status, these students put the most powerful leaders of the Carlisle Indian Industrial School on the defensive. They did so most dramatically in the case of two high-ranking members of the staff. One was bandmaster Claude Stauffer. Although the YMCA students were not directly responsible for the revelations of abuse against Stauffer, it is clear from his congressional testimony that a discourse of "civilization" provided an important weapon against him.

In a disturbing interrogation during the hearings, committee members asked Stauffer about a brutal beating that he inflicted upon an eighteen-year-old student named Julia Hardin (Pottawatomi). The committee had read Hardin's deposition before Inspector Linnen in which she had described a violent punishment that he had unjustly given. Hardin had been a good student at Carlisle, earning marks of "Excellent" and "Very Good" for her conduct.[49] She told Linnen that in June 1913, she expressed reluctance toward participating in the outing program until she had proper clothes and a trunk in which to carry them. She could not afford to buy either until the end of the month on the only day that students were allowed to withdraw money from their accounts. According to Hardin, she at first was told that she could wait and leave when she was ready, but later in the day was commanded to leave the next morning. After refusing, she was ordered to go to the office of Hannah Ridenour, the matron of the female quarters. After Hardin entered, Stauffer arrived at Ridenour's office and told her, "You are going to the country tonight on the five o'clock train," and asked her to sign a check that would draw from her savings account to cover the cost of her outing train fare. She refused, and when she did, according to Hardin, Stauffer slapped her in the face with an open hand. She said, "He only slapped me once, then I dodged back, and finally he says; 'You are not going to have your own way, you are going to the country if I have to stand the responsibility.' So he got a board from one of the windows and then he whipped me." She described the board as two and a half feet long, and four inches wide, and provided a graphic account of her beating.

Q: Which matrons held you?

A: Miss Ridenour was one and I won't say whether the other was Miss Austin or Miss Knight, but it was one of them.

Q: Where did he strike you?

A: I was on the floor. He hit me on the head, shoulders, and every place else.

Q: You were on the floor?

A: Yes, he had thrown me on the floor.

Q: Who had?

A: Mr. Stauffer. Finally I said I would not go if that was the way he would treat me. And he kept asking me, 'Now, will you go' I said, 'No, not as long as you are doing this. If you had asked me in the right way I would have went.'

Q: How long did he whip you?

A: I couldn't give you the time, but he would whip me and then he would say, 'Now are you going?' And I would say I wouldn't and he would throw me down again.

Q: About how many times do you think that he struck you?

A: I couldn't tell you but I know he must have been there for at least ten minutes. He would say, 'Now will you go?' and I would say, 'No,' and then he would throw me down again.

Q: Do you think he struck you as many as twenty-five times?

A: I know it was over that, for we were in there at least ten minutes.

Q: Do you think he struck you forty or fifty times?

A: That was more like it. Then they sent for Mr. Whitwell [the principal] and he came. I had just got through working for him in his office and he couldn't believe it. He came over to me. 'Now Julia,' he says, 'come and show them that you are a lady and sign this check, and you go out to the country and show them what you are.' And he spoke to me so nice I couldn't help it, so I got up, went over and signed the check for him. Then they took me up to the lock-up.[50]

Hardin showed incredible bravery in her deposition, a testimony that, fundamentally, neither Friedman nor Stauffer would contradict in any of their interviews with investigators. The congressional committee, in their own interrogations, seemed to be moved by her words. Yet in their questioning of Stauffer, they did not address the fundamental justice of an outing program that violently coerced students to work in the country, withheld students' money, and forced students to pay the transportation costs without their consent. Instead, they framed their discourse surrounding his violent assault and abuse of power in terms of his "civilized" manhood.

The Chairman: Did it occur to you that that was a manly and courageous thing to do?

Mr. Stauffer: I have regretted ever since that it was necessary for me to do it, but I did as my duty prompted me to.

The Chairman: You were moved solely by a sense of duty?

Mr. Stauffer: Yes, sir.

The Chairman: You mean you slapped a young lady in the face from a sense of duty, and expect anybody to believe it?

Mr. Stauffer: Well, that is my version of it, Senator Robinson.[51]

Hardin did not frame her testimony in terms of "civilization" or manliness. She provided a straightforward account of a terrifying experience of pain and powerlessness, one in which she showed a remarkable degree of strength and defiance. Yet the discourse of "civilization" provided a powerful lens through which to understand the injustice that Hardin experienced. When the committee chair asked Stauffer if slapping Harding was, "a manly and courageous thing to do," it was a rhetorical question tinged with biting sarcasm that Stauffer could not adequately answer. To the committee members, Stauffer would have resembled more an overly masculine beast than an agent of "civilization." Ultimately, the revelations of Stauffer's behavior ended up costing him his job.[52]

The second member of Carlisle's staff thrown on his heels was football coach Glenn "Pop" Warner. Warner not only had very little patience for the niceties of "civilized manliness"—he made no effort to hide it. Like other college football men of his age and

FIG. 15. Musical director Claude Stauffer. Testimony revealed that he had beaten a student because she refused to go on an outing assignment. He was fired after the congressional hearings. Photograph courtesy of the Cumberland County Historical Society, Carlisle, Pennsylvania.

FIG. 16. Left to right: Gus Welch, Alex Arcasa (Colville), Pop Warner, Stancil "Possum" Powell (Cherokee), and Jim Thorpe at practice in 1910. In 1914 Welch organized a petition from the football team to get Warner fired. In his deposition before the Indian Service inspector E. B. Linnen, he said about his coach, "As a man, I don't think very much of him." Photograph courtesy of the Cumberland County Historical Society, Carlisle, Pennsylvania.

class at the time, he embraced an excessively masculine posture to maintain authority. The student petitions of protest at Carlisle all, ultimately, condemned Friedman and called for his removal, but as mentioned, the athletes later submitted one of their own sharply critical of Warner. In this document, and during deposition interviews with Linnen, students painted a picture of the athletic director that contrasted sharply with that of the character-building coach so often touted in school media (and thoroughly unrecognizable later in the Hollywood portrayal of him as the patient mentor who castigates a morally weak Jim Thorpe for being a "powder puff" in *Jim Thorpe: All American*). With his crass and violent behavior, Warner became a potent symbol of corruption and "uncivilized" leadership at the school. Students had plenty of reason to protest against him. Warner was often violent toward the players and was even present at the whipping of four members of the band, and by 1914 several students were embittered by the role that he played when the International Olympic Committee had stripped Jim Thorpe of his gold medals.[53] Their central complaints against him in the petition, however, focused upon his lack of moral character and how this undermined the legitimacy of his authority.

The athletes' petition reads as if the football players had retained Richard Henry Pratt's original admonition to demonstrate restraint and manly self-control on the field. It states, "We are lovers of clean athletics and we believe that they are beneficial to young men if they are conducted in the proper manner." They call for Warner's removal, and cite as their reasons, among others, that "he possesses a weak moral character," "continually uses profane and abusive language in the presence of the boys," "has proven himself selfish by abolishing branches of athletics that he was not capable of coaching such as base-ball and basket-ball," had bet on a football game that Carlisle played against Dartmouth, and allowed officers of the Athletic Association to use funds for their own purposes.[54]

Gus Welch led the effort to accumulate athlete names for this petition of protest, one addressed to Commissioner of Indian Affairs Cato Sells, but submitted directly to Rep. A. R. Rupley. Before its release, however, Linnen deposed six football players whom he interviewed about Warner: Welch, Elmer Busch (Pomo; the captain of the football team), Edward Bracklin, Joseph Guyon, John Wallette (Ojibwe, Turtle Mountain), and Peter Calac (Mission). Welch took direct aim at Warner's manhood, acknowledging his masculinity but questioning his character: "In my opinion, Mr. Warner is a very good football coach and all that, but as a man I don't think very much of him. I think he is a man with no principle, and I think it is a fair statement from me that I don't think he is the man, he don't have the right influence to be over young boys that he is here. I think it is detrimental to their cause to have a man that uses them as he does."[55]

Welch then details how Warner used profane language toward members of the team. Importantly, Welch characterizes this as not just immoral, but abusive, publicly humiliating players by saying, "'You God damn bone head,' or 'You son of a bitch'" for "executing

FIG. 17. Joseph Guyon. Guyon and Edward Bracklin were among those who signed Welch's petition against Warner. In his deposition Bracklin accused Warner of physically abusing players and said, "He doesn't use [his players] as a man ought to use the boys." Photograph courtesy of the Robert R. Rowe private collection, Dickinson College Archives and Special Collections.

FIG. 18. Edward Bracklin. Photograph courtesy of the Robert R. Rowe private collection, Dickinson College Archives and Special Collections.

a play that wasn't perfect" and "making minor mistakes." Welch says that he witnessed Warner physically threaten Roy Large (Shoshone) and hit Wallette with a large stick, and that all members of the team knew that Warner regularly sold complimentary tickets meant to be given to family and friends and pocketed the proceeds. When asked if he thought of Warner as "dishonest," Welch answered, "I do. . . . All the boys that are not afraid of him in their own opinions will say he is not trustworthy and don't think any-

"Civilization" on Trial

thing of him." Welch noted that Warner had control over the secretive Athletic Association budget, and students suspected that he improperly enriched himself with its proceeds.[56]

Elmer Busch affirmed Welch's understanding of Warner as an abusive coach who used profanity, and a dishonest man who misappropriated funds from the Athletic Association budget for his own benefit. He stated that Warner allowed privileges to athletes, like permission to travel home, that overruled Friedman's directives. Edward Bracklin said of Warner, "Well, he is rather an abusive fellow in a way, when he's dealing with the boys on the field, and he doesn't use them as a man ought to use the boys, these boys that are just growing up. He is not a very desirable leader in ways. He has often used profane language among the boys." He concluded that he recognized that Warner had constructed a deeply fraudulent image of himself. He told Linnen of Warner's gambling, and also accused him of cheating, saying, "He claims to be, and the rest of the people of the country claim him to be, a true sportsman. But a true sportsman wouldn't send scouts out to see the other teams play and get all their plays and then bring them back here and show them to us."[57]

Students further accused both Stauffer and Warner of having had crates of beer delivered to their homes, connecting them to the problems of drinking on campus.[58] Even if the pair did not supply the students with alcohol, the allegation signified the extent of their power: alcohol was delivered to their homes without their fearing reproach. The students' attack assumed a superior moral ground and condemned these two men for their lack of manly self-control. It proved to be extremely effective. In his report to Congress, Linnen cited the students' complaints, and wrote, "Mr. Glenn S. Warner is not a proper person to longer be associated with said student body by reason of his domination over the athletic boys, [and] his foul language and cursing of the athletic boys in the presence of the student body and outsiders who happen to be present on such occasions." Linnen concludes that teachers, the industrial staff, and the principal all agreed that football had assumed an outsized role on campus, and that "the manner in which athletics have been conducted has been extremely bad for the academic and industrial training of the student body."[59]

Yet, while students may have turned the tables of "civilization" upon Carlisle's most powerful administrators, they also demonstrated their own ability to get dragged into racism, antisemitism, and misogyny through their own "civilization" discourse. From Carlisle's beginnings, Pratt had sought to separate Carlisle's students from the town's African American population. School documents reveal an attitude that portrayed Black residents who lived near the school as a morally corrosive influence. For example, shortly after Friedman had left Carlisle in the spring of 1914, a student disciplinary board "court marshalled" two male students for spending a night with women off campus. They charged the offending students for "associating with Negro women and white women of low and immoral character and indulging in fornication with them." They described one woman with whom they allegedly had sex as "a notorious bad character in the Negro section of Carlisle," and the other as "a Negress of low and immoral character."[60]

In testimony before the committee, students sometimes blamed the African American community for both drinking and sex among students. Bracklin, for example, testified that African American bootleggers were the primary source of alcohol for students on campus.[61]

> Representative Carter: Do you know anything about how these boys get this whisky?
>
> Mr. Bracklin: Not positively; only what I have heard.
>
> Representative Carter: What do you hear about it?
>
> Mr. Bracklin: Sometimes they go down here in town and get these bootleggers, of course. They are blacks mostly. They get them to go and get the whisky for them and the negroes bring it to them.[62]

Angel Decora Dietz echoed this testimony, saying that when she asked students where they had obtained alcohol, "they say they get it in town from negroes."[63] Yet in earlier testimony, Peter

Eastman suggested that it was, in fact, students' ability to pass as white (ironically demonstrating a success of Carlisle's mission) that allowed them to purchase liquor. He said students procured alcohol at the local Thadium House hotel.[64] Wallace Denny (Oneida), the disciplinarian, also commented that Carlisle students had actually become indistinguishable from other whites in town. He said that white barmen in Carlisle would not "knowingly" serve a student, prompting Linnen to suggest that students wear their uniforms at all times in order for them not to be mistaken as white.[65]

In fact, any Carlisle students who did not know where they stood within the country's racial hierarchy needed only to look to their school's leadership to tell them. Friedman had used the connection between race, "civilization," and manhood to undermine anyone who challenged him. He dismissed Montreville Yuda, the Carlisle graduate who had brought the students' original petition to Washington, as "more negro than Indian."[66] Elaborating, he said, "I don't know whether it is darky blood or not, but he is one of the shrewdest young chaps I have seen."[67] Little is known about Yuda's background, and he might very well might have had African American parentage.[68] If so, due to Carlisle's racial restrictions on enrollment, it would have disqualified him from having been allowed to attend and graduate from the school. From its beginnings, Carlisle's founders had baked a racial hierarchy into the school's very foundation. When it came to finding a scapegoat for drinking or sexual activity, some Carlisle students seemed to have learned very well whom to blame.[69]

If students drew upon a "civilization" discourse to accuse Stauffer and Warner of being overly masculine, they did the same to portray Friedman as not masculine enough. Students cited many incidences of Friedman's incompetence, including his subservience to Warner. Charges against the superintendent were not entirely new. Friedman had survived previous investigations, including for accusations of cruelty in 1909 and financial impropriety in 1911.[70] He had even alienated powerful members of staff, such as John Whitwell, Bertha Canfield, and Angel Decora Dietz. By the time the commission arrived, a large proportion of the student body and staff was against Friedman. Some students also accused Friedman of speaking to them in a derogatory manner. One of the unnamed female witnesses described how Friedman referred to them as savages, saying to the committee, "And the way Mr. Friedman yells at the girls. . . . And he said 'Oh, there you savages,' or 'Oh, you savages'—he called them savages anyhow, and I thought it was very rude of him."[71] As legitimate as their objections to him might have been, they frequently framed their attacks upon Friedman in terms of his manhood and his Jewishness.

Although Friedman converted to Christianity and joined the Carlisle Episcopalian church in 1912, his father was Jewish and he was raised as a Jew. He had a Jewish name and a Jewish physical appearance.[72] While staff and student attacks upon him were laced with antisemitism, many had issues with Friedman that were not necessarily connected to his ethnicity. He had moved Carlisle's identity dramatically away from Pratt's educational model, advocating practical manual training geared toward skills in modern industry, steering away from what he considered an anachronistic emphasis upon agricultural skills, and eliminating much of the academic curriculum (to which the school's principal, John Whitwell, strenuously objected).[73] Furthermore, Friedman drew heated criticism for his dismissal of the well-liked Walker, the leader of the school YMCA.[74] Friedman was, in the words of Genevieve Bell, "anathema to Pratt. He was not a military man. He was a bureaucrat."[75] While he had a looser style of leadership than that of Pratt and Mercer, some of his actions conflicted with this posture. He had students follow a strict calendar that all had to carry at all times, and that scheduled nearly every waking hour. As we have seen, despite his stated aversion to corporal punishment, he seemingly allowed it to happen under his watch on several occasions. Especially damaging to his reputation, accounting audits showed that he had embezzled money from the school and the Athletic Department when taking trips with his wife to watch the football team play.[76] Yet if his deviance from the kind of military identity that Pratt and Mercer cultivated undermined his masculine posture, so did his Jewish identity, and attacks upon his manhood often took on an anti-Semitic form.

During the hearings, staff and students alike denigrated Fried-man for his Jewish identity. Rep. Robinson, the committee chair, noted in his report that students often called Friedman "Old Jew" as a sign of disrespect.[77] During the hearings, Eastman testified that, when students threw shoes at Friedman, they called him "Jew," "Christ-killer," and "pork-dodger."[78] In many respects, they might have been taking their cues from other figures of author-ity at the school.

Bertha Canfield stated that Carlisle needed a "strong moral Christian man at the head as superintendent," implying that Fried-man held none of these qualities. [79] In his love letter addressed to student Anna La Fernier, employee C. B. Behney wrote, "Anna, if you loved me just half as much as I hate the 'Israelite' we would be married by this time. Don't you think it would make the 'Jew' sit up and take notice?"[80] In Friedman's Jewish identity, students found an easy attack upon his authority.

The derogatory comments toward Friedman received little response from the commissioners, except to serve as evidence of Friedman's unsteady grip on his authority over students. This should surprise nobody, for antisemitism, and in particular stereotypes that Jewish men were unmanly, would have been firmly rooted in the "civilization" that students had been taught in white schools even before coming to Carlisle. Anti-Semitic stories appeared in the *McGuffey Reader* texts that were standard fare for rural schools in the nineteenth century.[81] English literature, in particular, had a long history of stereotyping Jewish men as effeminate and lack-ing in masculine character traits since the beginning of the mod-ern era.[82] Rather than offending the committee, its members much more likely would have recognized and understood the students' anti-Semitic attitudes.

As evidence of Friedman's deviation from masculine expecta-tions, students also mentioned his marriage in their testimonies. They portrayed him as lacking an adequately manly authority over his wife, Mary Friedman, a gentile woman and active mem-ber of the Suffrage League of Carlisle.[83] Mary held regular meet-ings at the superintendent's house in support of a constitutional amendment that would guarantee a woman's right to vote, and which were promoted in the school newspaper.[84] The movement to allow women a vote challenged the idea of naturally separate spheres and argued that women should be included in the public political domain.[85] Students who testified before the hearings, heavily influenced by the teachings of the YMCA and YWCA, did not mention her activism, but they demonstrated anti-feminist and masculinist judgments, at once castigating Mary Friedman for taking what they portrayed as an inappropriate role in public life and portraying her as contributing to the feminization of her husband.[86]

Students mentioned intimate and embarrassing stories about the Friedmans that painted a picture of Moses Friedman feminized and unable to control his wife. One female student described a game that she saw them play with one another at their house. "Mr. Friedman got up on the porch they started to play peek-a-boo around those pillars there, and they acted what I would call silly for a man that was ruling over the students that are here."[87] This story portrayed both as immature and temperamentally unfit to serve as figures of authority over students. Another female student who testified claimed that Mary was an inappropriate figure for emulation, saying, "Every time I see her she is carrying on somewhat simple. She does not carry herself as a woman ought to for us to follow an example by, but she always has those simple ways about her."[88] Although the student did not state what she meant by "simple," the context implies that she behaved in a childlike and unwomanly manner, challenging her husband's manhood. Others portrayed Mary Friedman as a loose woman who publicly exhibited her sexuality. A female student provided the following testimony.

> Miss ——: Yes, sir. In the first place, his wife is not the woman that ought to be on the grounds for we girls to follow the example, because the way she goes around here on the campus sometimes is simply disgraceful. We girls have seen her time and again when the boys were playing on their instruments over here, when they happened to be coming from the club she would

go out here and skirt-dance and kick until you could see up to her knees. Mr. Denny was standing there one time when she was performing these acts.

Senator Lane: Was her husband around?

Miss ——: Once, that I remember of. He was coming up here when he had just come out of the dining hall, and he was coming up, and he called out to her, "Oh, honey, I will pay for it," and she said, "I have paid for it already." And it just happened some of the boys were playing on their trombones, and she started on her skirt-dance, and she went on—well, she carried it a little too far.[89]

This student expressed shock and outrage when Mary demonstrated her sexual freedom. Senator Lane's question in which he asked, "Was her husband around?" demands that Moses Friedman be held ultimately responsible for his wife's sexuality. The fact that Friedman was present during this incident illustrated his inability to control Mary, and further portrayed him as lacking manly authority. One might very much expect students—living in an institution that barred them from engaging in any measure of sexual activity at a moment well into their adult lives, that labeled sexually active women as "ruined" and "immoral," and that dangerously nailed windows shut in the women's dormitory to prevent late night liaisons between them and men among the student body—to have recognized the hypocrisy of the Friedmans' behavior. Yet by labeling Mary Friedman a bad moral example, students also spoke in ways that the committee would surely have understood. It is hard to imagine a congressional committee reacting well if students attempted to justify their own claims to their own sexual identities, as legitimate as these might have been. Instead, their attack upon Friedman's manhood cut deep, providing powerful ammunition to a case against the superintendent that would effectively end his career. In his final report, Linnen supported the students' demand for Friedman's immediate dismissal from Carlisle.[90] Shortly following the hearings, this threat was carried out.[91] Yet it left untouched ideas about manliness and "civilization" that gave the Carlisle Indian School authority over their lives in the first place.

Student testimony that employed a "civilization" discourse proved effective in many ways, but it also took the investigation in unexpected directions, particularly with regard to the athletic program. Linnen and Carlisle staff used the petition campaign against the school and the student testimony to condemn the athletic department. In their comments before the full committee, the students rarely touched on athletics. Edward Bracklin never discussed sports, even though he was a member of the football team and had ample opportunity to do so.[92] The football players certainly received special privileges, and Warner was definitely a corrupt and narcissistic leader. Yet Linnen devoted a disproportionate amount of his final report to the athletic program. His critique of the athletes totaled seven pages of evidence while his analysis of corporal punishment lasted only two.[93] He stated that students at Carlisle most objected to the misuse of the athletic fund even though students did not mention this as one of their most important concerns in either their testimonies or in their depositions.[94]

In her dissertation Bell speculates that investigators really came to Carlisle looking for a scapegoat for the scandal that cost Jim Thorpe his Olympic medals. Even with the Carlisle Indian School unraveling, with its educational standards in decline, and with its legitimacy having been undermined years earlier when the federal government abandoned Pratt's original mission, "sports were really the prime concern" of the committee.[95] This is certainly true, but supporters of boarding school education also provided pressure from outside the government, portraying football as overly masculine and antithetical to "civilized" manliness for Indigenous students. Following the 1914 hearings, the Society of American Indians published a post-mortem in which they castigated football as appropriate only for elite universities. They argued that the pressure to win led Carlisle administrators to engage in ethical lapses, unfairly privilege athletes, and to neglect the educational mission of the school. The SAI also encouraged Carlisle to double down on its "civilizing" mission, providing preference to "the full-blood Indian student" since "mixed bloods reared more or less in civilized surroundings do not need the schools supported by the federal Government nearly as much as the real Indians for whom they were devised." Their commentary ended with praise for Carlisle's legacy, stating, "The good the school has done in the teaching of manhood and industry can not be measured."[96] Given the associations of athletics at Carlisle with debasement, the student petitions, and particularly the petition from the athletes, all constructed from a position of "civilization," would have played right into the government's hands.

So would staff members who resented the power and position of athletics on campus. Whitwell, for example, complained to the committee, "I have seen five and six teams playing at once and a number on the side lines. It looks like practically the whole school is over there."[97] Whitwell believed that the football team dominated concerns over the students' actual education, to the detriment of the latter. He said to the committee that Thorpe did not attend classes, and he lamented the appointment of assistant coach William "Lone Star" Dietz as teacher of mechanical trades. William H. Miller, the school's financial clerk, also discredited the athletic department. He found that Friedman had abused the athletic fund by claiming money for railroad expenses from it.[98] Warner also used the fund without any oversight to support his own and the athletes' extravagant lifestyle: the players all received an overcoat, a suit of clothing, and a watch each year.[99] These were all serious allegations, but in a real sense, they were symptomatic. Linnen had found in the sports programs not only a convenient example of corruption, but an allegory for the school's declension from its mission of "civilization."

Although students testified that their peers across campus engaged in drinking, sexual activity, and other deviations from the school's moral code, Linnen and Carlisle staff specifically blamed athletes for these diversions from discipline. Whitwell implicated Gus Welch as a heavy drinker.[100] Welch often drank with Thorpe, and was accused of drinking with the assistant quartermaster.[101] Welch was football captain and a leader among protesting students.

By mentioning him as a primary offender, Whitwell suggested that Welch influenced other athletes, branding the athletic program as hedonistic overall. To make matters worse, because of Warner's power at the school, athletes received preferential treatment when found guilty of offenses.[102] Carlisle staff placed most students who became drunk in the school's guardhouse, sentences ranging from a week to twelve days.[103] While athletes received a similar punishment for drunkenness, they often were released before a game.[104]

Similarly, because athletes received special treatment, some accused them of being particularly sexually active. In a letter to M. K. Sniffen, head of the Indian Rights Association, former student Louis Schweigman claimed that Friedman allowed the athletes to engage in sexual activity.[105] Schweigman made no such accusation in his testimony, and there is ample reason to doubt his original account. Friedman did not have the power to influence the behavior of the athletes directly. In fact, other than the case of Sampson Burd, no record of other athletes who were sexually active emerged during the hearings.[106] Yet staff witnesses like Canfield made sensational accusations about athletes, claiming in testimony that "ruined" female students traveled with the football team.[107] Canfield and Schweigman provided powerful accounts that helped to conflate athletes and sex. Neither, however, proved that athletes were any more sexually active than students as a whole. More to the point, their testimony spoke to an inspector and congressional committee that would already have connected masculinity to savagery and sexuality.

Ironically, despite Linnen's focus upon corruption in the athletic department, only Friedman and Stauffer were dismissed following the investigation. Because Warner drew his salary from the athletic fund and not the government, the congressional commission did not have the power to force his removal.[108] Warner decided to continue as athletic director for the 1914 football season, leaving him unpunished for his violent behavior and his financial malfeasance. By remaining as athletic director, Warner branded all athletes with his misbehavior. In the days following the hearings, the athletes submitted their petition to Linnen for Warner's dismissal, hoping to exert external pressure, but in the end, they could not force Warner out.[109]

For Carlisle's administrators and the federal government, the congressional hearings exposed the risks that they encountered when they committed to a big time football program. Carlisle's famous athletes and winning team certainly generated publicity, but, particularly after the Jim Thorpe scandal, they exposed a school that was badly failing at its "civilizing" mission. It did not take long after Friedman's ouster for school publications to espouse a new role for sports, one that echoed Pratt's earliest admonition for football players to serve as examples of "civilized" manhood. A June 1914 article printed in the *Red Man* heralded the new direction of the athletic department. The author, a prominent athlete at a different institution, stated: "As a consequence of this over-emphasizing of athletics, I feel that in many ways my college career has been a failure. I have failed to see the opportunities which most college men at some time consider; I have failed to come face to face with the deepest things of life, which, compared to athletics in importance, are as a mountain and a grain of sand."[110]

By this time colleges and universities had already begun to construct or expand their own football stadiums, creating seating capacities in the tens of thousands. As Brian Ingrassia has noted, these spectacular playing venues erased any doubt that college football had become commercial popular culture.[111] The author of the *Red Man* piece told both students and Carlisle's supporters that virtuous football had become an impossibility. Its publication in the *Red Man* announced that athletics would only be a small part of the Carlisle student's education. Students could still play sports, but athletics would no longer define the institution.

The article also criticized prominent leaders of the athletic department. The unnamed author directly condemned a coach's influence on the players: "Often an athlete must associate with or compete against men who are foul-mouthed and evil-minded. Sometimes a bad example or a few evil words by a man whose physical powers he admires are enough to knock a young fellow off his balance and to start him on the wrong track. Again, one is sometimes harmed by the low moral standards which control the team. When a coach's or captain's principles allow dirty play, unfairness or crookedness, their pupils are of necessity in danger of becoming tainted."[112]

Although the author ostensibly was not a Carlisle student, this paragraph clearly served as a reference to Warner. It reads as if it were lifted directly from Linnen's report. Warner, presuming he read the article, must have understood the intention of the message, perhaps making it more remarkable that he stayed at Carlisle for the 1914 season. The author proposed to limit the influence of coaches like Warner over athletes, encouraging players to resist "evil-minded" coaches. According to the author, athletes who did so gained agency over their future. They were able to avoid the influences of vice and violence.

The unnamed author also challenged the predominance of drinking in athletics. Commenting on traditions in college sport, the author stated, "Also, in many colleges, it is the custom to 'celebrate' after a big athletic victory, to 'drown sorrow' after a defeat. . . . In these cases it is showing school spirit and patriotism to get drunk and do things which at any other time would be tabooed by student sentiment. . . . These are some of the principal temptations which I would advise a man entering scholastic or collegiate athletics to be ready for and guard against."[113]

A white athlete at a Big Four university might associate drinking with local patriotism and college pride, thus making abstinence difficult for some. A non-drinker might even find himself marked as un-American, someone who has little nationalistic pride and deserves belittling. And most certainly, as with football, heavy drinking allowed elite white college men to demonstrate their masculinity. The author of this article, however, seems to be speaking very much to an Indian student at Carlisle, admonishing him to demonstrate control and manliness. What for a student at Princeton or Yale might exhibit virility and strength would, for a Carlisle student, symbolize an unmanly lack of self-control.

The author, however, offered a solution to students attracted to vice: membership in the YMCA. Referring to the athletes' influence

"Civilization" on Trial

over others, the author remarked, "When an athlete gets up in a Christian Association or religious gathering and makes a stand for right living, he has, in all probability, made a deeper impression than any other man, no matter how good, could make."[114] The author urged athletes to join and contribute to the YMCA, for by doing so they would persuade others to follow a similar route. As the YMCA promoted sport, athletes could still play football while learning and demonstrating manliness. A student could continue to play sports, but only within institutions that tempered an athlete's masculinity with the "civilizing" influence of Christianity. The author recounted that he had, "expended all my energy and enthusiasm on athletics, and as a result had none left for the mental and moral things which are absolutely necessary to a man's life if he is ever to attain *real* manhood" (italics author's own).[115] If athletics insufficiently taught "real" manhood, according to the author, the YMCA produced both men and athletes.

The *Red Man* article condemning sports signaled the end of an era at Carlisle. It represented the school's turn away from athletics and football, clearly in response to the congressional hearings and the investigation into the school. It is important to remember that this entire incident began with petitions that students generated. It is difficult to know the true motivations for who chose to sign these documents and rebel against Carlisle. Some might have been genuinely concerned with declining moral standards. Others may have resented a school administration that failed to practice the level of disciplined, "civilized" behavior that it demanded of students. Certainly corporal punishment and capricious enforcement of senseless rules motivated students like Julia Hardin. Ultimately, however, students appropriated a discourse of "civilization," portraying a school run by men severely lacking in the qualities of "civilized" manhood, limited men who had been empowered to enforce standards of "civilization" over others.

Audre Lourde, when criticizing affluent white heterosexual feminists for narrowly defining their movement around their own experiences, famously said, "The master's tools will never dismantle the master's house." All systems of domination have tools at their disposal to maintain the status quo and enforce hierarchies. Those who invaded the Americas had guns and germs among theirs, but they also had powerful ideologies. European settlers in North America included a diverse set of tribes, languages, nations, and cultures, but just as powerfully, they carried with them ideologies that allowed these assorted populations to merge together under a common mission. As Gail Bederman has shown in her scholarship so influential to this book, whiteness and "civilization" were central to allowing European Americans to create a collective identity that they believed was unique and superior. This is a mighty tool, and one that Carlisle students used in 1914, if not against their "masters" then certainly against their invaders who also had labeled themselves their "trustees." But it also came with significant risks. Lourde cautioned that such tools might allow subordinated peoples to beat their oppressors "at their own game," but they never allow the creation of "genuine change."[116] In their rebellion against their school, Carlisle students in many ways were remarkably successful. Yet their "civilization" discourse also caught them in a powerful undertow of patriarchal racism. What is more, they unwittingly created a backlash against the school's athletic program that had become a significant source of pride for students. Instead of being the showcase for Indian heroics, sports now were portrayed as a cauldron of hedonism and vice. For the football team's indiscretions, the students paid a much higher price than did their violent and corrupt coach. With that being said, Carlisle students never had a great many tools at their disposal in the first place, and if their "civilized" rebellion did not reverse the legacy of conquest, it did at least bring down the house of Carlisle.

5

The Aftermath

The 1914 congressional investigation devastated Carlisle's reputation. At its inception, Pratt created the Carlisle Indian Industrial School as an institution that would remove young Indigenous Americans from their homes and completely assimilate them into white Anglo-Protestant society. The federal government had long since abandoned this agenda. Instead, the hearings and investigative report pulled the veil off a school where corrupt leaders exploited its resources to enrich themselves, where students received insufficient industrial education and experienced brutal and capricious punishments, and where a shining athletic program served as a deceptive façade covering a decaying Potemkin village.[1]

Considering that Commissioner of Indian Affairs Cato Sells had already expressed his disinterest in off-reservation boarding schools, Carlisle's future looked grim.[2] The appointment of Oscar Lipps as superintendent did provide the school with a fresh start and an opportunity to save its tarnished reputation. Other than Warner continuing as athletic director, Lipps began his time at Carlisle with a clean slate. Key figures from the school's staff found themselves humiliated and no longer on campus. After Claude Stauffer was fired, he found work as conductor for the Loysville Girls Orphan Band in remote Perry County on the other side of North Mountain from Carlisle (still remarkable, considering the charges against him).[3] Linnen and the congressional committee recommended that Hannah Ridenour, the matron involved in the Julia Hardin incident, be transferred.[4] John Whitwell was sent to the Cushman Indian School in Washington.[5]

Friedman's career was in ashes. Once an outside candidate for commissioner of Indian Affairs, he now found himself in serious legal trouble. In May 1915 a federal grand jury in Sunbury, Pennsylvania, indicted him and his clerk, Siceni Nori (Laguna), for embezzling school funds, and Friedman for misappropriation of Athletic Department funds. Nori ended up pleading guilty to the embezzlement and to charges of destroying evidence, and he testified against Friedman. A federal jury in Williamsport believed Friedman's denials and acquitted him while Nori went to the penitentiary. Friedman ended up as the superintendent for the Anchor Ranch School for Defective Boys in New Mexico, and then for the United States Vocational School in Pocono Pines, Pennsylvania.[6] Little is known of his life after 1921.

It is sadly fitting that Nori, one of the few students who actually graduated from Carlisle, ended up taking the fall for Friedman's corruption, for as much as Carlisle's reputation suffered, and as much as its former staff found their careers in ruins, the investigation also damaged the standing of Carlisle students. Before the report, Pratt's grandstanding and the athletic program's success created an image of Carlisle as producing the foremost Indian students in the country. Although students initiated the investigation with their petitions and protests, the government report ridiculed them as drunkards and immoral. When the new superintendent Oscar Lipps reflected upon his 1914 arrival at Carlisle after the investigation, he expressed disdain for the returning students, saying, "Many of them were Indian boys fifteen to eighteen years of age, and as I knew them they were average boys without any bad habits. You can imagine my disappointment two or three years later when they came home moral degenerates."[7] Pratt had once hoped that his athletic department and football team would produce an unassailable example of his male students' manly character. Now Carlisle's detractors saw it as evidence of their depravity.

Lipps drastically downgraded the position of football at Carlisle as soon as he took office. Warner remained as athletic director for the 1914 football season, but after an unsuccessful effort that year, he departed. Lipps hired as Warner's replacement one of his former players, Victor M. Kelley (Choctaw), who had been coaching at Texas A&M. In November 1915, however, the players rebelled against Kelley in favor of Gus Welch, the assistant coach. Indian Commissioner Cato Sells stepped in and ordered football abolished at the school. The administration reintroduced football in 1916, allowing for a hastily assembled six-game football schedule under the command of M. L. Clevett, a coach who did Carlisle's reputation no favors when, after a match at Conshohocken Athletic Club, he ended up in jail for failing to return the guarantee money. Football continued for the 1917 season with a full schedule, this time with Leo F. "Deed" Harris, a former scout for Warner, as coach, but before the team could play a game in 1918, Carlisle Indian Industrial School closed down and was transformed into an army hospital.[8]

In his letter hiring Welch as assistant coach, Lipps emphasized conduct and manliness over victories on the field. As the second term of his employment, Lipps writes that Welch would be expected to "use your utmost endeavor to influence the students of the school to obey all the rules of the school, to practice cooperation and mutual self-help, not only in athletics but along the lines that makes for real manhood." Lipps also admonished Welch to be "governed by high ideals," and to serve as an example of "high standards and conduct" for the players. This language places student athletes as responsible for the tarnished image of athletics at the school, even though it was actually Welch who, a year earlier, had petitioned the government about corruption under Warner's leadership and within the Carlisle Indian School's athletic program.[9]

By decreasing the significance of football, Lipps clearly aimed to reestablish Carlisle as an institution that acquainted students with "civilized" self-control. He reintroduced the YMCA. He invited Pratt back onto campus to promote uplift and "civilized" character. He not only condemned alcohol, but enlisted student support for the prohibition movement to criminalize alcoholic beverage consumption, even having school media print articles deriding the negative influence of alcohol on manhood. Yet even though he set out to reestablish Pratt's "civilization" agenda, Lipps's plan was quite different. He had a very narrow outlook for what his students could achieve, limiting their education even more strictly than it had already been to vocational training. Lipps launched a new curriculum that eliminated virtually all liberal arts subjects and concentrated solely on preparing students for manual, industrial, or service work.[10] Lipps espoused "civilization" but disavowed Pratt's ambitions for uplifting Carlisle students to a status equal to that of middle-class whites.

Unlike a decade earlier, however, when Carlisle first overhauled its curriculum to advance a more vocational orientation, Lipps did not aggressively deploy the football team to project a winning image of the school. Warner may have still been coach, but he no longer controlled the school. He still had the clout to schedule games against prominent opposition such as Pittsburgh and the emerging powerhouse, Notre Dame, but following his departure at the end of that year, Pittsburgh constituted the only major opposition to agree to play Carlisle, and even that was more than likely due to Warner's appointment there as athletic director and coach.[11] The remainder of the schedule featured games against non-elite local football colleges, such as Lehigh and Bucknell, and the 1917 season included only one game against a prominent college team: Army.[12] No longer did the Carlisle schedule feature the majority of the "Big Four" or any other football powerhouse.

Over this same time period, football also became less prominent in the school media. The 1913 football season, Friedman's last as superintendent, ended with a front-page report in the *Carlisle Arrow* celebrating the achievements of the team.[13] In 1914 Carlisle recorded a losing season for the first time since 1901.[14] Early in the fall, school publications featured football reports prominently on the second page, but by the end of the season, with the team losing their contests, they published fewer articles about games. The *Arrow* devoted a single paragraph to the matchup against Brown as well as to three end-of-season matchups.[15] The game against Auburn did not even merit a report. There was no end-of-season article celebrating the team's achievements, mainly because there was little to celebrate. Even the report on the annual football ban-

The Aftermath

quet managed to avoid discussing the actual season.[16] In 1915, except for front page coverage of games against Dickinson and West Virginia Wesleyan, the *Arrow* dispatched football reports to between pages two and five, and buried the end-of-season summary as well.[17] The *Arrow* did not sugarcoat its coverage, calling the game against Pittsburgh "disastrous."[18]

In 1917 the *New York Tribune* seemed to make an attempt to put Carlisle back in the national college football spotlight. In March the paper reported that the school had once again upgraded its schedule, adding games against Harvard, Princeton, and Penn, and, in the process, had successfully begun drafting players from reservations around the United States. The article framed the discussion of a revived Carlisle football program in familiar terms of masculine combat and "civilized" uplift.[19] The reporter opined: "Football attracts the Indian. It has that element of personal conflict that he loves." He then went on to quote captain Jake Hermann (Sioux), sounding like the Pratt of old, as saying, "'Education is the salvation of my people, and Indians are human beings. The same wind chills us, and the same fire warms us. If we are cut, we bleed red blood. Education has done wonders for us thus far, and the Indians—the Western Indians—are a young and undeveloped race. The uplift of our race interests us, and if football may be used as a means of uplifting, since it attracts boys to school, surely the end justifies the means."[20] In reality Carlisle scheduled games that season against only two top-shelf teams, Army and a diminished Penn.[21] Lipps did not want to recreate Carlisle's football glory of either the Pratt or Warner years. He had little to gain from masculine exhibitions of Indians in "personal conflict" to entertain *New York Tribune* readers, and little ambition for any dramatic "uplifting" among his students.

When he did reference the football team, Lipps attempted to discuss the sport as a means to develop "civilized" manly character. Shortly after his arrival, Lipps presented the Carlisle players with their varsity letters as recognition of their participation in school athletics. His speech was recorded for posterity in the *Carlisle Arrow*. Lipps remarked, "Of course 'C' stands for Carlisle; it also occurred to me that 'C' stands for courage. It has taken courage to earn those C's; it has taken courage to win a football game and to win races. . . . There is another form of courage that I want to impress upon you and that is courage to stand for those principles that you know to be right and which is often lacking among men—moral courage."[22]

This speech could not have contrasted more sharply with Warner's hyper-masculinity. Lipps defined the athletes' manhood in terms of "moral courage." He might just as well have added "civilization" to his words beginning with the letter C. Markedly, his understanding of sports never mentions the aggression and strength necessary for a winning team. While not directly codified in terms of demonstrating "civilization," the players' manhood still promoted the "civilized" ideal of self-control.

Nevertheless, football players found it difficult to shake the reputation of masculine hedonism that Linnen's report and the 1914 investigation had tagged to them. In at least one instance, the legacy of the football team's sullied image impacted a female student even more profoundly than it hurt any player. During the summer of 1915 a female student returned to Carlisle from her outing assignment in Bala Cynwyd, a suburb of Philadelphia, where she had worked for a family doing domestic labor. She was pregnant. Immediately the school expelled her. Despite this, Lipps decided to investigate the circumstances of her pregnancy, for she had claimed to have been raped during her outing. The matron of the home where the student worked was outraged. She accused the student of fabricating the rape story and in a letter to Lipps suggested that the real father was a Carlisle Indian School football player. "She was very fond of one of the young men in the football squad and wrote me on Nov. 23rd of her delight at having been his selected one to go to the Penn-Indian game in Phila," the matron wrote. The student's file, in fact, contains a letter from a football player from a road trip with the team. He wrote, "I cannot think of anything else but my little girl," and signed, "xxxxxxx and then some."[23]

In the end, the outing manager could find no evidence that

the female student was lying. He wrote, "Last evening I had [the female student] over in my room for about an hour, but I failed to get any other story from her, than that story which she had already told others. The child adheres to this story in such a way that we cannot doubt her word."[24] There is no report as to whether the school pressed charges against the young man whom this student accused of being the rapist. She paid the price for his violation, and the matron knew precisely whom to blame to deflect guilt away from her son. In the wake of the 1914 hearings, she had no problem pointing a finger at a boyfriend on the football team.

Later in 1915, when Lipps, Sells, and Secretary of Interior Franklin Lane abolished the football team following the argument between Kelley and Welch, school media portrayed players as needing lessons in "civilized" manhood. A student-written article printed in the *Carlisle Arrow* entitled, "How to Become a Good Athlete," provided some advice for the potential football player. Much like Lipps's speech to the team, the author promoted manliness as essential for athletes, framed in terms of self-control. The author admonished players to refrain from alcohol and smoking, and to curb aggressive behavior. About the argument between Welch and Kelley, the student wrote, "These are some of the faults with our athletes in school. They get angry at each other easily. It is because they are not training in the right way. No young man has a right to be considered an athlete until he has made good and has qualified himself in the ways that I have mentioned."[25] The author portrays players as unable to control their emotions and to curb aggression. He attributes these alleged character traits to the downfall of football at Carlisle. Ironically, popular sports writers, like the author of the *New York Tribune* piece, attributed to Indigenous football players these very same masculine qualities, yet cited them as reasons for Indian school football success.

Despite Lipps's attempts to downgrade football, the team still remained popular among the student body. During the Friedman era the football team had attracted sixty male students.[26] Prior to the 1915 season the *Carlisle Arrow* reported that the football squad numbered seventy-five.[27] Although students could still play lacrosse or baseball after football was abolished, they eagerly desired the return of football as it brought the most national attention and crowds.[28] When Lipps allowed the sport to return for the 1916 season, it excited not only students but national media outlets, which continued to portray the team in sensational terms to grab the attention of readers. The *New York Tribune* celebrated the return of the "aborigines," calling Carlisle "one of the most picturesque teams on the gridiron."[29]

As we saw in chapter 2, students interviewed for oral histories years after their time at Carlisle fondly remembered football, and sports more generally, and likely also welcomed the fact that Lipps reinstated the team. Yet when they did so, they did not necessarily frame their memories of the team within narratives of masculinity or manliness that defined white understandings of the game and of Carlisle's team. They sometimes offered critical insights about football and athletics, but in terms that reflected their experiences, not the moral expectations of white society. Delia Waterman (Oneida), who, after Carlisle, became an activist who worked to organize fellow Oneidas to fight for land claims on ancestral territory, had fond memories of sports, but when discussing them she also expressed particularly sharp criticisms of the school.

When she came to Carlisle, Waterman remembered, "The only one I was interested to know was Jim Thorpe." Yet she also recalled the story of two brothers with the last name of Godfrey, one of whom died playing football: "They was a good six feet maybe, and one of the brothers got hurt, broke his nose. Whether it was attended to, or he didn't get the attention or something, but it ran, he got an infection. Killed him. I think that was from a broken nose."[30]

Waterman may have been remembering Louis Godfrey (Ojibwe, Fond du lac) who entered Carlisle with his brother Frank at the age of eighteen in 1914. On November 27, 1917, a newspaper wire report stated that he left a game against Penn with "several contusions" and "bandaged around the head." In his letter informing the commissioner of Indian Affairs of Godfrey's death, the Carlisle superintendent Lipps wrote that, as Waterman remembered,

Louis had suffered a broken nose in the Carlisle game against Penn, and he had also sprained his knee. In the letter, the superintendent claims that Godfrey did not heed the advice of the school doctor, aggravated his injury by walking on his leg, developed phlebitis, and after surviving surgery, died of a blood clot that lodged in his brain.[31] Not only did Waterman recall a sports story that ended in the death of a player, but, unlike the superintendent, she did not blame Godfrey for disobeying a doctor's orders. Instead, she portrayed school officials as negligent, a narrative about neither masculine prowess nor manly "civilization," but instead about the incompetence and indifference of the school's administration.

At least one parent expressed similar concerns about the risks and utility of football. In a 1917 letter to the superintendent, the father of George May (Wichita) wrote, "I wish that George would learn something more useful than playing in the band or football. I would like for him to work at a certain trade of which he can make his living by it. I don't approve of him playing ball as he is liable to get hurt and playing in the band might give him consumption or other lung diseases."[32]

Waterman also remembered that whites did not want Indian athletes to become too famous. Referring to the Olympic Committee stripping Jim Thorpe of his medals, she said that Indians who achieved great success were "pulled down off the ladder." She compared Thorpe to Ira Hayes (Pima), one of the six marines photographed by Joe Rosenthal raising the American flag over Iwo Jima during World War II. After the war Hayes became an alcoholic and died of alcohol poisoning in 1955. When asked if Hayes died because of "personal weakness," a question that implied a lack of manly character, Waterman said no. "Because when he first came back, he was so famous that they wanted him here and there. And he didn't think it was anything to him to be shown into big banquets and all that. There was other things he was more interested in. Something for his people. He wanted water irrigation on his reservation."[33] When her story veered into an interpretation of Ira Hayes's death, Waterman explicitly rejected a narrative that explained it in terms of manly "civilization." Instead, she expressed a sense of solidarity with an Indigenous man's experiences, connecting her own identity as a member of a northeastern North American nation to someone from the plains and someone else from the desert Southwest, all of whom shared similar experiences as racialized and colonized people in the United States.

John Alonzo, quoted in chapter 2, also had complicated recollections of football at Carlisle. Despite his pride in the team, he also remembered corruption associated with it. For example, he recalled that the University of Pennsylvania once hired Frank Hudson away to play a game against Harvard. He also echoed Waterman's sentiments about the government and white society holding back Indians. He praised Pratt and said that when Carlisle's founding superintendent left, the school was allowed to fall into ruin. About the closing of Carlisle, Alonzo said, "I think Congress didn't want Indians to get too smart at the time. Keep the Indians from getting ahead. Keep the Indian on the reservation."[34] Alonzo echoes many of Pratt's sentiments, but like Waterman, he expresses solidarity with Indigenous people outside his own Pueblo confederacy of nations. Waterman and Alonzo both enjoyed sports at Carlisle, but they did not seem to be caught up in narratives of manliness or masculinity. They cared much more about the competence of those who ran Carlisle, the integrity of their education, and the advancement of Indigenous people as a group.

Students at other boarding schools did not necessarily frame them as forums in which to exhibit Victorian notions of manhood and masculinity. As we have seen in discussions of sports like running and basketball in earlier chapters, Indigenous North Americans have a deep history of sporting traditions dating back centuries before contact with Europeans.[35] As Peavy and Smith show in their research on women's basketball at the Fort Shaw Indian School, during the first years of the twentieth century, these female players became so dominant at the game that they drew far more attention from nearby fans and students than did their school's all male football team.[36] The Fort Shaw female basketball team also actively ignored what were known as "girls' rules," and played the same game that men played at the time.[37] Playing in front of male and female fans in crowded gymnasiums and auditoriums, they introduced a fast-paced style of play to this newly invented game. As young women, their involvement in basketball had little to do with manliness. Their passion for the sport reflected the desire of female students to test their talents, engage in exciting physical culture, and win games.[38]

In reality, Carlisle school administrators did not seem to have much regard for what sports meant to students. They used sports to sustain the institution over which they had assumed responsibility. When Pratt was fired in 1904, the new superintendent, Mercer, drew upon his students' passion for football to keep Carlisle in the public eye and maintain its relevance, but Lipps did not have this option. The football team had become a major source of embarrassment, exposing a decadent and corrupt administration. Lipps quickly moved to manage the institution's impression by deflecting blame toward students, expelling thirty-five in the first six months after his appointment.[39] This was more than Mercer achieved during his entire tenure. In total, Lipps expelled fifty-seven students during his short period at Carlisle. He portrayed these students as particularly incorrigible. Yet he also clearly used his power to expel as a tool of retribution. For example, he dismissed Julia Hardin, the student whom Stauffer had beaten. Despite the fact that she simply reported being the victim of abuse, he sent her home in June 1914. Her greatest "crime" had been to tell a truth that embarrassed the adults responsible for running the school.[40]

Lipps also attempted to restore Carlisle's reputation by addressing student behavior. He campaigned to eradicate both drinking and sexual activity among students. In the case of drinking, he employed a kind of public relations assault that addressed both students and any interested body off campus. Importantly, calls for students to abstain from drinking relied heavily upon reorienting understandings of manliness. Unlike football, which elevated masculine power as an ideal manly trait, temperance highlighted self-control and responsibility, core characteristics of "civilized" manhood. During Lipps's short period as superintendent, he put great effort into promoting prohibition in a variety of ways.

In March 1914, only a few months after Lipps's arrival, the *Red Man* published a special prohibition issue. It contained articles discussing the evils of drinking and its impact upon the Indian population. All the featured writers were vehemently opposed to alcohol and supported prohibition. Their ideals mirrored the wider campaign in America to introduce prohibition as a constitutional amendment, which eventually took place in 1919 with the ratification of the 18th Amendment. Taken together, the articles paternalistically promoted denial of one's passions as essential for a "civilized" society, and they did so emphasizing gendered themes of manhood and womanhood.[41]

In the issue Reverend Sherman Coolidge argued, "You must eradicate whiskey from your land if you want to preserve manhood and womanhood in America."[42] Gabe E. Parker considered alcohol "a curse which corrupts manhood."[43] For these authors, men proved their manhood not by their ability to handle heavy drinking, but rather through manly self-control. They portrayed alcohol as causing the destruction of manliness and morality. Parker commented that under the influence of alcohol, "perception is diminished and intellectual power is weakened; personal responsibility is disregarded and the moral standard is lowered."[44] In Parker's interpretation, all other forms of vice stemmed from alcohol. Thus, sexually active students were influenced by drinking, as alcohol had influenced their "personal responsibility . . . and the moral standard."[45] The other authors continued this theme by arguing that abstinence was the only method of guaranteeing self-control.[46]

The school's weekly newspaper, the *Carlisle Arrow*, also regularly published articles calling for prohibition. Shortly after the hearings, it featured an article by Calvin Lamoureaux (Lakota), who spoke out against the use of alcohol in Native communities and its damaging effect upon families.[47] All of his examples featured men behaving in an "uncivilized" manner. Drinking men turned to crime and became homeless because they were not breadwinners who provided for their families. Alcohol, according to Lamoureaux, led to sexual promiscuity, weakened health, and, in effect, denied manliness.[48]

The Aftermath

In April 1915 the *Carlisle Arrow* reprinted excerpts from the Haskell Indian School's newspaper, the *Indian Leader*, denouncing alcohol. An anonymous author portrayed an alcohol addicted man as someone who could not handle the responsibilities of manhood: "A drunkard can't have a home, can't keep money, is always in debt, never at home, never happy, can't stay home, never tries to farm, all of his stock might die, can't be in love with girls, can't get married, nobody likes him, nobody can trust him, always hated by everybody, he just bums around, he hasn't any clothes of good kind to wear, if he is married his wife don't like him much, and hardly ever a drunkard or hobo is married."[49]

In other words, men who drank excessively sabotaged their manhood, making it impossible to provide an income for a family, obtain a job, farm, or earn a living in any skilled occupation. Drunken men could not support a family and, as a result, could not attract a woman. They could not earn enough to purchase proper clothing and maintain a manly appearance. For a hard drinking man, his masculine toughness only served as a façade. For Lipps self-control was the true measure of a man.

Lone Star Dietz helped the school embrace temperance during his employment at Carlisle with two of his drawings in the *Carlisle Arrow*. One portrayed a bar scene, featuring various drinkers and violence with the caption "full of personal liberty."[50] The caption referenced anti-prohibition arguments that drinking was the choice of the individual. The second picture was of an Umatilla man voting for prohibition.[51] The bar scene represents a distinctly Indian man firing a pistol into the ceiling. Dietz draws the bar as a scandalous location with a sign in the background that reads, "Minors can have all the booze they want." A collapsed man is also partly hidden behind the bar. The image suggests that the bar owner prefers money over social responsibility, and it equates masculinity with unhinged and violent behavior.

A few months later, the *Red Man* published Dietz's cartoon of the Umatilla man voting in favor of prohibition. He submits his ballot while carrying a book marked "knowledge" under his arm. Dietz portrays a man using his intelligence, someone who has log-

FULL OF PERSONAL LIBERTY

FIGS. 19 AND 20. Pro temperance political cartoons by Lone Star Dietz that appeared in the *Carlisle Arrow* on November 20, 1914, and March 5, 1915, respectively. Reproduced with permission of the Cumberland County Historical Society, Carlisle, Pennsylvania.

The State of Oregon has voted out the saloon. The Umatilla Indians, men and women, voted the dry ticket unanimously.—*News Item*.

ically and sensibly come to support prohibition. The drawing idealizes the restrained and controlled prohibition voter as the ideal man, someone who, unlike the drinkers in the bar, represents a role model for others.

Lipps even encouraged students to surveil one another to promote abstinence. In March 1915 Reverend Patterson spoke to the school. He called on students to form small groups, recruit members, pledge to practice temperance, and report on anybody who did not comply with the pledge. According to Patterson, a male student in such gatherings would be among those "who are watching him and measuring his manhood."[52] Patterson's talk garnered a pledge of abstinence from the entire crowd.[53]

While Lipps addressed student drinking as a public, ideological crusade, he addressed student sexual activity very differently. The congressional testimonies had brought unwelcome attention to student sexuality, and Lipps seemed reluctant to employ school publications, create sex education curriculum, or invite speakers who potentially might further embarrass the school. Instead, Lipps expelled and disciplined students who engaged in sex, using administrative power and bureaucratic tools to enforce his understandings of individual morality and self-control.[54]

Lipps was the first superintendent to record sexually transmitted infections (STIs) on the students' record cards.[55] Such a plan had twofold objectives: to improve student health and to expel those found to have venereal disease. Students treated for STIs now had their history of sexual activity as part of their permanent record, information available to anyone inquiring about them.

Lipps codified sexuality as a failure of manliness, not evidence of masculine prowess. In 1914 Lipps expelled George May after the student was diagnosed with an STI. In a letter of explanation to May's parents, Lipps commented, "Unless a boy has some backbone and strength of character, he is going to go wrong in this world, and our aim has been to appeal to their honor and pride and show them the evils that will come to them if they do not heed our advice."[56] Later in the same letter, Lipps commented, "I feel disposed to everything in my power to get George to see the error in his ways and to change his ideals and views of life and make a man of himself."[57]

May's mother did not buy any of this. She wrote a sharply worded letter protesting his expulsion. "You are to blame for the condition that my son George is in," she said. "He had a good reputation and was respected wherever he went. I send [sic] him there thinking he would receive a good education as I had heard of Carlisle

The Aftermath

so often as being a good school and taken good care of. I am not very glad that he has to come home with a disgrace on him self from Carlisle."[58] Her letter convinced Lipps to give May a second chance, something not likely available to a female student found to be "ruined" by "immorality." May remained at Carlisle until 1917, when he first went on an outing to Detroit to work at the Ford Motor Company, and then joined the army. By November of that year the *Arrow and Red Man* printed a letter that he sent from camp. May was now a model of manly sacrifice and discipline.[59] Lipps's campaign against sexuality, however, did not appear overly successful. Since student records only tell us who was diagnosed with an STI, they provide a very narrow understanding of how many were sexually active. Between 1914 and 1915, nineteen students in total contracted STIs, fifteen of whom were expelled, two female and thirteen male.[60]

In an effort to steer students away from vice, Lipps supported institutions that promoted Protestant visions of manhood. He worked to return the YMCA to its former glory, reversing its near collapse under Friedman prior to the congressional investigation.[61] By the late nineteenth century in the United States, the YMCA had promoted physical culture among its members, helping to popularize sports like basketball. Under Lipps, however, the organization at Carlisle focused much more upon its mission to develop "civilized" young men. In March 1914, shortly after Lipps arrived as superintendent, the *Carlisle Arrow* reported, "Supervisor Lipps again assured us he would do all in his power to help along the work" of the YMCA.[62] In the school media there were weekly reports on the YMCA meetings, speakers, and various organizational decisions.

Clearly Lipps placed a high priority upon reforming students' manhood, for although he also promoted the YWCA for girls, notes on the YMCA's boys' activities almost always appeared first and most prominently in school publications. The organization's principles and mission dovetailed neatly with Lipps's vision that students needed to cast their gender identities within a Victorian mold. The *Arrow* reported in March 1914 that Lipps told assembled students, "We should aim for a nobler and higher life. True living means right living, right motives, high aims, and Christian manhood and womanhood."[63] If only to underscore the heightened significance of a self-controlled manhood, directly below this report on Lipps's comments, the *Arrow* printed a blurb from Andrew Carnegie entitled, "The Exceptional Young Man." In the excerpt, Carnegie defines the ideal young adult male as a disciplined and devoted employee who looks out for the interests of his employer above his own, and "is always improving himself during his spare time for larger things."[64]

Lipps also turned to the Boy Scouts of America to promote his vision of manliness among the male students. He chaired the Scouts committee. He allowed Red Fox James, a Native scout and Boy Scout field worker, to became the principal organizer of the troop, which was heralded as the "first Indian troop of Boy Scouts in the world."[65] A total of eighteen students became members at a ceremony on January 23, 1915. James became the acting scoutmaster until his departure in March 1915.[66] The school provided Carlisle's troop with significant space in the newspaper.

Like the YMCA, the Boy Scouts provided male students with lessons in self-control. During the Lipps administration the Boy Scouts expanded to a significant extent. The school media readily reported on the organization's activities, often on the front page.[67] Lipps provided the Boy Scouts with their own headquarters on campus, and in a symbolically powerful move, he placed it in the Gymnasium's trophy room. Doing so suggests that Lipps valued the Scouts' disciplined and virtuous model of manliness over the victories and glories that masculine athletes brought to Carlisle.[68]

Indeed, Lipps brought a missionary-style return to Pratt's "civilization" agenda when he arrived at Carlisle. In September 1914 Lipps said to those assembled for the Carlisle Indian School Christian Union, "Christ was the perfect man. He is the ideal for the whole civilized world. While we will not reach this perfection, we can strive for it."[69] Like many others during this era, Lipps constructed a Jesus who served as a colonial model of "civilized" manliness, one appropriate to "the whole civilized world."

The Aftermath

For Lipps, Carlisle needed to reset its identity, and this meant returning to the basic, "civilizing" mission of the Pratt era. Yet Lipps did not return entirely to Pratt's formula. Unlike Pratt, he could not direct the curriculum in a way that would have stamped out all traces of Indigenous identity. By the time Lipps arrived at Carlisle, the school had long since abandoned its goals for total assimilation and even had a curriculum that included Native arts and crafts. In the same speech in which he espoused Christ as the ideal man, Lipps said, "We can strive for it (the perfection of Christ), and in striving, develop the kind of character that will perpetuate the noble qualities that have made the American Indians famous," such as not asking for "favors without returning full value."[70] It is hard to imagine an Indigenous audience taking such a backhanded gesture as genuine praise, but it still goes much further in acknowledging Native identities than Pratt ever would have. In addition, with Carlisle's strictly vocational course offerings, Lipps made no pretense, as Pratt had, of providing his students with the tools that they needed to propel themselves into the highest levels of white society in a single generation. Nevertheless, Lipps shared with Pratt a belief in the superiority of white, Anglo-Protestant "civilization" and a sense that Carlisle existed to pass this along to its Indigenous students.

Not surprisingly, Lipps regularly invited Pratt to visit the campus and to speak before the student body. Although Pratt had not visited the school for ten years, very little of his rhetoric had changed. During one of his speeches to the student body, Pratt asked the audience to repeat after him, proclaiming, "the way to civilize an Indian is to get him into civilization; the way to keep him civilized is to let him stay."[71] The statement, a Pratt favorite, echoed his stubborn attitude toward Indian education and manhood, one encapsulated in his comment, "The men who have mental power are the men who are going to manage the country."[72] For Pratt, manly intelligence demonstrated that the student was superior to other men. In his attempt to find a post-athletic identity for Carlisle, Lipps returned to the discourse of "civilization," something that the students had appropriated for their rebellion.

Lipps's tenure as superintendent of Carlisle, however, was short-lived. Halfway through the 1916–17 academic year, Lipps was promoted to the supervisor of Indian schools.[73] John Francis Jr. replaced Lipps until the school's closure in 1918. The appointment of Francis signaled the waning of Carlisle's influence. Unlike previous superintendents, Francis had little experience of actually teaching students. He had been mostly a bureaucrat throughout his career in Indian education and had only moved into the Indian Education Department as chief in 1912.[74] As the United States entered World War I, the school began to idealize a version of manhood very much consistent with the militaristic model that the Boy Scouts promoted.

Up until 1917 the school media only briefly mentioned the war in Europe. Following American involvement from 1917, the school newspaper invoked a more militaristic and patriotic manhood in order to persuade students to enlist in the armed forces.[75] The school newspaper printed an honor roll of enlisted students.[76] Many ex-students joined as well, and some, such as Gus Welch, were promoted to serve as officers.[77] After leaving Carlisle, Lewis Braun/Brown, the student who testified about disciplinarian Denny's physical abuse of students, became a first lieutenant in Company D of the Seventh Engineer Battalion of the United States Army. He was killed in fighting on October 14, 1918, near Cunel, France, after leading his platoon over the top of his trench in an attack upon the enemy.[78] The newspaper heavily promoted patriotism, printing quotes from President Woodrow Wilson on the inevitability of American victory alongside songs about the American flag.[79] In a letter printed in the school newspaper, H. P. McCain, adjutant general of the American army, outlined the main reasons for rejections at officers' training camps, writing, "Perhaps the most glaring fault noted in aspirants to the officers' reserve corps . . . might be characterized by the general word 'slouchiness.' I refer to what might be termed a mental and physical indifference."[80] For McCain, the ideal officer possessed both intelligence and physical health—in short, the officer demonstrated "civilized" manliness. To stand out for promotion in the masculine arena of warfare, the

Indian Officer in Army

CAPTAIN "GUS" WELCH.

"Gus" Welsh, Indian athlete and
graduate of Carlisle school, who has
been made a captain in the United
States cavalry, is the first Indian to
receive this honor. He was an official
at the Carlisle school when the war
broke out, and received his military
training at the first Fort Niagara
camp.

FIG. 21. Gus Welch as army captain during World War I. National Archives
and Records Administration. Reproduced with permission of the
Dickinson College Archives and Special Collections.

aspiring officer required the ability to lead men and provide a positive example. McCain codified this ideology with his comment, "It should become second nature with them to walk and carry themselves with the bearing of an officer and a gentleman."[81] Of course, for Carlisle students, almost none could achieve the status of officer. Except for a few notable exceptions, the vast majority of students listed in Carlisle's "roll of honor" were rank and file.[82]

By the time Carlisle closed in 1918, reformers no longer considered it a beacon of Indian education.[83] Despite reforms implemented after the congressional hearings, political leaders increasingly saw the off reservation boarding school as a legacy of antiquated, failed policies. While the school's dying days saw a return to the Victorian values of the Pratt era, its leaders had no faith in Pratt's commitment to an idealistic vision of uplift and equality. Realistically, Carlisle had been a rudderless institution since Pratt had left. The football team, which Pratt had originally envisioned as a vehicle to promote the school's "civilizing" mission, had come to symbolize much of what the school had supposedly been created to eradicate. With the school's reputation in shambles, the once legendary football team had, at best, lost its significance. The very nature of football, its foundation in the masculine culture of white college men, served as a reaction against the "civilized" manliness that the new administrators at Carlisle sought to restore.

Carlisle football players, and more vicariously, Carlisle students, found both pain and glory in competing against and defeating these future elites. Yet, as a consequence of their rebellion, they also took the blame for the corrupting aspects of the football team that they themselves exposed. Importantly, however, the end of the Carlisle Indian Industrial School did not mean the end of high profile football or sports at Indian boarding schools, or within Indigenous communities. After Carlisle closed, Haskell's football team took the baton and, like Carlisle's, achieved national recognition by defeating the top teams in the country. In 1926 Haskell's alumni funded the construction of a ten-thousand-seat stadium, and their team played games at venues like Yankee Stadium, drawing thousands of fans. Indigenous athletes would continue to win boxing matches, running races, and basketball games into the indefinite future.

A half century after the congressional inquiry into mismanagement of the Carlisle Indian School, Haskell graduate Billy Mills (Lakota) won a gold medal in the 10,000-meter race during the 1964 Olympics in Tokyo, the only American to win an Olympic gold medal in this event, and along with Carlisle's Louis Tewanima, one of only three Americans even to have medaled in it. The Indigenous athletes who went to Carlisle, or to Haskell, or even who simply carried on the athletic traditions begun at boarding schools, deserve credit for the sense of pride that they inspired among Indigenous people, but perhaps even more so for the happiness that they brought to Native communities. When the federal government exposed corruption within the Carlisle Indian School football program, it did virtually nothing to end corruption within interscholastic athletics in the United States. Congress and the Indian Service did, however, destroy a significant source of satisfaction for Indigenous Americans. Yet neither body could prevent Native Americans from picking up the ball on their own and generating joy through sports. As Mills writes in his inspirational allegory, *Lessons of a Lakota*, "Happiness is a wonderful thing. It makes you feel good in any situation. It gives you hope in times of despair. It makes you feel peace in a world of turmoil."[84]

Epilogue

D uring the fall of 2020, the time of this book's revision, the streaming service Apple TV debuted the comedy television series *Ted Lasso*, a show about an American football coach hired to manage the fictionalized A. F. C. Richmond, a soccer team in the English Premier League. Lasso, played and partially written by actor and comedian Jason Sudeikis, is a goofy yet smart midwesterner with a folksy twang who maintains a relentless optimism even among his most cynical British acquaintances. As the show progressed over two seasons, its story lines became more complicated. The male characters central to the show find that masculine posturing, so central to sports cultures on both sides of the Atlantic, impedes their ability to form honest and meaningful human relationships.

Like Ted Lasso, Matthew Bentley made a trip across the ocean to explore a kind of football different from that with which he was familiar. Granted, Bentley and Lasso traveled in opposite directions, and from the time that he began his work on the Carlisle Indian Industrial School football team, Bentley knew far more about the American game than the fictional Lasso seems to have known about soccer. Yet he shared Lasso's curiosity. Along with Lasso, he asked questions about the relationship of sports to ideas about manhood. More important, he applied his critical understanding of sports and gender to the Carlisle Indian Industrial School's football team, revealing a story where the protagonists understood masculinity, race, and empire as interdependent concepts. Sadly, he did not live long enough to prepare his dissertation for final publication. Yet Bentley's insights into the history of masculinity, his passionate interest in sports, and his keenly in-depth research are the bedrock and foundation for this book. His energy and insight shine through on every page.

In *The Great Gatsby*, F. Scott Fitzgerald's epic novel of 1920s hedonism, Tom Buchanan infamously rants in the first chapter about the perilous condition of the white race. Over cocktails, he asks the book's narrator, Nick Carraway, whether he has read *The Rise of the Colored Empires* "by this man Goddard."[1] He says, "If we don't look out the white race will be—will be utterly sub-merged." As if to underscore the centrality of white masculinity to this process, he continues, "It is up to us, who are the domi-nant race, to watch out or these other races will have control of things." Appropriately, Fitzgerald writes Buchanan as also having been a star football player at Yale.

Fitzgerald portrays Buchanan in a satirical fashion, a blowhard impressed by his own masculinity who, in the end, proves to be an extremely limited man. Yet Fitzgerald also writes Buchanan as accurately voicing what prominent Americans like Teddy Roos-evelt and G. Stanley Hall said when they embraced football as a training ground for young, elite, white men. Students at the Carl-isle Indian Industrial School who played football not only played a sport, but they stepped into a much bigger and more consequen-tial drama about manhood, race, and "civilization." In this story they were the ones who were supposed to have been kept in line so that they did not "have control of things." This book has exam-ined the legacy of the Carlisle Indian School by focusing upon the way that it institutionalized ideas of manhood, race, and "civili-zation," and the role that football, perhaps the most remembered aspect of the school, played in all of this. Yet it is vitally important to recognize that terms and ideas like manliness, masculinity, and "civilization" say much more about those who created and ran the Carlisle Indian Industrial School than they do about the Indige-nous girls/women and boys/men whose lives were most affected by it. They are relevant to issues of race and gender that permeate the American sports environment to the present day.

Richard Henry Pratt did not consider himself to be a racist. In fact, the *Oxford English Dictionary* credits him with being the first person to use the term "racism" publicly when, in a 1903 speech before the Lake Mohonk Conference of the Friends of the Indian, he railed against segregation.[2] Pratt idealistically hoped that football could serve as valuable evidence supporting what he believed to be his anti-racist philosophy. If Carlisle students could show self-control while playing football, Pratt assumed they could prove that Indigenous young men were capable of elevating themselves to a higher tier of manly "civilization." Yet Pratt placed at the very core of his missionary faith a concept of "civilization" that elevated the ideas, social formations, legal statutes, ideologies, cultures, languages, and expressions of people whose ancestry originated in northern and western Europe as superior to those of anybody in the rest of the world. In short, Pratt's concept of "civilization" was inherently deeply racist.

Understanding the interplay between race, gender, and ideas about "civilization" can help us understand more deeply several important aspects of football at Carlisle. For example, it is easier to see now why Congress and Inspector Linnen would focus so much of their report about corruption at Carlisle upon the athletic program. The students had effectively appropriated a discourse of "civilization," and it ended up taking down their superintendent, band leader, and ultimately the school itself. Yet when students revealed the corrupt state of the football team, they also made themselves vulnerable. As Carlisle began to develop into a powerhouse on the gridiron, popular media had already begun to portray their Indigenous players in racialized terms as hypermasculine and overly physical. It was not a leap for the committee to frame the football team's indiscretions as a reflection of its players, and of a student body in need of being controlled.

In contrast, Warner continued with his coaching career unscathed. He would find that his past as a white leader of Indigenous players would only add to his mystique as a coach. After leaving Carlisle for the University of Pittsburgh after the 1914 season, he eventually ended up coaching Stanford from 1924 to 1932. There, in 1930, the student government adopted "Indians" as the team name. The name stayed until 1972, when, in response to protests and a petition from the Stanford American Indian Organization, the university president, Board of Trustees, and student body agreed to remove the moniker, along with the degrading mascot imagery that accompanied it.[3]

One can apply a similar analysis to the double standard that the athletic program faced when caught breaking the rules of amateur sport. As Sally Jenkins points out in her book, *The Real All Americans*, during the first decades of the twentieth century, the Big Four schools faced their own accusations of professionalism. Yet they did not face the level of shame that Carlisle did, and they continued with their football programs, which represented the apex of the college football world well into the 1930s.[4] While unfair, it should surprise nobody. Popular media accounts had always portrayed Carlisle players as "natural" warriors who could easily translate a supposedly innate combativeness into victories on the gridiron. It seems that sports fans thrilled at watching a team packaged and branded as descending from people they believed had posed a perilous danger to the civil order. While elite schools were not supposed to break the rules, their cheating at least betrayed a spirit of masculine competitiveness and cunning necessary for their survival as a dominant race.

Scott L. Morgensen defines such double standards and hypocrisies as central features of what he terms "colonial masculinity." To Morgensen, this term applies not only to relations between white and Indigenous American populations but also to settler colonial societies more widely. He recognizes a pattern whereby modern settler populations from Europe have desired to "go primitive." This has two effects. First, as Bederman discusses in her work, by performing violence, white settler societies reassure themselves that they have the necessary tools to defend "civilization." In Morgensen's words, "*their* 'savage' violence, as white men defending civilization, could become a sign of having *achieved* civilization" (Morgensen's italics). In a more subtle and insidious way, colonial masculinity also transforms immorality into a racial trait that needs to be policed. If gentlemen are, by definition, "civilized" and moral, then by "playing Indian," to use Philip Deloria's phrase, white men would have constructed Indigenous Americans as an undifferentiated, "uncivilized," and immoral racial group.[5]

In writing about his grandfather, Vine Deloria Sr. (Lakota), Deloria makes many of the same observations about football, manhood, and masculinity at Carlisle that we have in this book. Vine Deloria Sr. played football and baseball for St. Stephens College (now Bard College) in upstate New York, where he is still recognized as the school's "Greatest Athletic Hero." As we do, Philip Deloria writes of Pratt's expectations for his football players, how Pratt equated becoming manly with becoming white. Yet Deloria's grandfather held his memories of football close to his heart in ways that confound a simple story of masculinity and manliness. He had desperately wanted to play and coach professional football, but followed the wishes of his father and became an Episcopalian minister. Football games comprised some of Deloria's grandfather's last memories as his mind sank into dementia. As with Jim Thorpe, the game allowed him to win adulation from both white society and Lakota, and to build memories and experiences that often overlapped with those of whites. Yet sports also allowed him to develop deeply positive experiences with his body and build a life as a Lakota in twentieth-century America, something that he would pass along to his family. As Deloria points out, the last half of the twentieth century saw fewer American Indian athletes achieve the kind of success that they did at Carlisle, but sports became an important part of many local reservation and urban Indian communities.[6] In the example of his grandfather, Deloria sees sports for Indigenous Americans as being "not simply performance or pleasure, but a way of serving, a special gift that informed his intellect, spirituality, and moral sensibility."[7]

Sports in general, and football in particular, look very different a century after Carlisle's closing. Over the course of the twentieth century, working-class communities would embrace football as an outlet for expressions of masculine prowess. A few decades after Carlisle's final season, the very idea that Yale football might represent the sport's elite would become laughable. After the 1981 season, the National Collegiate Athletic Association (NCAA) relegated the former Big Four schools, each of whom had, in 1954, joined the eight-college Ivy League, to the second tier Division 1-AA (later renamed the Football Championship Subdivision, or FCS). At the time of this writing, none of the Ivy League Schools even participate in the FCS playoff at the end of the season, and no school in the Ivy League has even played in a post-season game since Columbia's victory over Stanford in the 1934 Rose Bowl.

Top tier college football teams, particularly in the South, worked hard to maintain their game as a proving ground for white masculinity well into the twentieth century, some remaining all white as late as the 1970s. However, as of 2019, whites comprised only 37 percent of players in the elite Football Bowl Subdivision (FBS) of college football. Just as school officials and media accounts portrayed Carlisle's players as needing guidance from a white coach like Pop Warner, one hundred years later white coaches dominate in a game in which white players do not. In 2019, despite the fact that white players make up a minority of those on college teams, only 20 percent of head coaches were people of color.[8] The Carlisle Indian School's history of collegiate football, and its legacy of colonial masculinity, have remained long after the school played its last game. When the most prominent football programs did integrate, players of color confronted many of the same ideas about race and gender that Carlisle players experienced years earlier. Perhaps one can see this most starkly in the popularity of the "white savior" narrative in twenty-first-century cinematic portrayals of American sports.

A brief digression into the 2009 hit movie *The Blind Side* perhaps best illuminates how remarkably durable football narratives of colonial masculinity have been. The film stars Sandra Bullock as Leigh Anne Tuohy, a tough, affluent, and attractive white mother living in suburban Memphis, who adopts a physically large, homeless African American teenager named Michael Oher, played by Quinton Aaron. Over the course of the film she rescues Oher, portrayed from the outset as a physical specimen with low intelligence, from his Black community. Scenes of the housing projects where Oher's mother lived portray her as an irresponsible, drug-addicted woman, and the men who live nearby as violent predators. Their leering glances and suggestive comments directed toward Tuohy/Bullock portray men living in African American communities as hypersexual, overly masculine threats to white women. On the football team at an otherwise all-white, private Wingate Christian School, Coach Cotton, played by Ray McKinnon, and Tuohy/Bulloch teach Oher/Aaron not only how to play the game but how to channel and tame his base passions by elevating his supposedly innate protective instincts. One can use the same adjectives to describe the film's portrayal of Oher's background that Richard Henry Pratt used to describe Indigenous communities, and—like Carlisle, Pratt, and Warner—the film frames Wingate, the Tuohys, and Cotton as three pillars of "civilization" who elevate Oher above his upbringing.[9]

Alongside *Jim Thorpe: All-American*, the movie *The Blind Side* takes a number of liberties with actual events that, collectively, elevate the moral stature of its white characters. Briarcrest, Oher's actual school, upon which Wingate is based, is a southern private school founded as a segregation academy in 1973, created not to elevate the status of poor African Americans but as a destination for white families to send their children after Memphis integrated its public schools. Similarly, as with *Jim Thorpe*'s sanitized representation of Warner, *The Blind Side* presents its viewers with a carefully varnished portrait of Oher's football coach. Briarcrest's Danny Hugh Freeze Jr., the actual head coach under whom Oher played in high school and at the University of Mississippi, ended up getting fired from Ole Miss after violating NCAA rules for recruiting athletes, and after using a university cell phone to call escort services on several occasions.[10]

Judging by its success at the box office, audiences loved *The Blind Side*. The film grossed almost 306 million dollars, and an additional 128 million dollars in DVD and Blu-ray sales.[11] The film's creators seemed to have understood how to tell a story about race, gender, and football by tapping powerful narratives that viewers would recognize and enjoy. For many audiences, it might seem to present an anti-racist message celebrating the uplift of an underprivileged individual who is led to develop his untapped personal potential. Yet the film's creators grounded their story in the same model of manhood that Richard Henry Pratt used to guide his mission at the Carlisle Indian Industrial School. White men of privilege drew upon this same Victorian gender formation, one that bifurcated male identity into "civilized" manliness and "savage" masculinity, to justify their conquest of land and violation of treaties, their ownership of other human beings, their power to determine the lives of women, and their control of wealth and property. As this book approaches publication, movements like Indigenous Lives Matter and Black Lives Matter ask everybody to imagine a revolution in racial and gender identities that would allow human beings truly to live as equals.

Richard Henry Pratt intended to use football as a performance of colonial manliness. He believed in equality, but he could not envision Indigenous people as equal unless they accepted a status as inferior. Of course, after Pratt left, subsequent Carlisle administrations abandoned even a pretense of promoting equality. Compared to the overt exploitation and corruption that took place after Pratt left, his years as superintendent might have seemed like a golden age. Perhaps this is why many former students remembered Pratt fondly.[12] Ex-students regularly wrote back proclaiming "my dear Carlisle." Former student and player Albert Exendine considered Pratt the most charismatic man he ever met.[13] A group of students even contributed to the headstone on Pratt's grave in Arlington National Cemetery, which reads, "erected in Loving Memory by his Students and other Indians," and, "Friend and Counselor of the Indians. Founder and Superintendent of the Carlisle Indian School 1879–1904."[14] Deloria's writing about his grandfather, however, shows how complex such sentiments might have been. Whatever their praise of Pratt, it does not mean that former students, and former athletes, saw themselves through Pratt's eyes. For the superintendent, a football game might have told a story about manhood, but for students, the football team recorded a remarkable series of wins during a painful era in Indigenous American history when victories were few and far between.

APPENDIX

Carlisle American Football Results, 1893–1917

The vast majority of results are taken from the Carlisle newspaper. However, the school media, especially during football's early and late years, did not print the results. As such, the source of the match report is included within the appendix. If no report is featured, the result is taken from either the College Football Data Warehouse (http://www.cfbdatawarehouse.com) or the football schedule printed in the school newspaper.

Key

A: the *Arrow*
CA: *Carlisle Arrow*
CA & RM: *Carlisle Arrow and Red Man*
IH: *Indian Helper*
PA: Points against
PF: Points for
RM: *Red Man*
RM & H: *Red Man and Helper*

1893

COACH: W. G. Thompson
RECORD: 2 wins, 1 defeat

Date	Opposition	PF	PA	Venue	Report
Oct. 11	Dickinson College	0	16	Carlisle	
Nov. 11	Harrisburg High School	10	0	Carlisle	
Nov. 30	Edu. Home of Philadelphia	50	0	Carlisle	

1894

COACH: Vance McCormick
RECORD: 1 win, 6 defeats, 2 ties
CAPTAIN: Benjamin Caswell

Date	Opposition	PF	PA	Venue	Report
Oct. 6	Harrisburg High School	14	0	Harrisburg	
Oct. 13	Dickinson College	12	12	Carlisle	
Oct. 20	Lehigh	12	22	Bethlehem	
Oct. 24	Navy	0	8	Annapolis	
Nov. 3	Franklin and Marshall	18	28	Lancaster	
Nov. 10	Bucknell	0	10	Williamsport	
Nov. 15	Pittsburgh Athletic Club	0	8	Pittsburgh	
Nov. 25	Columbia Athletic Club	0	18	Washington	
Nov. 28	York YMCA	6	6	York PA	

1895

COACH: Vance McCormick
RECORD: 4 wins, 4 defeats
CAPTAIN: Bemus Pierce

Date	Opposition	PF	PA	Venue	Reports
Oct. 5	Gettysburg	10	0	Gettysburg	IH, Oct. 11, 1895
Oct. 12	Duquesne Athletic Club	16	4	Pittsburgh	RM, Sept.–Oct. 1895
Oct. 16	University of Pennsylvania	0	36	Phila.	RM, Sept.–Oct. 1895
Oct. 20	Navy	0	34	Annapolis	RM, Nov.–Dec. 1895
Nov. 6	Yale	0	18	New Haven	RM, Nov.–Dec. 1895

Nov. 16	Bucknell	4	18	Lewisburg	RM, Nov.–Dec. 1895
Nov. 21	York YMCA	42	0	York PA	RM, Nov.–Dec. 1895
Nov. 28	Manhattan YMCA	16	4	New York	RM, Nov./Dec. 1895

1896

COACH: William Hickok
RECORD: 5 wins, 5 defeats
CAPTAIN: Bemus Pierce

Date	Opposition	PF	PA	Venue	Report
Sept. 26	Dickinson College	28	6	Carlisle	RM, Sept.–Oct. 1896
Oct. 3	Duquesne	18	0	Pittsburgh	RM, Sept.–Oct. 1896
Oct. 14	Princeton	6	22	Princeton	RM, Sept.–Oct. 1896
Oct. 24	Yale	6	12	East Orange	RM, Nov. 1896
Oct. 31	Harvard	0	4	Cambridge	RM, Nov. 1896
Nov. 7	University of Pennsylvania	0	21	Philadelphia	RM, Nov. 1896
Nov. 14	University of Cincinnati	28	0	Cincinnati	
Nov. 21	Penn State	48	5	Harrisburg	
Nov. 26	Brown	12	24	Chicago	
Dec. 19	University of Wisconsin	18	8	Chicago	

1897

COACH: William Bull
RECORD: 6 wins, 4 defeats
CAPTAIN: Bemus Pierce

Date	Opposition	PF	PA	Venue	Report
Oct. 2	Dickinson	36	0	Carlisle	
Oct. 9	Bloomsburg Normal School	26	0	Bloomsburg	
Oct. 16	Princeton	0	18	Princeton	
Oct. 23	Yale	9	24	New York	
Oct. 30	Gettysburg	82	0	Gettysburg	
Nov. 6	University of Pennsylvania	10	20	Philadelphia	*IH*, Nov. 12, 1897
Nov. 13	Brown	14	18	New York	
Nov. 20	Illinois University	23	6	Chicago	
Nov. 25	University of Cincinnati	10	0	Cincinnati	
Nov. 27	Ohio Medical College	20	12	Columbus	

1898

COACH: John Hall
RECORD: 6 wins, 4 defeats
CAPTAIN: Frank Hudson

Date	Opposition	PF	PA	Venue	Report
Sept. 24	Bloomsburg	43	0	Carlisle	*RM*, Dec. 1898
Oct. 1	Susquehanna University	48	0	Carlisle	*RM*, Dec. 1898
Oct. 6	Cornell	6	23	Ithaca	*RM*, Dec. 1898
Oct. 15	Williams College	17	6	Carlisle	*RM*, Dec. 1898
Oct. 22	Yale	5	18	New Haven	*RM*, Dec. 1898
Oct. 29	Harvard	5	11	Cambridge	*RM*, Dec. 1898
Nov. 5	Dickinson	48	0	Carlisle	*RM*, Dec. 1898

Date	Opposition	PF	PA	Venue	Report
Nov. 12	University of Pennsylvania	5	35	Philadelphia	RM, Dec. 1898
Nov. 19	University of Illinois	11	0	Chicago	RM, Dec. 1898
Dec. 3	Dartmouth	17	6	Carlisle	RM, Dec. 1898

1899

COACH: Glenn "Pop" Warner
RECORD: 9 wins, 2 defeats
CAPTAIN: Martin Wheelock

Date	Opposition	PF	PA	Venue	Report
Sept. 23	Gettysburg	21	0	Gettysburg	
Sept. 30	Susquehanna	56	0	Selinsgrove	RM, Sept.–Oct.–Nov. 1899
Oct. 14	U. of Pennsylvania	16	5	Philadelphia	RM, Dec. 1899
Oct. 21	Dickinson	16	5	Carlisle	
Oct. 28	Harvard	10	22	Cambridge	
Nov. 4	Hamilton College	32	0	Utica	
Nov. 11	Princeton	0	12	Princeton	
Nov. 25	Oberlin University	81	0	Carlisle	
Nov. 30	Columbia	45	0	New York	RM, Dec. 1899
Dec. 25	U. of California	2	0	San Francisco	
Dec. 27	Phoenix Indian	104	0	Phoenix	

1900

COACH: Glenn "Pop" Warner
RECORD: 6 wins, 4 defeats, 1 tie
CAPTAIN: Edward Rogers

Date	Opposition	PF	PA	Venue	Report
Sept. 22	Lebanon Valley	34	0	Carlisle	*RM & H*, Sept. 28, 1900
Sept. 26	Dickinson	21	0	Carlisle	*RM & H*, Sept. 28, 1900
Sept. 29	Susquehanna	46	0	Carlisle	*RM & H*, Oct. 5, 1900
Oct. 6	Gettysburg	45	0	Carlisle	*RM & H*, Oct. 12, 1900
Oct. 13	U. of Virginia	16	2	Washington	*RM & H*, Oct. 19, 1900
Oct. 15	U. of Maryland	27	0	Baltimore	*RM & H*, Oct. 19, 1900
Oct. 27	Harvard	5	17	Cambridge	*RM & H*, Nov. 2, 1900
Nov. 10	Yale	0	35	New Haven	*RM & H*, Nov. 16, 1900
Nov. 17	U. of Pennsylvania	6	16	Philadelphia	
Nov. 24	Wash. & Jefferson	5	5	Pittsburgh	
Nov. 29	Columbia	6	17	New York	

1901

COACH: Glenn "Pop" Warner
RECORD: 5 wins, 7 defeats, 1 tie
CAPTAIN: Martin Wheelock

Date	Opposition	PF	PA	Venue	Report
Sept. 21	Lebanon Valley	28	0	Carlisle	
Sept. 28	Gallaudet College	19	6	Carlisle	*RM & H*, Oct. 4, 1901
Oct. 2	Gettysburg	5	6	Harrisburg	
Oct. 5	Dickinson	16	11	Carlisle	*RM & H*, Oct. 11, 1901
Oct. 12	Bucknell	6	5	Williamsport	*RM & H*, Oct. 18, 1901
Oct. 16	Haverford	29	0	Carlisle	
Oct. 19	Cornell	0	17	Buffalo	
Oct. 26	Harvard	0	29	Cambridge	*RM & H*, Nov. 1, 1901
Nov. 2	University of Michigan	0	22	Detroit	*RM & H*, Nov. 8, 1901
Nov. 9	Navy	5	16	Annapolis	*RM & H*, Nov. 15, 1901
Nov. 16	U. of Pennsylvania	14	16	Philadelphia	*RM & H*, Nov. 22, 1901
Nov. 23	Washington and Jefferson	0	0	Pittsburgh	*RM & H*, Nov. 29, 1901
Nov. 28	Columbia	12	40	New York	*RM & H*, Dec. 6, 1901

1902

COACH: Glenn "Pop" Warner
RECORD: 8 wins, 3 defeats
CAPTAIN: Charles Williams

Date	Opposition	PF	PA	Venue	Report
Sept. 20	Lebanon Valley	48	0	Carlisle	*RM & H*, Sept. 26, 1902
Sept. 27	Gettysburg	25	0	Carlisle	*RM & H*, Oct. 3, 1902
Oct. 11	Bucknell	0	16	Williamsport	*RM & H*, Oct. 17, 1902
Oct. 15	Bloomsburg	50	0	Carlisle	*RM & H*, Oct. 17, 1902
Oct. 18	Cornell	10	6	Ithaca	*RM & H*, Oct. 24, 1902
Oct. 25	Medico-Chi	63	0	Carlisle	*RM & H*, Oct. 31, 1902
Nov. 1	Harvard	0	23	Cambridge	*RM & H*, Nov. 7, 1902
Nov. 8	Susquehanna	24	0	Carlisle	
Nov. 16	University of Pennsylvania	5	0	Philadelphia	*RM & H*, Nov. 21, 1902
Nov. 22	University of Virginia	5	6	Norfolk VA	*RM & H*, Nov. 28, 1902
Nov. 27	Georgetown	21	0	Washington	*RM & H*, Dec. 5, 1902

1903

COACH: Glenn "Pop" Warner
RECORD: 11 wins, 2 defeats, 1 tie.
CAPTAIN: James Johnson

Date	Opposition	PF	PA	Venue	Report
Sept. 19	Lebanon Valley	28	0	Carlisle	*RM & H*, Sept. 25, 1903
Sept. 26	Gettysburg	46	0	Carlisle	*RM & H*, Oct. 2, 1903
Oct. 3	Bucknell	12	0	Williamsport	*RM & H*, Oct. 9, 1903
Oct. 10	Franklin and Marshall	30	0	Lancaster	*RM & H*, Oct. 16, 1903
Oct. 17	Princeton	0	11	Princeton	*RM & H*, Oct. 23, 1903
Oct. 24	Swathmore	12	5	Carlisle	*RM & H*, Oct. 30, 1903
Oct. 31	Harvard	11	12	Cambridge	*RM & H*, Nov. 7, 1903
Nov. 7	Georgetown	28	6	Washington	*RM & H*, Nov. 13, 1903
Nov. 14	U. of Pennsylvania	16	6	Philadelphia	*RM & H*, Nov. 20, 1903
Nov. 21	University of Virginia	6	6	Norfolk VA	*RM & H*, Nov. 27, 1903
Nov. 26	Northwestern University	28	0	Evanston	*RM & H*, Dec. 4, 1903
Dec. 19	University of Utah	22	0	Salt Lake City	
Dec. 25	All-California Reliance	23	0	San Francisco	*RM & H*, Jan. 8, 1904
Jan. 1	Sherman Indian School	12	6	Riverside	

1904

COACH: Edward Rogers

RECORD: 10 wins, 2 defeats

CAPTAIN: Arthur Sheldon

Date	Opposition	PF	PA	Venue	Report
Sept. 17	Lebanon Valley	28	0	Carlisle	A, Sept. 22, 1904
Oct. 1	Gettysburg	41	0	Carlisle	A, Oct. 6, 1904
Oct. 5	Susquehanna	53	0	Carlisle	A, Oct. 6, 1904
Oct. 8	Bucknell	10	4	Lewisburg	A, Oct. 13, 1904
Oct. 15	Albright College	100	0	Carlisle	A, Oct. 20, 1904
Oct. 22	Harvard	0	12	Cambridge	A, Oct. 27, 1904
Oct. 29	University of Virginia	14	6	Norfolk VA	A, Nov. 3, 1904
Nov. 5	Ursinus	28	0	Carlisle	A, Nov. 10, 1904
Nov. 12	University of Pennsylvania	0	18	Philadelphia	A, Nov. 17, 1904
Nov. 19	Susquehanna	12	6	Selinsgrove	
Nov. 24	Ohio State	23	0	Columbus	
Nov. 26	Haskell Institute	38	4	St. Louis	A, Dec. 1, 1904

1905

COACH: George Woodruff (advisory). Following Army game, coached by Bemus Pierce and Frank Hudson

RECORD: 10 wins, 4 defeats

CAPTAIN: Nicholas Bowen

Date	Opposition	PF	PA	Venue	Report
Sept. 23	Penn. Railroad YMCA	71	0	Carlisle	A, Sept. 29, 1905
Sept. 30	Villanova	35	0	Carlisle	A, Oct. 6, 1905
Oct. 4	Susquehanna	47	0	Carlisle	A, Oct. 6, 1905
Oct. 7	State College	11	0	Harrisburg	A, Oct. 13, 1905
Oct. 14	University of Virginia	12	0	Richmond	A, Oct. 20, 1905
Oct. 21	Dickinson	36	0	Harrisburg	A, Oct. 27, 1905

Oct. 28	University of Pennsylvania	0	6	Philadelphia	A, Nov. 3, 1905
Nov. 4	Harvard	11	23	Cambridge	A, Nov. 10, 1905
Nov. 11	Army	6	5	West Point	A, Nov. 17, 1905
Nov. 15	Massillon Tigers	4	8	Cleveland	A, Nov. 17, 1905
Nov. 18	University of Cincinnati	34	5	Cincinnati	A, Nov. 24, 1905
Nov. 22	Canton Athletic Club	0	8	Canton	
Nov. 25	Washington and Jefferson	11	0	Pittsburgh	A, Dec. 1, 1905
Nov. 30	Georgetown	76	0	Washington	A, Dec. 8, 1905

1906

COACH: Bemus Pierce
RECORD: 9 wins, 3 defeats
CAPTAIN: Albert Exendine

Date	Opposition	PF	PA	Venue	Report
Sept. 26	Villanova	6	0	Carlisle	A, Sept. 28, 1906
Sept. 29	Albright	82	0	Carlisle	A, Oct. 5, 1906
Oct. 3	Susquehanna	48	0	Carlisle	A, Oct. 5, 1906
Oct. 6	State College	0	4	Williamsport	A, Oct. 12, 1906
Oct. 20	W. U. of Pennsylvania	22	0	Pittsburgh	A, Oct. 26, 1906
Oct. 27	University of Pennsylvania	24	6	Philadelphia	A, Nov. 2, 1906
Nov. 3	Syracuse	9	4	Buffalo	A, Nov. 9, 1906
Nov. 10	Harvard	0	5	Cambridge	A, Nov. 16, 1906
Nov. 17	Minnesota University	17	0	Minneapolis	A, Nov. 23, 1906
Nov. 22	Vanderbilt	0	4	Nashville	
Nov. 24	University of Cincinnati	18	0	Cincinnati	A, Nov. 30, 1906
Nov. 29	University of Virginia	18	17	Norfolk VA	A, Nov. 30, 1906

1907

COACH: Glenn "Pop" Warner
RECORD: 10 wins, 1 defeat
CAPTAIN: Antonio Lubo

Date	Opposition	PF	PA	Venue	Report
Sept. 21	Lebanon Valley	40	0	Carlisle	A, Sept. 27, 1907
Sept. 28	Villanova	10	0	Carlisle	A, Oct. 4, 1907
Oct. 2	Susquehanna	91	0	Carlisle	A, Oct. 4, 1907
Oct. 5	State College	18	5	Williamsport	A, Oct. 11, 1907
Oct. 12	Syracuse	14	6	Buffalo	A, Oct. 18, 1907
Oct. 19	Bucknell	15	0	Carlisle	A, Oct. 25, 1907
Oct. 26	University of Pennsylvania	26	6	Philadelphia	A, Nov. 1, 1907
Nov. 2	Princeton	0	16	New York	A, Nov. 8, 1907
Nov. 9	Harvard	23	15	Cambridge	A, Nov. 15, 1907
Nov. 16	University of Minnesota	12	10	Minneapolis	A, Nov. 22, 1907
Nov. 23	University of Chicago	18	4	Chicago	A, Nov. 29, 1907

1908

COACH: Glenn "Pop" Warner
RECORD: 10 wins, 2 defeats, 1 tie.
CAPTAIN: Wauseka

Date	Opposition	PF	PA	Venue	Report
Sept. 19	Conway Hall	53	0	Carlisle	CA, Sept. 25, 1908
Sept. 23	Lebanon Valley	35	0	Carlisle	CA, Sept. 25, 1908
Sept. 26	Villanova	10	0	Carlisle	CA, Oct. 2, 1908
Oct. 3	State College	12	5	Wilkes-Barre	CA, Oct. 9, 1908
Oct. 10	Syracuse	12	0	Buffalo	CA, Oct. 16, 1908
Oct. 24	University of Pennsylvania	6	6	Philadelphia	CA, Oct. 30, 1908
Oct. 31	Navy	16	6	Annapolis	CA, Nov. 6, 1908
Nov. 7	Harvard	0	17	Cambridge	CA, Nov. 13, 1908
Nov. 14	W. U. of Pennsylvania	6	0	Pittsburgh	CA, Nov. 20, 1908
Nov. 21	University of Minnesota	6	11	Minneapolis	CA, Nov. 27, 1908
Nov. 26	St. Louis University	17	0	St. Louis	
Dec. 2	Nebraska University	37	6	Lincoln	CA, Dec. 11, 1908
Dec. 5	Denver University	8	4	Denver	CA, Dec. 11, 1908

1909

COACH: Glenn "Pop" Warner
RECORD: 8 wins, 3 defeats, 1 tie
CAPTAIN: Joseph Libby

Date	Opposition	PF	PA	Venue	Report
Sept. 18	Steelton Athletic Club	35	0	Carlisle	CA, Sept. 24, 1909
Sept. 22	Lebanon Valley	36	0	Carlisle	CA, Sept. 24, 1909
Sept. 25	Villanova	9	0	Carlisle	CA, Oct. 1, 1909
Oct. 2	Bucknell	48	6	Carlisle	CA, Oct. 8, 1909
Oct. 9	State College	8	8	Wilkes-Barre	CA, Oct. 15, 1909
Oct. 16	Syracuse	14	11	New York	CA, Oct. 22, 1909
Oct. 23	University of Pittsburgh	3	14	Pittsburgh	CA, Oct. 29, 1909
Oct. 30	University of Pennsylvania	6	29	Philadelphia	CA, Nov. 5, 1909
Nov. 6	George Washington U.	9	5	Washington	CA, Nov. 12, 1909
Nov. 13	Gettysburg	35	0	Carlisle	CA, Nov. 19, 1909
Nov. 20	Brown	8	21	New York	
Nov. 25	St. Louis University	32	0	St. Louis	CA, Dec. 3, 1909

1910

<small>COACH:</small> Glenn "Pop" Warner
<small>RECORD:</small> 8 wins, 6 defeats
<small>CAPTAIN:</small> Pete Hauser

Date	Opposition	PF	PA	Venue	Report
Sept. 21	Lebanon Valley	53	0	Carlisle	*CA*, Sept. 23, 1910
Sept. 24	Villanova	6	0	Harrisburg	*CA*, Sept. 30, 1910
Sept. 28	Muhlenburg	39	0	Carlisle	
Oct. 5	Dickinson	24	0	Carlisle	*CA*, Oct. 7 and 21, 1910
Oct. 8	Bucknell	39	0	Wilkes-Barre	*CA*, Oct. 14, 1910
Oct. 11	Gettysburg	29	3	Carlisle	*CA*, Oct. 14, 1910
Oct. 15	Syracuse	0	14	Syracuse	*CA*, Oct. 21, 1910
Oct. 22	Princeton	0	6	Princeton	*CA*, Oct. 28, 1910
Oct. 29	University of Pennsylvania	5	17	Philadelphia	*CA*, Nov. 4 and 11, 1910
Nov. 5	University of Virginia	22	5	Washington	*CA*, Nov. 11, 1910
Nov. 12	Navy	0	6	Annapolis	
Nov. 17	Harvard Law	0	3	Cambridge	
Nov. 19	Johns Hopkins University	12	0	Baltimore	
Nov. 24	Brown	6	15	Providence	*CA*, Dec. 2, 1910

1911

COACH: Glenn "Pop" Warner
RECORD: 11 wins, 1 defeat
CAPTAIN: Sampson Burd

Date	Opposition	PF	PA	Venue	Report
Sept. 23	Lebanon Valley	53	0	Carlisle	CA, Sept. 29, 1911
Sept. 27	Muhlenburg	32	0	Carlisle	CA, Oct. 6, 1911
Sept. 30	Dickinson	17	0	Carlisle	CA, Oct. 6, 1911
Oct. 7	Mount St. Mary's College	46	5	Carlisle	CA, Oct. 13, 1911
Oct. 14	Georgetown	28	5	Washington	CA, Oct. 20, 1911
Oct. 21	University of Pittsburgh	17	0	Pittsburgh	CA, Oct. 27, 1911
Oct. 28	Lafayette	19	0	Easton	CA, Nov. 3, 1911
Nov. 4	University of Pennsylvania	16	0	Philadelphia	CA, Nov. 11, 1911
Nov. 11	Harvard	18	15	Cambridge	CA, Nov. 17 and 24, 1911
Nov. 17	Syracuse	11	12	Syracuse	CA, Nov. 24, 1911
Nov. 22	Johns Hopkins University	29	6	Baltimore	
Nov. 30	Brown	12	6	Providence	CA, Dec. 8, 1911

1912

COACH: Glenn "Pop" Warner
RECORD: 12 wins, 1 defeat, 1 tie
CAPTAIN: Jim Thorpe

Date	Opposition	PF	PA	Venue	Report
Sept. 21	Albright	50	7	Carlisle	
Sept. 25	Lebanon Valley	45	0	Carlisle	
Sept. 28	Dickinson	34	0	Carlisle	
Oct. 2	Villanova	65	0	Harrisburg	CA, Oct. 11, 1912
Oct. 5	Washington and Jefferson	0	0	Washington	CA, Oct. 11, 1912
Oct. 12	Syracuse	33	0	Syracuse	CA, Oct. 18, 1912
Oct. 19	University of Pittsburgh	45	8	Pittsburgh	CA, Oct. 25, 1912
Oct. 26	Georgetown	33	22	Washington	CA, Nov. 1, 1912
Oct. 28	Toronto All-Stars	49	7	Toronto	
Nov. 2	Lehigh	34	14	Bethlehem	CA, Nov. 8, 1912
Nov. 9	Army	27	6	West Point	CA, Nov. 15, 1912
Nov. 16	University of Pennsylvania	26	34	Philadelphia	CA, Nov. 22, 1912
Nov. 23	Springfield Training School	30	24	Springfield	CA, Nov. 29, 1912
Nov. 28	Brown	32	0	Providence	CA, Dec. 20, 1912

1913

COACH: Glenn "Pop" Warner
RECORD: 10 wins, 1 defeat, 1 tie
CAPTAIN: Gus Welch

Date	Opposition	PF	PA	Venue	Report
Sept. 20	Albright	25	0	Carlisle	CA, Sept. 26, 1913
Sept. 24	Lebanon Valley	26	0	Carlisle	CA, Oct. 3, 1913
Sept. 27	West Virginia Wesleyan	27	0	Carlisle	CA, Oct. 3, 1913
Oct. 4	Lehigh	21	7	Bethlehem	CA, Oct. 10, 1913
Oct. 11	Cornell	7	0	Ithaca	CA, Oct. 17, 1913
Oct. 18	University of Pittsburgh	6	12	Pittsburgh	CA, Oct. 24, 1913
Oct. 25	University of Pennsylvania	7	7	Philadelphia	CA, Oct. 31, 1913
Nov. 2	Georgetown	34	0	Washington	CA, Nov. 7, 1913
Nov. 8	Johns Hopkins University	61	0	Baltimore	CA, Nov. 14, 1913
Nov. 15	Dartmouth	35	10	New York	CA, Nov. 21, 1913
Nov. 22	Syracuse	35	27	Syracuse	
Nov. 27	Brown	13	0	Providence	

1914

COACH: Glenn "Pop" Warner
RECORD: 5 wins, 9 defeats, 1 tie
CAPTAIN: Elmer Busch

Date	Opposition	PF	PA	Venue	Report
Sept. 19	Albright	20	0	Carlisle	CA, Sept. 25, 1914
Sept. 23	Lebanon Valley	7	0	Carlisle	CA, Oct. 2, 1914
Sept. 26	West Virginia Wesleyan	6	0	Clarksburg	CA, Oct. 2, 1914
Oct. 3	Lehigh	6	21	Bethlehem	CA, Oct. 9, 1914
Oct. 10	Cornell	0	21	Ithaca	CA, Oct. 16, 1914
Oct. 17	University of Pittsburgh	3	10	Pittsburgh	CA, Oct. 23, 1914
Oct. 24	University of Pennsylvania	0	7	Philadelphia	CA, Oct. 30, 1914
Oct. 31	Syracuse	3	24	Buffalo	
Nov. 7	Holy Cross College	0	0	Manchester	CA, Nov. 13, 1914
Nov. 14	Notre Dame	6	48	Chicago	CA, Nov. 20, 1914
Nov. 21	Dickinson	34	0	Carlisle	
Nov. 26	Brown	14	20	Providence	CA, Dec. 4, 1914
Nov. 28	Boston All-Stars	6	13	Boston	CA, Dec. 4, 1914
Dec. 2	University of Alabama	20	3	Birmingham	CA, Dec. 4, 1914
Dec. 6	Alabama Polytechnic Inst.	0	7	Auburn	

1915

COACH: Victor M. Kelley

RECORD: 4 wins, 6 defeats, 2 ties

CAPTAIN: Peter Calac

Date	Opposition	PF	PA	Venue	Report
Sept. 18	Albright	21	7	Carlisle	CA, Sept. 24, 1915
Sept. 25	Lebanon Valley	0	0	Carlisle	
Oct. 2	Lehigh	0	14	Bethlehem	CA, Oct. 8, 1915
Oct. 9	Harvard	7	29	Cambridge	CA, Oct. 15, 1915
Oct. 16	University of Pittsburgh	0	45	Pittsburgh	CA, Oct. 22, 1915
Oct. 23	Bucknell	0	0	Carlisle	CA, Oct. 29, 1915
Oct. 27	Galluadet	52	0	Washington	
Oct. 30	W. Virginia Wesleyan	0	14	Carlisle	CA, Nov. 5, 1915
Nov. 6	Holy Cross	23	21	Worcester	CA, Nov. 12, 1915
Nov. 13	Dickinson	20	14	Carlisle	CA, Nov. 19, 1915
Nov. 20	Fordham University	10	14	New York	CA, Nov. 26, 1915
Nov. 25	Brown	3	39	Providence	CA, Dec. 3, 1915

1916

COACH: M. L. Clevett

RECORD: 3 wins, 4 defeats, 1 tie

CAPTAIN: George Mays

Date	Opposition	PF	PA	Venue	Report
Oct. 17	Lebanon Valley	20	6	Anville	CA, Oct. 20, 1916
Oct. 21	Conway Hall	20	0	Carlisle	
Oct. 28	Susquehanna	0	12	Susquehanna	

Nov. 4	Conshohocken Athletic Club	6	6	Conshohocken	
Nov. 11	Carson Long Institute	47	13	New Bloomfield	
Nov. 18	Lebanon Valley College	0	33	Annville	
Nov. 24	Alfred	17	27	New York	CA, Dec. 1, 1916
Dec. 12	Winchester Club	6	20	New Haven	

1917

COACH: Leo F. "Deed" Harris
RECORD: 3 wins, 6 defeats
CAPTAIN: George Tibbetts

Date	Opposition	PF	PA	Venue	Report
Sept. 29	Albright	59	0	Carlisle	CA & RM, Oct. 5, 1917
Oct. 6	Franklin & Marshall	63	0	Carlisle	CA & RM, Oct. 12, 1917
Oct. 13	University of West Virginia	0	21	Morgantown	
Oct. 20	Navy	0	61	Annapolis	
Oct. 27	Johns Hopkins University	15	7	Baltimore	CA & RM, Oct. 26, 1917
Nov. 3	Bucknell	0	10	Lewisburg	CA & RM, Nov. 9, 1917
Nov. 10	Army	0	28	West Point	CA & RM, Nov. 17, 1917
Nov. 17	Georgia Schl. of Tech.	0	98	Atlanta	
Nov. 24	University of Pennsylvania	0	26	Philadelphia	CA & RM, Nov. 30, 1917

NOTES

Specific government reports belonging to the series *Annual Report of the Commissioner of Indian Affairs* are cited in the notes only and by individual titles, which begin with a spelled-out numeral (e.g., *Annual Report of the Commissioner of Indian Affairs to the Secretary of the Interior, Fifty-First,1882*).

Preface

1. Email correspondence with Phil Bentley, November 13, 2020.

2. Email correspondence with Jonathan Bentley, November 21, 2020.

3. Scott, *Domination and the Arts of Resistance*, 3–4, 45–69.

4. Bentley cited the following sources as important to his use of the term *hegemony*: For Gramsci's concept of hegemony, see Gramsci, "Ethico-Political History and Hegemony," 194–95. For an analysis of Gramsci and hegemony, see Mouffe, "Hegemony and Ideology in Gramsci," 168–206.

Introduction

1. Pratt, "Advantages of Mingling," 261. As K. Tsianina Lomawaima shows, many misquote this phrase as "kill the Indian, save the man." Lomawaima points out that Indigenous Americans know all too well the violence embodied in Pratt's terrifying comment. In fact, Pratt said it in response to General Philip Sheridan's genocidal statement that "the only good Indian is a dead Indian." We use Pratt's words here to demonstrate how, in the minds of many with power and influence over Native Americans during the late nineteenth and early twentieth centuries, manhood was synonymous with a civilizing process and incompatible with their vision of indigeneity—(JB). See Lomawaima and Ostler, "Reconsidering Richard Henry Pratt," 79–100.

2. Prucha, *American Indian Policy in Crisis*; Hoxie, *Final Promise*.

3. For examinations of Carlisle, see Bell, "Telling Stories out of School." For the education movement, see Adams, *Education for Extinction*; Child, *Boarding School Seasons*; Fear-Segal, *White Man's Club*; Lomawaima, *They Called It Prairie Light*; Hoxie, *Final Promise*, 189–210; Prucha, *American Indian Policy in Crisis*, 265–91.

4. Before his death, Matthew Bentley published writing on the topics addressed in this book in academic journals as a single author. See Bentley, "Playing White Men"; Bentley, "Rise of Athletic Masculinity."

5. Pratt, *Battlefield and Classroom*, 9–103.

6. In this respect, it mirrored popular conceptions of the American frontier. See Slotkin, *Fatal Environment*, 53.

7. Lomawaima, *They Called It Prairie Light*; Trennert, "Educating Indian Girls," 271–90; Paxton, "Learning Gender," 174–86; Devens, "'If We Get the Girls,'" 219–37.

8. Paxton, "Learning Gender," 176.

9. Prucha, *American Indian Policy in Crisis*, 227–64; Hoxie, *Final Promise*, 75–81.

10. Prucha, *American Indian Policy in Crisis*, 30–71.

11. Dovie Thompson, "The Spirit Survives," in Fear-Segal and Rose, *Carlisle Indian Industrial School*, 318; and "Greeting," *Eadle Keatah Toh.*, January 1880, 2, accessed through the Carlisle Indian School Digital Resource Center, carlisleindian.dicinsson.edu.

12. For a study of Chilcot, see Lomawaima, *They Called It Prairie Light*.

13. Adams, *Education for Extinction*, 13–14; Slotkin, *Fatal Environment*, 51–80; Russett, *Sexual Science*, 140–44.

14. Adams, *Education for Extinction*, 12; Pearce, *Savagism and Civilization*, xix.

15. Berkhofer, *White Man's Indian*.

16. Hoxie, *Final Promise*, 22–23; Ryerson, "'Physical Value' of Races and Nations," 127–55.

17. Fear-Segal, *White Man's Club*, 23–24.

18. Fear-Segal, *White Man's Club*, 13; see also Nandy, *Intimate Enemy*, x–xi.

19. Kimmel, *Manhood in America*, 67; Dubbert, *Man's Place*, 81–114.

20. Segal, *Slow Motion*, 103–4.

21. Kimmel, *Manhood in America*, 82.

22. Bederman, *Manliness and Civilization*, 140–44.

23. Bederman, *Manliness and Civilization*, 239.

24. Gon, *Manly Art*; Hardy, *How Boston Played*.

25. Ingrassia, *Rise of Gridiron University*, 76–77; Bederman, *Manliness and Civilization*, 77–120.

26. Bederman, *Manliness and Civilization*, 7, 25–26.

27. Smits, "The 'Squaw Drudge,'" 281; Russett, *Sexual Science*, 143.

28. For sport at Carlisle see, Jenkins, *Real All Americans*; Anderson, *Carlisle vs. Army*. For a more academic approach to Carlisle sport, see Bloom, *To Show What an Indian Can Do*; Oriard, *Reading Football*, 229–47; Gamache, "Sport as Cultural Assimilation," 7–37; Adams, "More Than a Game," 25–53; Oxendine, *American Indian Sports Heritage*, 183–238; Deloria, *Indians in Unexpected Places*, 109–35. For general histories of American sport, see Rader, *American Sports*; Gorn and Goldstein, *Brief History of American Sports*; Lucas and Smith, *Saga of American Sport*.

29. For baseball at Carlisle, see Powers-Beck, "'Chief,'" 508–38; Powers-Beck, *American Indian Integration of Baseball*.

30. Adams, "More Than a Game," 42.

31. Adams, *Education for Extinction*, 307–21.

32. Reel, *Course of Study*; Adams, *Education for Extinction*, 315.

33. Adams, *Education for Extinction*, 315; Bell, "Telling Stories out of School," 73–92.

34. See Anderson, Swift, and Innes, "'To Arrive Speaking,'" 283–307.

35. Tegan, *Native Men Remade*.

36. See Hokowhitu, "Producing Elite Indigenous Masculinities," 23–48; and Hokowhitu, "Tackling Maori Masculinity," 259–84.

37. Gilbert, *Hopi Runners*, 74, 80.

38. Peavy and Smith, *Full Court Quest*; Davies, *Native Hoops*; Eby, "Building Bodies, (Un)Making Empire."

1. Manhood at Carlisle

1. "Answers to Questions Often Asked," *Indian Helper*, March 3, 1899, 1, 4.

2. Iverson, *Carlos Montezuma*, 5–9.

3. For an example of the journey to Carlisle, see Standing Bear, *My People the Sioux*, 123–32.

4. Carlos Montezuma, "An Apache: To the Students of Carlisle Indian School," *Indian Helper*, October 14, 1887, 1, 4.

5. Stele, "A Helpmate for Man Indeed," 25–41; Armitage, "Through Women's Eyes," 9–18. The history of femininity in the American West has only recently emerged in contrast to early historical analysis depicting women as either prostitutes or the "gentle tamers" of the "Wild West." Historians, such as Susan Armitage, have revealed a more complex picture. Women often travelled alone to the west as homesteaders. Women's trail diaries also reveal how they traded food with others to ensure the survival on the journey. (MB)

6. Adams, *Education for Extinction*, 82.

7. I have constructed my narrative of the Carlisle school from three main sources. Pratt, *Battlefield and Classroom*; Eastman, *Pratt, the Red Man's Moses*; and Bell, "Telling Stories out of School." Pratt's autobiography is a vital resource for understanding the man and the reasons behind his actions. It provides a fundamental insight into Pratt's reasoning and influences in defining manhood. Eastman's biography is a definite pro-Pratt piece of propaganda that mostly criticizes the ideology behind John Collier and the Indian New Deal of the 1930s. Bell's examination of Pratt and the student records is a much more balanced assessment of the educator's life and actions. Bell's thesis is particularly useful for the superintendents who followed Pratt. There is very little work on the later period of Carlisle's existence except for studies of the football team. I have also used my research to supplement these three sources where appropriate—(MB).

8. Eastman, *Pratt, the Red Man's Moses*, 14.

9. Timothy Smith, *Revivalism and Social Reform*.

10. Kaestle, "Ideology and American Educational History," 123–37.

11. Glancy, *Fort Marion Prisoners*.

12. Eastman, *Pratt, the Red Man's Moses*, 13–52; Pratt, *Battlefield and Classroom*, 1–115; Bell, "Telling Stories out of School," 52–54.

13. Eastman, *Pratt, the Red Man's Moses*, 53–63; Pratt, *Battlefield and Classroom*, 116–90; Bell, "Telling Stories out of School," 54–56.

14. For a comparison of Pratt and Armstrong, see Fear-Segal, "Nineteenth-Century Indian Education," 323–41.

15. The photographer used a whitening effect in the pictures so as to make the students appear whiter. See Malsheimer, "'Imitation White Man,'" 54–74. Students were also placed in stereotypical Indigenous clothing so as to enhance the effect of civilization. See Pfister, *Individuality Incorporated*, 20.

16. Eastman, *Pratt, the Red Man's Moses*, 64–75; Pratt, *Battlefield and Classroom*, 191–204; Bell, "Telling Stories out of School," 56–57.

17. Eastman, *Pratt, the Red Man's Moses*, 76–79; Pratt, *Battlefield and Classroom*, 212–29; Bell, "Telling Stories out of School," 57–61.

18. Standing Bear, *My People the Sioux*, 133–34.

19. See Bederman, *Manliness and Civilization*; Putney, *Muscular Christianity*; Macleod, *Building Character*.

20. On the concept of the "public transcript," see Scott, *Domination and the Arts of Resistance*, 3–4, 45–69. The "public transcript" of the dominant aims to reinforce their power while the subordinate tries to curry favor with the dominant. Conversely, the "hidden transcript" of the subordinate is what happens "off-stage," away from the eyes of the dominant. This represents their true feelings and can be seen in acts of resistance toward the dominant. Scott's idea of a "public" transcript is implemented into this study by defining it as the image of the school that Pratt, and later other superintendents, wanted the public to see. The school's public transcript was primarily portrayed through the school newspapers, which were edited by a white official at Carlisle. (MB)

21. Bederman, *Manliness and Civilization*.

22. Lee Baker, *From Savage to Negro*, 26–53. Brinton constructed a hierarchal classification of race in his *Races and Peoples: Lectures on the Science of Ethnography*, where he placed the white/European race at the top and the African at the bottom. Spencer is best known for popularizing the term "survival of the fittest." He also claimed to have "scientifically" confirmed the connection of "Black" with evil and savagery—(MB).

23. Lewis Morgan, *Ancient Society*, 3–44; Jacobson, *Whiteness of a Different Color*, 168.

24. Putney, *Muscular Christianity*, 28.

25. Pratt, "Advantages of Mingling," 268–69.

26. For the ideas behind environmentalism, see Thomas Morgan, "A Plea for the Papoose," 239–51.

27. Pratt, *Battlefield and Classroom*, 4–5.

28. McLoughlin, *Cherokee Renascence in the New Republic*, 58–91, 350–54, 396–401.

29. Pratt, "Advantages of Mingling," 264.

30. Standing Bear, *My People the Sioux*, 135. An interpreter was necessary during Carlisle's early days. For languages at boarding schools, see Spock, *America's Second Tongue*.

31. *Annual Report of the Commissioner of Indian Affairs to the Secretary of the Interior, Fifty-First, 1880* (Washington DC: Government Printing Office, 1882), 179.

32. *Annual Report of the Commissioner of Indian Affairs to the Secretary of the Interior, Forty-Ninth, 1880* (Washington DC: Government Printing Office, 1880), 179–82.

33. *Annual Report, Fifty-First*, 179.

34. *Annual Report, Fifty-First*, 179.

35. Adams, *Education for Extinction*, 233–34. This reward did not exist throughout Pratt's tenure. By 1904 English only schools had been introduced at a vast number of Native reservations, so Carlisle would no longer be the students' first introduction to the English education—(MB). See Hoxie, *Final Promise*, 189–90.

36. "Why the Indians Want Citizenship," *Indian Helper*, August 10, 1888, 4.

37. Adams, *Education for Extinction*, 16–17; Prucha, *American Indian Policy in Crisis*, 252.

38. Pfister, *Individuality Incorporated*, 60.

39. Lewis Morgan, *Ancient Society*, 19–27. This is despite the fact that for thousands of years, communities throughout the Americas had cultivated crops for complex societies, created surpluses, supported cities, and, in short, practiced high yield agriculture—(JB).

40. LaSalle A. Maynard, "Three Days among Indians," *Red Man and Helper*, March 13, 1903, 1.

41. *Annual Report, Forty-Ninth*, 179–82.

42. Richard Henry Pratt, "Seventh Annual Report of the Carlisle Indian Industrial School," *Morning Star*, October, 1886, 1–2; Richard Henry Pratt, "Twenty-Second Annual Report," *Red Man and Helper*, September 13, 1901, 4.

43. *Annual Report, Forty-Ninth*, 179.

44. *Annual Report, Fifty-First*, 180.

45. *Annual Report of the Commissioner of Indian Affairs to the Secretary of the Interior, Fifty-Third, 1884* (Washington DC: Government Printing Office, 1884), 188.

46. Slotkin, *Fatal Environment*, 53.

47. Richard Henry Pratt, "Fifteenth Annual Report," *Red Man*, September, October, and November 1894, 3–4.

48. This idea of worker servility was prominently discussed in nineteenth-century debates over racial slavery. By arguing that white workers were "free labour," worker servility was positively contrasted with African-American slavery. As such, white workers' servility was downplayed through comparison with the complete dominance of slaves—(MB). See Roediger, *Wages of Whiteness*, 43–94.

49. *Annual Report, Fifty-Third*, 186–89.

50. Bell, "Telling Stories out of School," 335.

51. Richard Henry Pratt, "Eleventh Annual Report of the Indian Industrial School, Carlisle, Pa," *Red Man*, November 1890, 1–3.

52. Richard Henry Pratt, "Seventh Annual Report of the Carlisle Indian Industrial School," *Morning Star*, October 1886, 1–2.

53. Hoxie, *Final Promise*, 221.

54. Prucha, *American Indian Policy in Crisis*, 328–51.

55. Pratt, "Twentieth Annual Report of the Indian Industrial School, Carlisle, Pa," *Red Man*, December 1899, 5–6.

56. Child, "Boarding School as a Metaphor," 37–57.

57. "Our 19th Anniversary Exercises and Tenth Graduating Class," *Red Man*, March 1898, 1–6.

58. *Annual Report of the Commissioner of Indian Affairs to the Secretary of the Interior, Fiftieth, 1881* (Washington DC: Government Printing Office, 1881), 188.

59. *Annual Report, Fiftieth*, 188.

60. Pratt, *Battlefield and Classroom*, 237.

61. Pratt, *Battlefield and Classroom*, 237. Spotted Tail did not want his children to be drilled like soldiers. After disagreeing with Pratt, he removed his children. Spotted Tail also wanted to use his son-in-law, Tackett, as an interpreter. Pratt refused as he wanted the students to speak English only—(MB).

62. Bell, "Telling Stories out of School," 249–50.

63. *Annual Report, Forty-Ninth*, 180.

64. *Indian Helper*, January 6, 1893, 2.

65. *Indian Helper*, April 25, 1890, 2.

66. "While Sentimentalists Dream, Practical Workers Accomplish Results," *Red Man and Helper*, August 9, 1901, 2. All Natives were granted American citizenship in 1924.

67. Baker, *From Savage to Negro*, 43.

68. Jacobson, *Whiteness of a Different Color*, 39.

69. Stearns, *Be a Man!*, 108–53. Whereas such men had previously owned a business, the rise of industrialization had damaged the ideal of the self-made man. Men found it more difficult to prove their individuality and manhood in an office. They were now controlled by others, an idea contradictory to the self-made man, who had power over his life. Industrialization also signified the death of the heroic artisan as a form of male identity among the middle class—(MB). Kimmel, *Manhood in America*, 58–59.

70. Stearns, *Be a Man!*, 134–39.

71. Stearns, *Be a Man!*, 55.

72. Standing Bear, *My People the Sioux*, 147.

73. *Annual Report, Forty-Ninth*, 179–80.

74. Adams, *Education for Extinction*, 277–83.

75. Standing Bear, *My People the Sioux*, 191–204; Jenkins, *Real All Americans*, 307.

76. "Industrial Training vs. Higher Education," *Red Man*, February 1900, 1.

77. Pfister, *Individuality Incorporated*, 38, 94.

78. Appleby, *Liberalism and Republicanism in the Historical Imagination*, 253–76.

79. Adams, *Education for Extinction*, 280–81.

80. Standing Bear, *My People the Sioux*, 147.

81. Shopes, "Fells Point," 126.

82. Prucha, *American Indian Policy in Crisis*, 147–55.

83. Prucha, *American Indian Policy in Crisis*, 138–55.

84. Higham, *Strangers in the Land*, 77–87.

85. *Indian Helper*, August 22, 1890, 2; Pratt, "Twelfth Annual," *Red Man*, October–November 1891, 1–2.

86. Antonetta, "Catholics, Carlisle, and Casting Stones," 267–87.

87. Lewis Morgan, *Ancient Society*, 5.

88. *Annual Report of the Commissioner of Indian Affairs to the Secretary of the Interior, Fifty-Second, 1884* (Washington DC: Government Printing Office, 1883), 164–65.

89. For an example, see "Let us Go Slow in Our Judgement of Indian Character," *Indian Helper*, June 19, 1891, 1.

90. Macleod, *Building Character*, 81.

91. "Is Civilization Dangerous?" *Indian Helper*, March 22, 1889, 1, 4.

92. "Is Civilization Dangerous?" 4.

93. The Man-on-the-Band-Stand (MOTBS) was the commentator of the *Indian Helper*, and later the *Red Man and Helper*. Created by newspaper editor Marianna Burgess, the invisible MOTBS spied on students and commented on various events. Jacqueline Fear-Segal has argued that the MOTBS was a form of surveillance to ensure that students behaved appropriately—(MB). Fear-Segal, "Man on the Bandstand," 99–122.

94. "Is Civilization Dangerous?," 1, 4.

95. "True Heroism," *Indian Helper*, March 22, 1889, 1.

96. According to Dyer, the "purity" of whiteness is challenged by the necessity of reproduction, an ideal considered bestial—(MB). Dyer, *White*, 26.

97. Smits, "The 'Squaw Drudge,'" 281.

98. Macleod, *Building Character*, 72.

99. Macleod, *Building Character*, 73.

100. Macleod, *Building Character*, 72–74; Putney, *Muscular Christianity*, 64–72.

101. Pratt, "Twelfth Annual," *Red Man*, October–November, 1891, 1–2.

102. Richard Henry Pratt, "Fifteenth Annual Report," *Red Man*, September, October, and November, 1894, 3–4.

103. Richard Henry Pratt, "Fifteenth Annual Report," 3–4.

104. *Indian Helper*, September 28, 1888, 2.

105. "A Bible Institute," *Indian Helper*, October 16, 1896, 2.

106. Putney, *Muscular Christianity*, 92–93.

107. "Dr. Leiper's Lecture," *Red Man and Helper*, March 13, 1903, 2.

108. W. G. Thompson, "Our Football Boys on Manhattan Field vs New York City Y.M.C.A. Team," *Indian Helper*, December 6, 1895, 1, 4.

109. Pratt, "Twentieth Annual Report," 5–6.

110. *Indian Helper*, May 8, 1891, 3.

111. Putney, *Muscular Christianity*, 127–43.

112. "Colonel Pratt at Buffalo," *Red Man and Helper*, July 26, 1901, 2.

113. Stoeltje, "A Helpmate for Man Indeed," 25–41.

114. Welter, "Cult of True Womanhood," 152.

115. *Annual Report, Forty-Ninth*, 180.

116. Kerber, "Republican Mother," 187–205.

117. *Annual Report, Fiftieth*, 188.

118. Hokowhitu, "Tackling Maori Masculinity," 259–84; Hokowhitu, "Producing Elite Indigenous Masculinities," 23–48; also see Tengan, *Native Men Remade*; Borrell, "Patriotic Games" 165–80.

119. Jemima Wheelock, "A Woman's Work in the World," *Red Man*, May 1890, 7.

120. Richard Henry Pratt, "Eighteenth Annual Report of the Indian Industrial School, Carlisle, Pa," *Red Man*, September, October, November, and December 1897, 2.

121. Richard Henry Pratt, "Twenty-Fourth Annual Report," *Red Man and Helper*, August 14, 1903, 1.

122. Richard Henry Pratt, "Twentieth Annual Report of the Indian Industrial School, Carlisle, Pa," *Red Man*, December 1899, 5–6; "Nineteenth Annual Report of the Indian Industrial School, Carlisle, Pa," *Red Man*, October–November 1898, 3.

123. Bell, "Telling Stories out of School."

124. Strober and Lanford, "Feminization of Public School Teaching," 212–35.

125. Strober and Lanford, "Feminization of Public School Teaching," 218.

126. Pratt, *Battlefield and Classroom*, 121.

127. Dubbert, *Man's Place*, 80–116.

128. "The New Woman and the Indian School Teacher," *Red Man*, August 1895, 5–6.

129. Putney, *Muscular Christianity*, 24–25.

130. Henry Van Dyke, "The Strenuous Life for Girls," *Red Man and Helper*, July 18, 1902, 2.

131. See Peavy and Smith, *Full Court Quest*; Peavy and Smith, "World Champions," 40–78; Peavy and Smith, "'Leav[ing] the White[s]'" 243–77.

132. "Man-on-the-band-stand," *Red Man and Helper*, January 9, 1903, 3.

133. Putney, *Muscular Christianity*, 148–50.

134. "Man-on-the-band-stand," *Red Man and Helper*, October 17, 1902, 3.

135. "Man-on-the-band-stand," *Red Man and Helper*, January 16, 1903, 4.

136. Pratt, "Twenty-Fourth Annual Report," 1.

137. Bell, "Telling Stories out of School," 64.

138. D'Emilio and Freedman, *Intimate Matters*, 70–71.

139. Smits, "The 'Squaw Drudge,'" 281–306; Lomawaima, *They Called It Prairie Light*, 90–94.

140. Bell, "Telling Stories out of School," 64.

141. Bell, "Telling Stories out of School," 276.

142. Bell, "Telling Stories out of School," 273.

143. "The New Woman and the Indian School Teacher," *Red Man*, August 1895, 5.

144. Bell, "Telling Stories out of School," 107–8.

145. "A Strange Indian Custom," *Indian Helper*, July 10, 1896, 1.

146. "A Strange Indian Custom," 1.

147. "Two Good Indians Who Are Not Dead," *Indian Helper*, March 4, 1892, 1, 4.

148. Smits, "The 'Squaw Drudge,'" 300.

149. *Indian Helper*, August 26, 1892, 2.

150. Pratt, "Twelfth Annual," 2.

151. The connection of reliance to femininity was also shown in the white portrayal of reservation Indians. Once they were forced to rely on the government for aid, white society visualized Indians as effeminate for lacking self-sufficiency—(MB).

152. *Annual Report of the Commissioner of Indian Affairs to the Secretary of the Interior, Fifty-Seventh, 1888* (Washington DC: Government Printing Office, 1888), 278.

153. *Annual Report, Fifty-Seventh,* 278.

154. Adams, *Education for Extinction*, 124–35; Fear-Segal, *White Man's Club*, 241–67.

155. Brandon Ecoffey, "Death Rate Cover-Up at Carlisle Indian School," *Native Sun News*, September 5, 2013, https://www.indianz.com/News/2013/09/05/native-sun-news-death-rate-cov.asp#:~:text=Previous%20estimates%20had%20surmised%20 that,been%20sent%20home%20from%20Carlisle; Jacqueline Fear-Segal notes that Richard Henry Pratt sent students home when mortally sick, and she also suspects that many other students died while on their outings and would have been buried in any number of rural cemeteries in Pennsylvania and the Mid-Atlantic—(JB). See Fear-Segal, "History and Reclamation of a Sacred Space," 155.

156. *Annual Report, Fifty-First,* 180.

157. *Annual Report, Forty-Ninth,* 189; *Annual Report of the Commissioner of Indian Affairs to the Secretary of the Interior, Fifty-Sixth, 1887* (Washington DC: Government Printing Office, 1887), 259.

158. *Indian Helper*, July 4, 1890, 4; Smits, "The 'Squaw Drudge,'"; Bloom, *To Show What an Indian Can Do*, 15–16.

159. Macleod, *Building Character*, 31.

160. "Colonel Pratt, on the Kind of Man to Succeed," *Red Man and Helper*, November 21, 1902, 2.

161. Jacobson, *Whiteness of a Different Color*, 48–49.

162. Jacobson, *Whiteness of a Different Color*, 49–53.

163. Jenkins, *Real All Americans*, 183. Pratt's relationship with Roosevelt was tumultuous at best. Pratt had alienated the president by constantly requesting a promotion. Pratt, who had had the ear of every president since Carlisle's creation, was largely ignored by Roosevelt. It was the beginning of the end for Pratt; Roosevelt secured his removal from Carlisle in 1904—(MB).

164. "Colonel Pratt, on the Kind of Man to Succeed," 2.

165. *Indian Helper*, September 4, 1896, 2.

166. Lomawaima and Ostler, "Reconsidering Richard Henry Pratt," 79–100.

167. Lomawaima, *They Called It Prairie Light*; Child, *Boarding School Seasons*; Adams, *Education for Extinction*, 209–38.

168. Bell, "Telling Stories out of School," 210.

169. Pratt, "Twenty-Second Annual Report," 4.

170. Pratt, "Twenty-Second Annual Report," 4.

171. Bell, "Telling Stories out of School," 220.

172. Pratt, "Twenty-Second Annual Report," 4.

173. Pratt, "Twenty-Second Annual Report," 4.

174. In this respect, it mirrors G. Stanley Hall's idea of children being "little savages." Bederman, *Manliness and Civilization*, 78. This is also reflected in Mark Twain's story of Huckleberry Finn. The character, as a child, wants to escape the attempts to "sivilise" him—(JB).

175. Pratt, *Battlefield and Classroom*, 308–9.

2. Playing White Men

1. Quoted in Jenkins, *Real All Americans*, 156.

2. Bell, "Telling Stories Out of School," 21.

3. Landis, "The Names," 101.

4. Pratt, *Battlefield and Classroom*, 317; for football at Carlisle, see Jenkins, *Real All Americans*; Lars Anderson, *Carlisle vs. Army*. For a more academic approach to Carlisle sport, see Bloom, *To Show What an Indian Can Do*; Oriard, *Reading Football*; Gamache, "Sport as Cultural Assimilation"; Adams, "More Than a Game"; Oxendine, *American Indian Sports Heritage*, 183–238.

5. *Indian Helper*, November 28, 1890, 3.

6. Pratt, *Battlefield and Classroom*, 317–18. Pratt's advice is remarkably similar to that given to Jackie Robinson by Branch Rickey. Shortly after meeting Robinson in 1945, Rickey lectured him on the abuse he might receive playing major league baseball. Exasperated, Robinson asked, "Mr. Rickey, do you want a ballplayer who's afraid to fight back?" Rickey responded, "I want a player with guts enough not to fight back!" Robinson, much like the Carlisle athletes, had to challenge the pervading racial stereotypes in order play major league baseball as an African American. In order to prove his "civilized" character, Robinson, like Carlisle's football players before him, faced an unimaginable level of abuse from fans and opposing players, but could never respond. In Robinson's case, this caused tremendous stress that took a deep physical and psychological toll. Robinson became a prolific columnist and activist for racial justice after he retired from baseball, but those who knew him believe that the pressures he faced as a player contributed to his early death in 1972 at the age of fifty-three—(MB). See Tygiel, *Baseball's Great Experiment*, 66.

7. Bloom, *To Show What an Indian Can Do*, 14–17.

8. See Ingrassia, *Rise of Gridiron University*; for some commentators, the violence of football was a necessary component of the sport. Oriard, *Reading Football*, 213–15.

9. Oriard, *Sporting with the Gods*, 16.

10. Oriard, *Reading Football*, 245–46.

11. Bederman, *Manliness and Civilization*.

12. Oriard, *Reading Football*, 229–33; Oriard, "Pigskin Pioneers," *Village Voice*, https://www.villagevoice.com/2000/10/10/pigskin-pioneers/, accessed March 4, 2011.

13. Quoted in Oriard, *Reading Football*, 229.

14. Quoted in Ingrassia, *Rise of Gridiron University*, 49–50.

15. This is not to say that all other players were white. Paul Robeson, who later became a famous Hollywood actor and communist, played football for Rutgers—(MB).

16. Oriard, *Reading Football*, 191–216.

17. Oriard, *Reading Football*, 244; Deloria, *Indians in Unexpected Places*, 123.

18. Quoted in Oriard, *Reading Football*, 212.

19. Oriard, *Reading Football*, 245–46.

20. Ingrassia, *Rise of Gridiron University*, 123.

21. Oriard, *Reading Football*, 207.

22. Ingrassia, *Rise of Gridiron University*, 123.

23. John Sayle Watterson, *College Football*, 10–18.

24. Watterson, *College Football*, 59.

25. "Foot Ball," *Red Man*, September–October 1895, 6–7.

26. "Foot Ball," 6–7.

27. "Foot Ball," 6–7.

28. "Foot Ball," 7.

29. See "Yale Had a Close Call," *New York Times*, October 25, 1896. The game is comprehensively covered in the November 1896 edition of the *Red Man* but also recollected by Pratt in his *Battlefield and Classroom*, 318–19.

30. "New York's Unstinted Applause," *Red Man*, November 1896, 2.

31. Quoted in Adams, "More Than a Game."

32. Pratt, *Battlefield and Classroom*, 319.

33. "Yale Had a Close Call."

34. Pratt, *Battlefield and Classroom*, 318. On the "Big Four," see Oriard, *Reading Football*, 58.

35. Fear-Segal, *White Man's Club*, 209.

36. "The Great Game," *Indian Helper*, November 12, 1897, 4.

37. "Colonel Pratt's Talk to the Students Last Saturday Evening, After the Cornell, 6–Carlisle, 10 Game," *Red Man and Helper*, October 24, 1902, 1.

38. "Gentlemanly Playing Wins," *Indian Helper*, October 25, 1895, 4.

39. Charlie "Hobo" Atsye, oral history interview transcript, June 22, 1973, interview by DeWitt Clinton Smith III, Carlisle Indian School Papers (1876–2007), MC 2008.4, box 1, folder 15.

40. Mr. and Mrs. George Serracino, oral history interview transcript, July 1, 1973, interview by DeWitt Clinton Smith III, Carlisle Indian School Papers (1876–2007), MC 2008.4, box 1, folder 15.

41. John Alonzo (Laguna), oral history interview transcript, October 1976, interview by DeWitt Clinton Smith III, Carlisle Indian School Papers (1876–2007), MC 2008.4, box 1, folder 15.

42. Adams, "More Than a Game," 42.

43. David MacFarland student file, NARA 1327 b136 f5347, accessed through the Carlisle Indian School Digital Resource Center, https://carlisleindian.dickinson.edu/ , August 31, 2020.

44. Oriard, *Reading Football*, 245.

45. "Picturesque Event," *Red Man*, November 1896, 6.

46. "Amateur Sport," *Harper's Weekly*, November 25, 1899, 1193–94.

47. Fear-Segal, *White Man's Club*, 24–25.

48. McCormick, Hickok, and Hall were all featured in Camp's All-America selection in 1892, 1893, and 1897 respectively. Bull played for Yale in the 1880s. "All-America Teams," Walter Camp Football Foundation, https://waltercamp.org/walter-camp-all-america-team-by-year/ , accessed August 20, 2009; Ronald Smith, *Sports and Freedom*, 39–95.

49. "The Great Game," *Indian Helper*, November 12, 1897, 1.

50. Jenkins, *Real All Americans*, 167.

51. *Red Man and Helper*, November 7, 1903, 2.

52. *Red Man and Helper*, November 7, 1903, 2. There is a narrative surrounding Carlisle trick plays concerning the role of the trickster. A predominant feature of Native and African American trickster stories and folklore is the defeat of a large animal by a smaller and more intelligent counterpart. In these respects, the larger animal is representative of the white man; the smaller animal is the wily Native or African American. According to Warner's reminiscences on Carlisle, the players enjoyed being able to "outsmart the palefaces." Trick plays are thus placed within the context of getting revenge on the dominant white society. Yet it is debatable whether Carlisle would have employed trick plays to a similar extent without Warner's arrival. Warner had created trick plays prior to his arrival at Carlisle; the hidden ball trick was supposedly tried by the Cornell scrubs team several years before. I suspect Carlisle would have used trick plays without Warner, but not to the extent they did—(MB). Warner, "The Indian Massacres," 8; Adams, "More Than a Game," 46–48; Gerald Gems, "Negotiating a Native American Identity through Sport," 1–21.

53. Caspar Whitney, "Amateur Sports," *Harper's Weekly*, October 21, 1899, 1074.

54. See Appendix, this volume.

55. "The Football Banquet," *Red Man and Helper*, December 12, 1902, 1.

56. Oriard, *Reading Football*, 244.

57. Camp's ideals, however, were based upon the amateur coach. The coach would ideally be a recently graduated player who would proceed into middle management. The professional coach, such as Warner and Amos Alonzo Stagg of the University of Chicago, would not move beyond coaching. As college football spread and became increasingly popular and professional, Camp's ideal started to fade. Indeed, what was the point of football training middle managers if a greater income could be gained through coaching?—(MB).

58. Bell, "Telling Stories out of School," 47; Hoxie, *Final Promise*, 190–97.

59. Warner, "The Indian Massacres," 8. Warner's articles in *Collier's Weekly* were an attempt to rewrite his and the players' history in a more favourable light. For example, Warner challenges the argument that Natives would quit when losing. As evidence, Warner uses Carlisle's 1913 match against Dartmouth. Carlisle was losing 10–7 at half-time. They emerged in the second half to win 34–10. What Warner neglects to mention is that he had bet on the match and promised the players a cut of the winnings if they turned the score around. Warner's analysis of his departure from Carlisle is suspect too. Warner argues that he left in 1914 because he saw "Carlisle's abolition as inevitable." He neglects to mention that the congressional commission recommended his dismissal and that the athletes revolted against him. This, alongside Lipps's disapproval of football, made Warner's position virtually untenable—(MB).

60. Warner, "The Indian Massacres," 8.

61. Warner, "The Indian Massacres," 8.

62. "The Football Banquet: Colonel Pratt," *Red Man and Helper*, December 12, 1902, 3.

63. Bell, "Telling Stories out of School," 402; Landis, "The Names," 100.

64. Jenkins, *Real All Americans*, 215; "The Picture Below," *Red Man and Helper*, February 19, 1904, 4.

65. "Football," *Red Man and Helper*, September 14, 1900, 2.

66. "We Have Made History," *Red Man*, November 1896, 5.

67. *New York Journal*, November 1, 1896.

68. "The Football Banquet," *Red Man and Helper*, December 12, 1902, 1.

69. According to Philip Deloria, "playing Indian" was largely acted out by supposedly civilized white men. Deloria, *Playing Indian*, 8.

70. Alfred Standing, "Home Pastimes of the Original Indians," *Red Man*, January 1898, 4.

71. Bemus Pierce, "Personnel of the Carlisle Indian Team," *Red Man*, January 1898, 6.

72. Again, well into twenty-first century, white coaches receive credit for the achievements of their players who happen to be people of color. Pierce's comments bring to mind a personal memory. In the spring of 1981, covering an Oakland A's game for my college radio station, I interviewed A's designated hitter Cliff Johnson, an African American, on the steps of his dugout before the game. Oakland had recently hired the temperamental, and white, manager Billy Martin. The A's had started the season with a series of impressive wins, and their management launched an ad campaign promoting the team's play as "Billy Ball." I asked Johnson what he thought about "Billy Ball," and he told me to turn off my tape recorder. Then he said, "I don't know a fucking player on this team named Billy, do you?"—(JB).

73. Pierce, "Personnel of the Carlisle Indian Team."

74. "Rogers Is Chosen Head Coach," *Red Man and Helper*, March 11, 1904, 2.

75. See Appendix, this volume.

76. Pratt and his successors kept meticulous records on ex-students. This was to challenge newspaper reports that frequently appeared concerning Carlisle graduates. The school managed to trace several of these fake stories to a single individ-

ual named Will R. Draper, or "The Wichita Liar." The journalist had reported that White Buffalo, an ex-Carlisle student, had been arrested for murder in Oklahoma. The school discovered that no murders had actually occurred nor had White Buffalo been arrested. Draper also attempted to portray a female Native student from another school as "possessed of a million dollars." The student faced proposals in her mail. The tracing of ex-students allowed Pratt to challenge news stories when they potentially damaged Carlisle's reputation—(MB). "That Wichita Liar," *Red Man and Helper*, December 5, 1902, 1; "The Same Old Fabricator," *Red Man and Helper*, December 5, 1902, 2.

77. Bell, "Telling Stories out of School," 335–39.

78. "The Football Banquet," *Red Man and Helper*, December 12, 1902, 1.

79. Quoted in Bloom, *To Show What an Indian Can Do*, 14.

80. "General Pratt Relieved," *Red Man and Helper*, June 17, 1904, 1.

81. Oriard, *Reading Football*, 241.

3. Athletic Masculinity

1. Fear-Segal, *White Man's Club*, 159.

2. The Carlisle Indian School printed a number of different publications, and its regular newspaper also went through transformations in format and title over the years. The former paper, the *Indian Helper*, had been absorbed into the *Red Man* during Pratt's final years. After he left, the school ceased its publication and, after a brief hiatus, introduced the *Arrow*, a paper, unlike its predecessors, with commercial sponsorship and lacking the details of daily life that had characterized the former paper—(JB). See Fear-Segal, *White Man's Club*, 228.

3. "Carlisle's Football Team One of the Most Remarkable of the Year," *Carlisle Arrow*, December 20, 1912, 7.

4. For the idea that masculinity was more natural for Native men, see Victoria Paraschak, "Doing Race, Doing Gender," 153–69.

5. Fear-Segal, *White Man's Club*, 123.

6. Reel, *Course of Study*, 54; Adams, *Education for Extinction*, 32; Hoxie, *Final Promise*, 195.

7. *Hearings before the Joint Commission of the Congress of the United States, Sixty-Third Congress, Second Session, to Investigate Indian Affairs, February 6, 7, 8, and March 25, 1914, Part II* (Washington DC: Government Printing Office, 1914), 1134.

8. Adams, *Education for Extinction*, 56–57, 309–15, 318.

9. Bell, "Telling Stories out of School," 80–84.

10. Bell, "Telling Stories out of School," 80–84. As Bell has observed, over the thirty-nine years of its existence, one can divide Carlisle's student body into three major cohorts. The first, between 1879 and 1890, were, in the words of Barbara Landis, "recruited to ensure the cooperation of their resisting parents and grandparents." The second cohort, enrolled between 1890 and 1904, had been enrolled in a primary education for at least four years before arriving at Carlisle. These were the first stu-

dents to have pressured Pratt to initiate a football program, and to have comprised the earliest successful Carlisle teams. The final cohort, according to Landis, were "orphans, troublemakers in the agency schools, second-generation offspring of former Carlisle students, or athletes recruited for their athletic ability"—(JB). See Barbara Landis, "The Names," 186–97. Using a theory of Carmelita Ryan, Bell argues that Mercer's dismissal may also have been due to a "serious moral offense." Although Bell does not state outright what the offense was, she states that Frank Hudson was dismissed during the same period for embezzling school funds—(MB).

11. Bell, "Telling Stories out of School," 88–90.

12. Hokowhitu, "Tackling Maori Masculinity," 259–84.

13. "Rogers Is Chosen Head Coach," *Red Man and Helper*, March 11, 1904, 2.

14. "Foot Ball," *Arrow*, September 8, 1905, 2.

15. "Indians Triumph over West Point," *Arrow*, November 17, 1905, 2.

16. "Athletic Notes," *Arrow*, September 21, 1906, 2.

17. Jenkins, *Real All Americans*, 224.

18. Jenkins, *Real All Americans*, 223–24.

19. Jenkins, *Real All Americans*, 227.

20. "Glenn S. Warner Returns to Carlisle," *Arrow*, December 21, 1906, 2.

21. Phil Smith, "Whiteness, Normal Theory, and Disability Studies," http://www.dsq-sds.org/article/view/491/668; Gould, *Mismeasure of Man*, 31–145.

22. "The Big Buffalo Game," *Carlisle Arrow*, October 16, 1908, 1.

23. "The Big Buffalo Game."

24. *Hearings Before the Joint Commission*, 1342.

25. "Glenn S. Warner Returns to Carlisle."

26. "The Story of the Defeat of Penn by the Carlisle Indians," *Carlisle Arrow*, November 10, 1911, 5–6.

27. An example within Carlisle's newspaper is "A Pawnee Medicine Dance," *Indian Helper*, November 11, 1887, 1, 4. Within this "story," a woman witnesses a medicine dance. When the dance starts, the woman comments, "He didn't look like a man, but more like the evil one. . . ." By referencing Satan, the woman portrayed the dance as evoking supernatural and evil forces beyond the comprehension of the viewer—(MB). Berkhofer, *White Man's Indian*, 28.

28. Warner, "The Indian Massacres," 7.

29. Adams, "More Than a Game," 30.

30. Benjamin H. Nuvamsa, "Louis Tewanima, Hopi (1882–1969)," Appendix A in Gilbert, *Hopi Runners*, 166–67.

31. Gilbert, *Hopi Runners*, 74.

32. Gilbert, *Hopi Runners*, 73.

33. Gilbert, *Hopi Runners*, 75.

34. Ronald Smith, *Sports and Freedom*, 168.

35. Oriard, *Sporting with the Gods*, 26; Ronald Smith, *Sports and Freedom*, 166–68.

36. Bloom, *To Show What an Indian Can Do*, 27–28.

37. Carlos Montezuma, "Carlisle's Athletic Policy Criticized by Dr. Montezuma," *Chicago Daily Tribune*, November 24, 1907, C2, quoted in Bloom, *To Show What an Indian Can Do*, 27–28.

38. Montezuma, "Carlisle's Athletic Policy Criticized by Dr. Montezuma."

39. W. G. Thompson to Carlos Montezuma, ca.1907, in *The Papers of Carlos Montezuma*, ed. John William Latimer Jr. (Wilmington DE: Scholarly Resources, 1984).

40. Thompson to Montezuma.

41. "The Explanation," *Arrow*, December 13, 1907, 2.

42. Gus Beaulieu, "Malicious Charges," *Arrow*, December 13, 1917, 4.

43. Beaulieu, "Malicious Charges," 4.

44. Despite this, Carlisle students watched a performance of Buffalo Bill's Wild West Show in 1898. The report noted that despite their difference in opinion, Pratt and William Cody remained good friends—(MB). "Buffalo Bill's Wild West Show," *Red Man*, June, July, and August 1898, 1, 8.

45. Slotkin, "Buffalo Bill's 'Wild West,'" 166.

46. Moses, *Wild West Shows and the Images of American Indians*.

47. Bell, "Telling Stories out of School," 83.

48. Goldwater, *Primitivism in Modern Art*, 8–13.

49. Newcombe, *Best of the Athletic Boys*, 112–13.

50. Newcombe, *Best of the Athletic Boys*, 111; *Hearings before the Joint Commission*, 1336.

51. "The New Athletic Quarters Finished," *Carlisle Arrow*, September 10, 1909, 1.

52. *Hearing before the Joint Commission*, 1335.

53. Watterson, *College Football*, 66–67. Ronald Smith, *Sports and Freedom*, 192–93. Shortly after the publication of Needham's articles, Endicott Peabody of the Groton Preparatory School called on Theodore Roosevelt to invite the "Big Three" (Yale, Harvard, and Princeton) to the White House to reform football. Roosevelt later remarked that reforming football was more difficult than obtaining peace between Russia and Japan following their war in 1902—(MB). Watterson, *College Football*, 68–70.

54. Watterson, *College Football*, 40–41.

55. Ronald Smith, *Sports and Freedom*, 171.

56. Smith, *Sports and Freedom*, 169.

57. *Hearings before the Joint Commission*, 1134–37; Letters from Major W. A. Mercer to Commissioner of Indian Affairs Leupp, NARA RG 75 b020 8195.

58. Caspar Whitney, "Amateur Sports," *Harper's Weekly*, January 23, 1897, 93–94.

59. Thompson to Carlos Montezuma (see preceding note 39).

60. This is not to say that some athletes did not run away. Prior to the 1901 match at the University of Michigan, Louis Leroy (Stockbridge) and Edward Demarr (Ojibwe) deserted Carlisle. Warner stated that the pair had "evidently tired of the discipline." Leroy went on to play for the New York Highlanders in the baseball majors in 1905 and 1906—(MB). "Deserted," *Red Man and Helper*, November 8, 1901, 2; Jenkins, *Real All Americans*, 191–92.

61. *Hearings before the Joint Commission*, 1336–43.

62. Bloom, *To Show What an Indian Can Do*, 31.

63. Thompson to Montezuma.

64. "Carlisle Toyed with Haskell, Running Up Large Score, 38 to 4," *Arrow*, December 1, 1904, 2. Emil Houser was often called Wauseka in the Carlisle match reports.

65. "Local Miscellany," *Arrow*, September 13, 1907, 3.

66. Newcombe, *Best of the Athletic Boys*, 111; Warner, "The Indian Massacres," 8.

67. *Hearings before the Joint Commission*, 1065.

68. "Carlisle's Great Football Record: *Philadelphia Public Ledger*," *Indian Craftsman*, December 1909, 9–18. The cover of this edition featured a drawing by "Lone Star" Dietz featuring an Indigenous man weaving, with a caption inside the cover celebrating Navajo blankets. For Pratt, the greatest sin Carlisle could commit would be to allow students to return to their former way of life, something that he called going "back to the blanket." Now, Carlisle administrators promoted Indigenous blanket making in their sanctioned publications—JB.

69. "Carlisle's Great Football Record."

70. "Carlisle's Great Football Record," 16.

71. Anderson, *Carlisle vs. Army*, 278. Of interest to note, future President Dwight Eisenhower played for Army.

72. For the idea of sportsmen representing the masculinity of an entire race, see Bederman, *Manliness and Civilization*, 41–42.

73. "W. U. P.–Indians," *Arrow*, October 26, 1906, 1.

74. "Indians Crush the U. P.," *Arrow*, November 2, 1906, 1, 4.

75. Adams, "More Than a Game," 31–32.

76. "Indians Scalp Harvard," *Arrow*, November 15, 1907, 1.

77. Oriard, *Sporting with the Gods*, 26.

78. "American Games," *Arrow*, October 25, 1907, 4.

79. "Carlisle's Football Players of the Past Also Make Good in Real Life," *Carlisle Arrow*, December 20, 1912, 12.

80. Correspondence from Major W. A. Mercer to Commissioner Leupp, NARA RG75_CCF_b0020_f12_8195.

81. Peavy and Smith, *Full Court Quest*, 62–71.

82. Peavy and Smith, *Full Court Quest*, 62–71.

83. Gilbert, *Hopi Runners*, 74, 80.

84. For the narrative of Thorpe's success and subsequent professionalism scandal, see Buford, *Native American Son*; Newcombe, *Best of the Athletic Boys*, 179–89, 207–11; Bruchac, *Jim Thorpe*, 213–23, 247–53; Wheeler, *Jim Thorpe*, 99–116, 141–52. For an academic study of Thorpe, see Mark Rubinfeld, "The Mythical Jim Thorpe," 167–89.

85. The only other study of a Carlisle player is Tom Benjey, *Keep A-Goin': The Life of Lone Star Dietz*. There is debate over whether Dietz was actually Native or white. Dietz was placed on trial for avoiding the draft for the First World War. He had written on the draft card that he was a non-citizen Indian. The prosecution argued that Dietz was actually from a white family. The first trial resulted in a hung jury. The second resulted in acquittal for Dietz. On further charges, Dietz admitted "no

contest," but this was due to financial restrictions; Dietz did not have the money to secure his defense witnesses for yet another trial—(MB).

86. Bloom, "No Fall from Grace," 228–44. Thorpe's success in the ABC sports poll was primarily due to the work of his daughter, Grace, in spreading knowledge of his feats—(JB).

87. Jenkins, *Real All Americans*, 228–29.

88. Newcombe, *Best of the Athletic Boys*, 140–49. Ironically, had Thorpe done a traditional outing, he would have made money and never been labeled a professional.

89. Newcombe, *Best of the Athletic Boys*, 193–94.

90. Wheeler, *Jim Thorpe*, 141–42.

91. Fred Bruce to Indian Rights Association, November 18, 1913, in Johnson Collection, Cumberland County Historical Society, Carlisle PA.

92. "A.A.U. Attacked for Its Methods of Registration," *Washington Times*, January 28, 1913, 11, accessed April 19, 2011, http://chroniclingamerica.loc.gov/lccn/sn84026749/1913-01-28/ed-1/seq-11/. The article includes a complete copy of Thorpe's letter of confession.

93. Wheeler, *Jim Thorpe*, 155. Thorpe was also offered fifty thousand dollars by Harry Edwards to become a professional boxer.

94. Newcombe, *Best of the Athletic Boys*, 237–38; Springwood, "Playing Football, Playing Indian," 123–42.

95. *Jim Thorpe: All-American*. Quoted in Bloom, "No State of Grace," 236.

96. "The World's Greatest Athlete," *Carlisle Arrow*, September 13, 1912, 9.

97. *Hearings Before the Joint Commission*, 1375.

98. "A.A.U. Attacked for Its Methods of Registration," 11; Wheeler, *Jim Thorpe*, 144–45.

99. "A.A.U. Attacked for Its Methods of Registration," 11.

100. Michael Neill and Joseph Harmes, "Torch Bearer," *People* 45:1 (January 8, 1996), 73.

101. "Carlisle's Day with a Vengeance," *Carlisle Arrow*, November 28, 1913, 4.

102. Bloom, "No Fall from Grace," 240.

103. N. Scott Momaday, "Stones at Carlisle," in Fear-Segal and Rose, *Carlisle Indian Industrial School*, 51.

104. Momaday, "Stones at Carlisle," 52.

4. "Civilization" on Trial

1. *Hearings before the Joint Commission*, 1017.

2. *Hearings before the Joint Commission*, 977–78.

3. "Congressman and Senators Here to Hold Investigation," *Carlisle Evening Herald*, February 7, 1914. My thanks go to Linda Waggoner for finding and transcribing newspaper reports on the congressional hearings and the aftermath. Welch, one of the instigators of the investigation, was romantically involved with Julia Carter, daughter of the Representative. Thus Carter's involvement in the hearings affected

him personally—(MB). *Hearings before the Joint Commission*; Bell, "Telling Stories out of School," 93; Jenkins, *Real All Americans*, 290.

4. *Hearings before the Joint Commission*, 1342.

5. See Child, *Boarding School Seasons*; Lomawaima, *They Called It Prairie Light*; Adams, *Education for Extinction*; Bell, "Telling Stories out of School."

6. Bederman, *Manliness and Civilization*, 45–76.

7. Adams, *Education for Extinction*, 308–9.

8. "The Y.M.C.A. Meeting," *Carlisle Arrow*, March 13, 1914, 1.

9. "General School News," *Carlisle Arrow*, December 5, 1913, 3.

10. "The Invincibles," *Carlisle Arrow*, October 10, 1913, 4.

11. *Hearings before the Joint Commission*, 1016–23, 1111–12.

12. *Hearings before the Joint Commission*, 1341.

13. *Hearings before the Joint Commission*, 1007.

14. *Hearings before the Joint Commission*, 977–78.

15. *Hearings before the Joint Commission*, 1006.

16. M. K. Sniffen to Cato Sells, November 24, 1913, in *The Papers of the Society of American Indians*, 1906–1946, Cumberland County Historical Society, Carlisle PA.

17. "Work for Indian Students," *Carlisle Arrow*, November 8, 1912, 1.

18. *Hearings before the Joint Commission*, 1161–62.

19. *Hearings before the Joint Commission*, 1056–57.

20. *Hearings before the Joint Commission*, 1192, 1017.

21. *Hearings before the Joint Commission*, 1066.

22. *Hearings before the Joint Commission*, 978.

23. Bell makes this observation as well in her dissertation, noting that it was very likely that many students at Carlisle were sexually active before arriving at school— (JB). See Bell, "Telling Stories out of School," 308.

24. *Hearings before the Joint Commission*, 1106. The names on this list have been erased from the record, and although they are now currently available in unredacted documents, we do not list them here out of respect for decedents to whom these names belong—(JB).

25. *Hearings before the Joint Commission*, 1060.

26. *Hearings before the Joint Commission*, 1290–91.

27. *Hearings before the Joint Commission*, 1059.

28. *Hearings before the Joint Commission*, 1372.

29. "Reception by Faculty to Greet New Students," *Carlisle Arrow*, October 24, 1913, 3; "The Mercer Reception," *Carlisle Arrow*, December 19, 1913, 1; Student Reporters, "General School News," *Carlisle Arrow*, October 9, 1914, 2.

30. *Hearings before the Joint Commission*, 1038–39; "The Band Makes a Hit with Governors," *Carlisle Arrow*, December 22, 1911, 2.

31. "Notes about ex-Students," *Carlisle Arrow*, April 4, 1913, 4.

32. Bell, "Telling Stories out of School," 264–80.

33. *Hearings before the Joint Commission*, 1289.

34. *Hearings before the Joint Commission,* 1289.

35. Ethel Williams's exact tribal origin is not known. She is not in the student records. Eleazer and Emma Williams are there but no Ethel. Without further evidence, I am wary of identifying her nation—(MB). Barbara Landis, "NARA RG 75 FILE 13 Carlisle Indian School Student Names and Folder Number," http://home.epix.net/~landis/nararonan.html, accessed April 11, 2012.

36. *Hearings before the Joint Commission,* 1351.

37. *Hearings before the Joint Commission,* 967. While individual acts of resistance were relatively common, mass rebellion was rare. At the Haskell Institute in 1919, students engaged in open rebellion. The electricity was cut and students looted the food supply and broke lights. One student, referencing the superintendent, allegedly yelled "string him up." Nine students were expelled as a result of the incident—(MB). Child, *Boarding School Seasons,* 93–94.

38. *Hearings before the Joint Commission,* 1248.

39. *Hearings before the Joint Commission,* 1050–53, 997.

40. *Hearings before the Joint Commission,* 1052.

41. Bell, "Telling Stories out of School," 109–10.

42. *Hearings before the Joint Commission,* 1177.

43. *Hearings before the Joint Commission,* 1000.

44. *Hearings before the Joint Commission,* 1002.

45. *Hearings before the Joint Commission,* 1001, 1226.

46. *Hearings before the Joint Commission,* 1370.

47. *Hearings before the Joint Commission,* 1000.

48. *Hearings before the Joint Commission,* 1001.

49. NARA RG 75 CCF b007 f04 10144; Julia Hardin student file, NARA 1327 b088 f4037, accessed through the Carlisle Indian School Digital Resource Center, http://carlisleindian.dickinson.edu/sites/all/files/docs-ephemera/NARA_1327_b088_f4037.pdf.

50. *Hearings before the Joint Commission,* 1102–3.

51. *Hearings before the Joint Commission,* 1245.

52. Fear-Segal and Rose, *Carlisle Indian Industrial School,* 360.

53. *Hearings before the Joint Commission,* 1350.

54. Petition to Cato Sells, Commissioner of Indian Affairs, March 21, 1914, NARA RG 75 CCF b007 f03 10144.

55. Gus Welch Deposition, February 16, 1914, NARA RG 75 CCF b007 f03 10144.

56. Gus Welch Deposition; *Hearings before the Joint Commission,* 1341.

57. Edward Bracklin deposition, February 16, 1914, NARA RG 75 CCF b007 f03 10144.

58. *Hearings before the Joint Commission,* 1343.

59. *Hearings before the Joint Commission,* 1335.

60. Bell, "Telling Stories out of School," 309.

61. *Hearings before the Joint Commission,* 1008.

62. *Hearings before the Joint Commission,* 1008.

63. *Hearings before the Joint Commission,* 1110.

64. *Hearings before the Joint Commission,* 1001.

65. *Hearings before the Joint Commission*, 1055, 1375.

66. *Hearings before the Joint Commission*, 1276.

67. *Hearings before the Joint Commission*, 1276.

68. Carlisle Student Record Card, Montreville Yuda Student Record file NARA RG 75 1329 b2.

69. Jacobson, *Whiteness of a Different Color*, 149–55.

70. "Investigates Indian School," *New York Times*, July 10, 1909; Bell, "Telling Stories out of School," 91–92. The 1909 investigation was launched after accusations of cruelty by James R. Wheelock. Investigator E. P. Holcomb conducted an investigation and cleared Friedman of wrongdoing. The 1911 investigation was conducted after the student rolls were revealed to be fraudulent. Graduated students had been kept on the record so as to boost government funding of Carlisle. One student on the roll had actually died. The names were immediately removed following the discovery—(JB).

71. *Hearings before the Joint Commission*, 1028.

72. December 15, 1912, Church and Cemetery Records, Microfilm #25, Cumberland County Historical Society, Carlisle PA; *Hearings before the Joint Commission*, 1037.

73. Bell, "Telling Stories out of School," 89–91.

74. *Hearings before the Joint Commission*, 1000.

75. Bell, "Telling Stories out of School," 89.

76. *Hearings before the Joint Committee*, 1301.

77. *Hearings before the Joint Commission*, 1388.

78. *Hearings before the Joint Commission*, 985.

79. *Hearings before the Joint Commission*, 1060.

80. *Hearings before the Joint Commission*, 1372.

81. In his biography of Henry Ford, Neil Baldwin provides an example of how the ubiquitously assigned *McGuffey Reader* circulated anti-Semitic tropes to American schoolchildren, including Henry Ford, in the nineteenth century—(JB). See Baldwin, *Henry Ford and the Jews*, 1–7.

82. See Biberman, *Masculinity, Anti-Semitism and Early Modern English Literature*.

83. Banks, *Becoming a Feminist*.

84. "A Delightful Party in the Interest of Suffrage," *Carlisle Arrow*, January 9, 1914, 6.

85. Banks, *Becoming a Feminist*.

86. Kimmel, "Men's Responses to Feminism at the Turn of the Century," 261–83.

87. *Hearings before the Joint Commission*, 1027.

88. *Hearings before the Joint Commission*, 1030.

89. *Hearings before the Joint Commission*, 1027.

90. *Hearings before the Joint Commission*, 1334.

91. "School Troubles," *Adams County News*, May 16, 1914.

92. *Hearings before the Joint Commission*, 1003–9.

93. *Hearings before the Joint Commission*, 1334–43, 1349–50.

94. *Hearings before the Joint Commission*, 1336.

95. Bell, "Telling Stories out of School," 95.

96. "Lessons of the Carlisle Investigation," 97–98.

97. *Hearings before the Joint Commission*, 1064.

98. *Hearings before the Joint Commission*, 1348.

99. *Hearings before the Joint Commission*, 1336.

100. *Hearings before the Joint Commission*, 1066. The reaction of Congressman Carter, the father of Welch's girlfriend Julia Carter, to such news is not recorded.

101. *Hearings before the Joint Commission*, 1066.

102. *Hearings before the Joint Commission*, 1342.

103. *Hearings before the Joint Commission*, 1189.

104. Newcombe, *Best of the Athletic Boys*, 135–36.

105. M. K. Sniffen to Cato Sells, November 24, 1913.

106. *Hearings before the Joint Commission*, 1060.

107. *Hearings before the Joint Commission*, 1359.

108. *Hearings before the Joint Commission*, 1223.

109. *Hearings before the Joint Commission*, 1386.

110. "The Temptations of an Athlete: By One of Them," *Red Man*, June 1914, 438–41.

111. Ingrassia, *Rise of Gridiron University*, 139–70.

112. "The Temptations of an Athlete."

113. "The Temptations of an Athlete."

114. "The Temptations of an Athlete."

115. "The Temptations of an Athlete."

116. Lorde, "Master's Tools," 100–103.

5. The Aftermath

1. *Hearings before the Joint Commission*, 1146.

2. "Will Not Move Indian School," *Adams County News*, February 7, 1914.

3. "Friedman Suspended," *Evening Sentinel*, February 13, 1914; Claude Stauffer's Obituary, Flower Necrology Scrapbook, 1916–1963, Cumberland County Historical Society, Carlisle PA.

4. *Hearings before the Joint Commission*, 1335.

5. "Prof. Whitwell Popular Here," *Carlisle Arrow*, May 8, 1914, 1.

6. "Clean Slate for Moses Friedman," *Adams County News* (Gettysburg PA), October 23, 1915. Bell, "Telling Stories out of School," 97. Friedman's time in New Mexico is shrouded in mystery. He was ordered to become the superintendent of the Anchor Ranch School for Defective Boys by the New York Supreme Court. Yet I have been unable to discover any mention of the school or Friedman's time in New Mexico except for a 1969 report in the *Albuquerque Journal*, mentioning that he purchased a local house, and his First World War draft card. Friedman's draft card holds particular interest. It lists his occupation as "Special work as stockman for NY Supreme Court." I presume this was for the Anchor Ranch School, but there is no mention of it anywhere. I contacted the local historical society, who had never heard of it. Anchor Ranch is now part of the Los Alamos military base, which only deepens the mystery. But it raises some intriguing questions. What was meant by "defective"? Was it mentally, physically, or emotionally related? What was Fried-

man's involvement in the school, if it indeed existed? Unfortunately, the answers to these questions will have to wait for further research—(MB). "Old Events," *Albuquerque Journal*, June 12, 1969, A4; Ancestry.com, "World War I Draft Registration Cards 1917–1918 for Moses Friedman" in Ancestry.com, accessed January 10, 2009.

7. Bell, "Telling Stories out of School," 99.

8. For a narrative of Carlisle's post-hearings football history, see Benjey, "End of Carlisle's Trail of Glory," 7–11.

9. Gus Welch student file, RG 75, Series 1327, box 133, folder 5234. Accessed through the Carlisle Indian School Digital Resource Center, http://carlisleindian.dickinson.edu/, accessed December 4, 2020.

10. "Outline of Courses," *Carlisle Arrow*, February 5, 1915, 1–3.

11. "Football Schedule for 1914," *Carlisle Arrow*, September 4, 1914, 2; Jenkins, *Real All Americans*, 294; See Appendix, this volume.

12. See Appendix.

13. "Carlisle's Football Team Closes Its Most Successful Season," *Carlisle Arrow*, December 12, 1913, 1.

14. See Appendix.

15. John McGillis, "Athletics," *Carlisle Arrow*, December 4, 1914, 2.

16. John McGillis, "Annual Banquet and Reception," *Carlisle Arrow*, January 8, 1915, 4.

17. "West Virginia Wesleyan, 14–Carlisle, 0," *Carlisle Arrow*, November 5, 1915, 1; "The Dickinson-Indian Game," *Carlisle Arrow*, November 19, 1915, 1. A victory was just as likely to be toward the front of the newspaper as a defeat. The front page featured the victory over Dickinson as well as the loss to West Virginia. The second page also featured a single win and one defeat. Yet the heavy defeats to Harvard and Pittsburgh were confined to page five—(MB). "The Football Season of 1915," *Carlisle Arrow*, December 3, 1915, 5, 8.

18. "The Football Season of 1915."

19. Frank O'Neill, "Carlisle Indians Lay Plans for Strong Football Team," *New York Tribune*, March 4, 1917, 3, accessed April 11, 2011, http://chroniclingamerica.loc.gov/lccn/sn83030214/1917-03-04/ed-1/seq-17.

20. O'Neill, "Carlisle Indians Lay Plans for Strong Football Team."

21. "Herman to Captain Carlisle on Gridiron," *Evening Public Ledger*, August 29, 1917, 13, accessed April 12, 2011, http://chroniclingamerica.loc.gov/lccn/sn83045211/1917-08-29/ed-1/seq-13.

22. "Mr. Lipps Presents 'C's," *Carlisle Arrow*, April 10, 1914, 7.

23. Student Record file. NARA RG 75, file 1327, Carlisle Indian School Student Records, folder 364, box 8.

24. Student Record file, folder 364, box 8.

25. Francis J. Auge, "How to Become a Good Athlete," *Carlisle Arrow*, March 3, 1916, 8.

26. *Hearings before the Joint Commission*, 1224.

27. "School Athletics," *Carlisle Arrow*, September 10, 1915, 3.

28. This is not to say that the Carlisle lacrosse schedule did not feature prominent opponents. The 1915 lacrosse schedule, for example, featured games against Johns Hopkins, Lehigh, and Swarthmore College, all national champions. Despite this, football was still a far more popular sport in national discourse. This can clearly be seen in the records of ticket revenue for Carlisle games. The 1913 lacrosse match against Swarthmore College, for example, earned Carlisle only eighty-three dollars in ticket sales. By comparison, the football match against Muhlenburg College, a minor team on the schedule, earned Carlisle one hundred and fifty dollars. Lacrosse never came close to matching the popularity and income provided by football—(MB). *Hearings before the Joint Commission*, 1139; "Lacrosse Schedule for 1915," *Carlisle Arrow*, February 5, 1915, 6. For a history of lacrosse, see Fisher, *Lacrosse*.

29. "Football at Carlisle Big Boost to Sport," *New York Tribune*, October 22, 1916, 2, accessed April 11 2011, https://chroniclingamerica.loc.gov/data/batches/dlc_self_ver02/data/sn83030214/00206532075/1916102202/0492.pdf.

30. Delia Waterman (Oneida), oral history interview transcript, December 10, 1976, interview by DeWitt Clinton Smith III, Carlisle Indian School Papers, Dickinson College (1876–2007), MC 2008.4, box 1, folder 15.

31. Louis Godfrey student file, NARA RG 75 Series 1327, box 150, folder 5838, accessed through https://carlisleindian.dickinson.edu/.

32. George May student file, NARA RG 75 Series 1327, box 116, file 4707, accessed through https://carlisleindian.dickinson.edu/, October 19, 2020.

33. Delia Waterman (Oneida), oral history.

34. John Alonzo (Laguna), oral history.

35. Peavy and Smith, *Full Court Quest*.

36. Peavy and Smith, *Full Court Quest*, 126–28.

37. Peavy and Smith, *Full Court Quest*, 103–4.

38. Peavy and Smith, *Full Court Quest*, 66.

39. Bell, "Telling Stories out of School," 283–84.

40. Bell, "Telling Stories out of School," 290.

41. See *Red Man* (vol. 6, no. 7), March 1914.

42. Sherman Coolidge, "American Indians for the Honor of Their Race," *Red Man*, March 1914, 251–55.

43. Gabe E. Parker, "Intemperance a National Vice," *Red Man*, March 1914, 268–70.

44. Parker, "Intemperance a National Vice, 268."

45. Parker, "Intemperance a National Vice, 268."

46. M. R. Patterson, "Why I Changed Front on the Liquor Question," *Red Man*, March 1914, 276.

47. Calvin Lamoureaux, "Alcohol," *Carlisle Arrow*, April 24, 1914, 1.

48. Lamoureaux, "Alcohol."

49. "Who Wants to Be One?," *Carlisle Arrow*, April 2, 1915, 3.

50. *Carlisle Arrow*, November 20, 1914, 5.

51. *Carlisle Arrow*, March 5, 1915, 5.

52. The School Printer, "Total Abstinence for Carlisle Indians," *Carlisle Arrow*, March 19, 1915, 3.

53. School Printer, "Total Abstinence for Carlisle Indians."

54. Bell, "Telling Stories out of School," 100.

55. Bell, "Telling Stories out of School," 264–65.

56. Quoted in Bell, "Telling Stories out of School," 269; George May Student File, accessed through https://carlisleindian.dickinson.edu/, October 19, 2020.

57. Quoted in Bell, "Telling Stories out of School," 269; George May student file.

58. George May student file, accessed through https://carlisleindian.dickinson.edu/, October 19, 2020.

59. Bell, "Telling Stories out of School," 269. Despite his sexually transmitted infection, May joined the army. Carlisle reprinted one of his letters home—(JB). George H. Mays [*sic*], "A Letter from One of Our Soldier Boys," *Carlisle Arrow and Red Man*, November 2, 1917, 7. Note that the letter printed in the *Carlisle Arrow and Red Man* spells his name as "Mays," but on his student identification his name is spelled "May"—(JB).

60. Bell, "Telling Stories out of School," 264.

61. *Hearings before the Joint Commission*, 1002–3.

62. Moses Komah, "The Y.M.C.A. Meeting," *Carlisle Arrow*, March 13, 1914, 1.

63. Lucy Charles, "Notes from Mr. Lipps' Talk," *Carlisle Arrow*, March 13, 1914, 2.

64. "The Exceptional Young Man," *Carlisle Arrow*, March 13, 1914, 2.

65. Zeph. Simons, "First Indian Troop of Boy Scouts in the World," *Carlisle Arrow*, January 15, 1915, 1; Boy Scout, https://carlisleindian.dickinson.edu/, October 20, 2020.

66. Juan Guterres, "A Surprise Party," March 12, 1915, 2.

67. An example is Zeph. E. Simons, "Indian Boy Scouts of America," *Carlisle Arrow*, January 29, 1915, 1.

68. Student Reporters, "General School News," *Carlisle Arrow*, February 5, 1915, 4.

69. "The Christian Union Meeting," *Carlisle Arrow*, September 4, 1914, 1.

70. "The Christian Union Meeting."

71. "Indian School Founder Talks on Anniversary," *Carlisle Arrow*, October 16, 1914, 5–6.

72. Scott Dewey and Others, "Notes from General Pratt's Talks," *Carlisle Arrow*, March 26, 1915, 1.

73. Bell, "Telling Stories out of School," 102.

74. Bell, "Telling Stories out of School," 102.

75. Britten, *American Indians in World War I*; Mead, *Doughboys*.

76. "Carlisle's Roll of Honor," *Carlisle Arrow and Red Man*, December 21, 1917, 11.

77. Jenkins, *Real All Americans*, 296–98.

78. Lewis Brown student file, RG 75, Series 1327, box 91, folder 4110. Accessed through http://carlisleindian.dickinson.edu/ on December 3, 2020.

79. Henry Holcomb Bennett, "The Flag Goes By," *Carlisle Arrow and Red Man*, December 21, 1917, 12.

80. "Real Causes of Rejections at Officers' Training Camps," *Carlisle Arrow and Red Man*, October 5, 1917, 14.

81. "Real Causes of Rejections."

82. "Carlisle's Roll of Honor."

83. Adams, *Education for Extinction*, 324.

84. Mills with Sparks, *Lessons of a Lakota*, 1.

Epilogue

1. Fitzgerald, *Great Gatsby*, 11. Fitzgerald was making a not so thinly veiled reference to Lothrop Stoddard's *The Rising Tide of Color: The Threat Against White World Supremacy*, a book that, like Buchanan's comments, portrays the central crisis of the post–Great War era as a battle of Europeans for racial supremacy around the colonial world—(JB).

2. "The Ugly, Fascinating History of the Word 'Racism.'" *Code Switch: Word Watch*. NPR, January 6, 2014. https://www.npr.org/sections/codeswitch/2014/01/05/260006815/the-ugly-fascinating-history-of-the-word-racism.

3. Hannah Knowles, "Fraught Mascot," *Stanford Daily*, September 20, 2018; "Stanford Mascot Timeline," Stanford Native American Cultural Center, https://nacc.stanford.edu/about-nacc/history-timelines/stanford-mascot-timeline.

4. Jenkins, *Real All Americans*.

5. Morgensen, "Cutting the Roots of Colonial Masculinity," 38–61; Deloria, *Playing Indian*.

6. Deloria, *Indians in Unexpected Places*, 109–35.

7. Deloria, *Indians in Unexpected Places*, 134.

8. "N.C.A.A. Demographics Database Spreadsheet."

9. John Lee Hancock, Director, *The Blind Side*, United States, Warner Brothers, 2009.

10. Ross Dellenger, "'When Can We Move On?': The Past, Present and Future of Hugh Freeze," *Sports Illustrated*, https://www.si.com/college/2020/11/05/hugh-freeze-past-present-future-liberty-ole-miss.

11. "The Blind Side (2009)," *The Numbers*, https://www.the-numbers.com/movie/Blind-Side-The#tab=summary.

12. Adams, "Beyond Bleakness," 35–64.

13. An example is the *Indian Helper*, February 27, 1891, 2; Jenkins, *Real All Americans*, 218.

14. Bell, "Telling Stories out of School," 51.

BIBLIOGRAPHY

Archives and Manuscript Materials

Carlisle Indian School Newspapers. Cumberland County Historical Society, Carlisle PA.

1900 and 1910 Carlisle Indian School Census. Cumberland County Historical Society, Carlisle PA.

Carlisle Church and Cemetery Records. Cumberland County Historical Society, Carlisle PA.

Carlisle Oral History Project. Cumberland County Historical Society, Carlisle PA.

Carlisle YMCA Folder. Cumberland County Historical Society, Carlisle PA.

Flower Necrology Scrapbook, 1916–1963. Cumberland County Historical Society, Carlisle PA.

Johnson Collection. Cumberland County Historical Society, Carlisle PA.

The Papers of Carlos Montezuma, M.D. John William Larner Jr., Editor, Scholarly Resources Inc. (microfilm).

The Papers of the Society of American Indians. John William Larner Jr., Charles E. Gillette, and Hazel W. Hertzberg, Editors, Scholarly Resources Inc. (microfilm).

Carlisle Indian School Football Team Depositions. National Archives and Records Administration, NARA RG 75 CCF b007 f 03.

Oral History Interviews with Former Carlisle Indian School Students by DeWitt Clinton Smith III. Carlisle Indian School Papers, Dickinson College Special Collections (1876–2007), MC 2008.

Thorpe, Grace (Sac and Fox). Phone interview with John Bloom. February 16, 2001.

Published Works

Adams, David Wallace. "Beyond Bleakness: The Brighter Side of Indian Boarding Schools." In *Boarding School Blues: Revisiting American Indian Educational Experiences*, edited by Clifford E. Trafzer, Jean Keller, and Lorene Sisquoc, 35–64. Lincoln: University of Nebraska Press, 2006.

———. *Education for Extinction: American Indians and the Boarding School Experience, 1875–1928*. Lawrence: University Press of Kansas, 1995.

———. "More Than a Game: The Carlisle Indians Take to the Gridiron, 1893–1917." *Western Historical Quarterly* 32 (Spring 2001): 25–53.

Adelman, Marvin. *A Sporting Time: New York City and the Rise of Modern Athletics*. Champaign: University of Illinois Press, 1986.

Anderson, Kim, John Swift, and Robert Alexander Innes. "'To Arrive Speaking': Voces from the Bidwewidam Indigenous Masculinities Project." In *Indigenous Men and Masculinities: Legacies, Identities, Regeneration*, edited by Robert Alexander Innes and Kim Anderson. Winnipeg: University of Manitoba Press, 2015.

Anderson, Lars. *Carlisle vs. Army: Jim Thorpe, Dwight Eisenhower, Pop Warner, and the Forgotten Story of Football's Greatest Battle*. New York: Random House, 2007.

Annual Report of the Commissioner of Indian Affairs. Washington DC: GPO, 1879–1918.

Appleby, Joyce. *Liberalism and Republicanism in the Historical Imagination*. Cambridge MA: Harvard University Press, 1992.

Armitage, Susan. "Through Women's Eyes: A New View of the West." In *The Women's West*, edited by Susan Armitage and Elizabeth Jameson, 9–18. Norman: University of Oklahoma Press, 1987.

Baker, Lee D. *From Savage to Negro: Anthropology and the Construction of Race, 1896–1954*. Berkeley: University of California Press, 1998.

Baker, William J. "To Pray or to Play? The YMCA Question in the United Kingdom and the United States, 1850–1900." In *A Sports-Loving Society: Victorian and Edwardian Middle-Class England at Play*, edited by J. A. Mangan, 198–216. Abingdon: Routledge, 2006.

Baldwin, Neil. *Henry Ford and the Jews: The Mass Production of Hate*. New York: Public Affairs, 2001.

Banks, Olive. *Becoming a Feminist: The Social Origins of 'First Wave' Feminism*. Brighton, UK: Wheatsheaf, 1986.

Barker-Benfield, G. J. *The Horrors of the Half-Known Life: Male Attitudes towards Women and Sexuality in Nineteenth Century America*. New York: Harper and Row, 1976.

Bederman, Gail. *Manliness and Civilization: A Cultural History of Gender and Race in the United States, 1880–1917*. Chicago: University of Chicago Press, 1995.

Bell, Genevieve. "Telling Stories out of School: Remembering the Carlisle Indian Industrial School, 1879–1918." PhD diss., Stanford University, 1998.

Benjey, Tom. "End of Carlisle's Trail of Glory." *College Football Historical Society Newsletter* 20, no. 1 (2006): 7–11.

——— . *Keep A-Goin': The Life of Lone Star Dietz*. Carlisle PA: Tuxedo Press, 2006.

Bentley, Matthew. "'Playing White Men': American Football and Manhood at the Carlisle Indian School, 1879–1904." *Journal of the History of Childhood and Youth* 3, no. 2 (Spring 2010): 187–209.

——— . "The Rise of Athletic Masculinity at the Carlisle Indian School, 1904–1913." *International Journal of the History of Sport* 29, no. 10 (July 2012): 1466–89.

Berkhofer, Robert F. *Salvation and the Savage: An Analysis of Protestant Missions and American Indian Response, 1787–1862*. Lexington: University of Kentucky Press, 1965.

————. *The White Man's Indian: Images of the American Indian from Columbus to the Present*. New York: Vintage Books, 1979.

Biberman, Matthew. *Masculinity, Anti-Semitism and Early Modern English Literature: From the Satanic to the Effeminate Jew*. New York: Routledge, 2004.

Bird, Sharon R. "Welcome to the Men's Club: Homosociality and the Maintenance of Hegemonic Masculinity." *Gender and Society* 10, no. 2 (April 1996): 120–32.

Bloch, Ruth H. "Untangling the Roots of Modern Sex Roles: A Survey of Four Centuries of Change." *Signs* 4, no. 2 (Winter 1978): 237–52.

Blocker, Jack S. *Retreat from Reform: The Prohibition Movement in the United States, 1890–1913*. Westport CT: Greenwood Press, 1976.

Bloom, John. "No Fall from Grace: Grace Thorpe's Athlete of the Century Campaign for Her Father." In *Native Athletes in Sport and Society: A Reader*, edited by C. Richard King, 228–44. Lincoln: University of Nebraska Press, 2005.

————. *To Show What an Indian Can Do: Sports at Native American Boarding Schools*. Minneapolis: University of Minnesota Press, 2000.

Borrell, Phillip. "Patriotic Games: Boundaries and Masculinity in New Zealand Sport." In *Indigenous Men and Masculinities: Legacies, Identities, Regeneration*, edited by Robert Alexander Innes and Kim Anderson, 165–80. Winnipeg: University of Manitoba Press, 2015.

Bowden, Henry Warner. *American Indians and Christian Missions: Studies in Cultural Conflict*. Chicago: University of Chicago Press, 1981.

Branch, Taylor. "The Shame of College Sports." *Atlantic Magazine*. http://www.theatlantic.com/magazine/archive/2011/10/the-shame-of-college-sports/8643. Accessed July 23, 2012.

Brinton, Daniel G. *Races and Peoples: Lectures on the Science of Ethnography* (New York: N. D. C. Hodges, 1890). https://www.nature.com/articles/044124a0.

Britten, Thomas A. *American Indians in World War I: At Home and at War*. Albuquerque: University of New Mexico Press, 1997.

Bruchac, Joseph. *Jim Thorpe: Original All-American*. New York: Dial Books, 2006.

Buford, Kate. *Native American Son: The Life and Sporting Legend of Jim Thorpe*. New York: Alfred A. Knopf, 2010.

Bundgaard, Axel. *Muscle and Manliness: The Rise of Sport in American Boarding Schools*. Syracuse: Syracuse University Press, 2005.

Butler, Judith. *Gender Trouble: Feminism and the Subversion of Identity*. New York: Routledge, 1999.

Calloway, Colin G. *First Peoples: A Documentary Survey of American Indian History*. 2nd ed. Boston: Bedford—St. Martin's, 2004.

Carlisle Indian School Digital Resource Center. https://carlisleindian.dickinson.edu/.

Child, Brenda J. "Boarding School as a Metaphor." *Journal of American Indian Education* 57, no. 1 (Spring 2018): 37–57.

————. *Boarding School Seasons, American Indian Families 1900–1940*. Lincoln: University of Nebraska Press, 1999.

Clark, David Anthony Tyeeme, and Joane Nagel. "White Men, Red Masks: Appropriations of "Indian" Manhood in Imagined Wests." In *Across the Great Divide: Cultures of Manhood in the American West*, edited by Matthew Basso, Laura McCall, and Dee Garceau, 109–30. New York: Routledge, 2001.

Clifford, James. "Indigenous Articulations." In *The Post-Colonial Studies Reader*, edited by Bill Ashcroft, Gareth Griffiths, and Helen Tiffin, 2nd ed., 180–83. Abingdon: Routledge, 2006.

Connell, R. W. "Cool Guys, Swots and Wimps: The Interplay of Masculinity and Education." *Oxford Review of Education* 15, no. 3 (1989): 291–303.

———. *Gender and Power: Society, the Person and Sexual Politics*. Cambridge: Polity in association with Blackwell, 1987.

———. *Masculinities*. Cambridge: Polity, 1995.

———. *The Men and the Boys*. Cambridge: Polity, 2000.

———. *Which Way Is Up?: Essays on Sex, Class and Culture*. London: Allen & Unwin, 1983.

Coward, John. *The Newspaper Indian: Native American Identity in the Press, 1820–90*. Urbana: University of Illinois Press, 1999.

Dasgupta, Romit. "Performing Masculinities? The 'Salaryman' at Work and Play." *Japanese Studies* 20, no. 2 (2000): 189–200.

Davidoff, Leonore, and Catherine Hall. *Family Fortunes: Men and Women of the English Middle Class, 1780–1850*. London: Routledge, 2002.

Davies, Wade. *Native Hoops: The Rise of American Indian Basketball, 1895–1970*. Lawrence: University Press of Kansas, 2020.

De Beauvoir, Simone. *The Second Sex*. London: Vintage Books, 1997.

Deloria, Philip. *Indians in Unexpected Places*. Lawrence: University Press of Kansas, 2004.

———. *Playing Indian*. New Haven CT: Yale University Press, 1998.

Demetriou, Demetrakis Z. "Connell's Concept of Hegemonic Masculinity: A Critique." *Theory and Society* 30, no. 3 (June 2001): 337–61.

Devens, Carol. "'If We Get the Girls, We Get the Race': Missionary Education of Native American Girls." *Journal of World History* 3, no. 2 (Fall 1992): 219–37.

D'Emilio, John, and Estelle B. Freedman. *Intimate Matters: A History of Sexuality in America*. 2nd ed. Chicago: University of Chicago Press, 1997.

Dippie, Brian W. *The Vanishing American: White Attitudes and U.S. Indian Policy*. Middletown CT: Wesleyan University Press, 1982.

Donaldson, Mike. "What Is Hegemonic Masculinity?" *Theory and Society* 22, no. 5 (October 1993): 643–57.

Dyreson, Mark. "The 'Physical Value' of Races and Nations: Anthropology and Athletics at the Louisiana Purchase Exposition." In *The 1904 Anthropology Days and Olympic Games: Sport, Race, and American Imperialism*, edited by Susan Brownell, 127–55. Lincoln: University of Nebraska Press, 2008.

Dubbert, Joe. *A Man's Place: Masculinity in Transition*. Englewood Cliffs NJ: Prentice-Hall, 1979.

Dyer, Richard. *White*. London: Routledge, 1997.

Eastman, Elaine Goodale. *Pratt, the Red Man's Moses*. Norman: University of Oklahoma Press, 1935.

Eby, Beth. "Building Bodies, (Un)Making Empire: Gender, Sport, and Colonialism in the United States, 1880–1930." PhD diss., University of Illinois at Urbana-Champaign, 2019.

Ecoffey, Brandon. "Death Rate Cover-Up at Carlisle Indian School." *Native Sun News*. September 5, 2013. https://www.indianz.com/News/2013/09/05/native-sun-news-death-rate-cov.asp#:~:text=Previous%20estimates%20had%20surmised%20that,been%20sent%20home%20from%20Carlisle.

Fear-Segal, Jacqueline. "The History and Reclamation of a Sacred Space." In *Carlisle Indian Industrial School: Indigenous Histories, Memories, & Reclamations*, edited by Jacqueline Fear-Segal and Susan D. Rose, 853–55. Lincoln: University of Nebraska Press, 2016.

———. "The Man on the Bandstand at Carlisle Indian Industrial School: What He Reveals about the Children's Experiences." In *Boarding School Blues: Revisiting American Indian Educational Experiences*, edited by Clifford E. Trafzer, Jean Keller, and Lorene Sisquoc, 99–122. Lincoln: University of Nebraska Press, 2006.

———. "Nineteenth-Century Indian Education: Universalism versus Evolutionism." *Journal of American Studies* 33, no. 2 (1999): 323–41.

———. *White Man's Club: Schools, Race, and the Struggle of Indian Acculturation*. Lincoln: University of Nebraska Press, 2007.

Fear-Segal, Jacqueline, and Susan D. Rose, eds. *Carlisle Indian Industrial School: Indigenous Histories, Memories, & Reclamations* Lincoln: University of Nebraska Press, 2016.

Filene, Peter. *Him/Her/Self: Sex Roles in Modern America*. Baltimore MD: Johns Hopkins University Press, 1986.

Fitzgerald, F. Scott. *The Great Gatsby*. New York: Scribner, 1925.

Fisher, Donald M. *Lacrosse: A History of the Game*. Baltimore MD: Johns Hopkins University Press, 2002.

Flink, James. *America Adopts the Automobile, 1895–1910*. Cambridge MA: MIT Press, 1970.

Forth, Christopher. *Masculinity in the Modern West: Gender, Civilization and the Body*. Basingstoke, UK: Palgrave Macmillan, 2008.

Foucault, Michel. *Discipline and Punish: the Birth of the Prison*. London: Penguin Books, 1991.

———. *The History of Sexuality, Volume I*. New York: Random House, 1978.

———. *Power*. London: Allen Lane, 2000.

Frank, Stephen. *Life with Father: Parenthood and Masculinity in the Nineteenth-Century American North*. Baltimore: Johns Hopkins University Press, 1998.

Freedman, Estelle B. "Separatism as Strategy: Female Institution Building and American Feminism, 1870–1930." *Feminist Studies* 5, no. 3 (Fall 1979): 512–29.

———. "'Uncontrolled Desires': The Response to the Sexual Psychopath, 1920–1960." *Journal of American History* 74, no. 1 (June 1987): 83–106.

Gamache, Ray. "Sport as Cultural Assimilation: Representations of American Indian Athletes in the Carlisle School Newspaper." *American Journalism* 26, no. 2 (Spring 2009): 7–37.

Gems, Gerald. *The Athletic Crusade: Sport and American Cultural Imperialism.* Lincoln and London: University of Nebraska Press, 2006.

———. "Negotiating a Native American Identity through Sport: Assimilation, Adaptation, and the Role of the Trickster." In *Native Athletes in Sport and Society,* edited by C. Richard King, 1–21. Lincoln: University of Nebraska Press, 2005.

Gilbert, Matthew Sakiestewa. *Hopi Runners: Crossing the Terrain between Indian and American.* Lawrence: University Press of Kansas, 2018.

Glancy, Diane. *Fort Marion Prisoners and the Trauma of Native Education.* Lincoln: University of Nebraska Press, 2014.

Glenn, Myra C. "The Naval Reform Campaign Against Flogging: A Case Study in Changing Attitudes Toward Corporal Punishment, 1830–1850." *American Quarterly* 35, no.4 (Autumn 1983): 408–25.

Goldwater, Robert. *Primitivism in Modern Art.* Cambridge MA: The Belknap Press of Harvard University Press, 1986.

Gorn, Elliott. *The Manly Art: Bare Knuckle Prize Fighting in America.* Ithaca NY: Cornell University Press, 1989.

Gorn, Elliot J., and Warren Goldstein. *A Brief History of American Sports.* New York: Hill and Wang, 1993.

Gould, Stephen Jay. *The Mismeasure of Man.* New York: W. W. Norton, 1981.

Gramsci, Antonio. "Ethico-Political History and Hegemony." In *The Antonio Gramsci Reader: Selected Writings, 1916–1935,* edited by David Forgacs, 194–95. London: Lawrence and Wishart, 1999.

———. *Selections from the Prison Notebooks of Antonio Gramsci.* Edited by Quinton Hoare and Geoffrey Nowell Smith. London: Lawrence and Wishart, 1971.

Green, Harvey. *Fit for America: Health, Fitness, Sport and American Society.* Baltimore MD: Johns Hopkins University Press, 1988.

Gossett, Thomas F. *Race: the History of an Idea in America.* New York: Oxford University Press, 1997.

Haller, Beth A. "Cultural Voices or Pure Propaganda?: Publications of the Carlisle Indian School, 1879–1918." *American Journalism* 19, no. 2 (Spring 2002): 65–86.

Haller Jr, John S. *Outcasts from Evolution: Scientific Attitudes of Racial Inferiority, 1859–1900.* Chicago: University of Illinois Press, 1971.

Hantover, Jeffrey P. "The Boy Scouts and the Validation of Masculinity." In *The American Man,* edited by Elizabeth Pleck and Joseph Pleck, 285–99. Englewood Cliffs NJ: Prentice-Hall, 1980.

Hardy, Steven. *How Boston Played: Sport, Recreation, and Community, 1865–1915.* Boston: Northeastern University Press, 1982.

Hawkins, Mike. *Social Darwinism in European and American Thought 1860–1945.* Cambridge: Cambridge University Press, 1997.

Haywood, Chris and Mac an Ghaill, Mairtin. "Schooling Masculinities." In *Understanding Masculinities: Social Relations and Cultural Arenas,* edited by Mairtin Mac an Ghaill, 50–60. Buckingham: Open University Press, 1996.

Hearings before the Joint Commission of the Congress of the United States, Sixty-Third Congress, Second Session, to Investigate Indian Affairs, February 6, 7, 8, and March 25, 1914, Part II. Washington DC: Government Printing Office, 1914.

Higham, John. *Strangers in the Land: Patterns of American Nativism, 1860–1925.* New York: Atheneum, 1977.

Hoch, Paul. *White Hero, Black Beasts: Racism, Sexism and the Mask of Masculinity.* London: Pluto Press, 1979.

Hokowhitu, Brendan. "Producing Elite Indigenous Masculinities." *Settler Colonial Studies* 2, no. 2 (2012): 23–48.

———. "Tackling Maori Masculinity: A Colonial Genealogy of Savagery and Sport," *The Contemporary Pacific* 16, no. 2 (Fall 2004): 259–84.

Horsman, Reginald. *Race and Manifest Destiny: The Origins of American Racial Anglo-Saxonism.* Cambridge MA: Harvard University Press, 1981.

Hoxie, Frederick. *A Final Promise: The Campaign to Assimilate the Indians, 1880–1920.* Lincoln: University of Nebraska Press, 1984.

Hylton, Kevin. *Race and Sport: Critical Race Theory.* London: Routledge Publishers, 2009.

Ingrassia, Brian M. *The Rise of Gridiron University: Higher Education's Uneasy Alliance with Big-Time Football.* Lawrence: University of Kansas Press, 2012.

Iverson, Peter. *Carlos Montezuma and the Changing World of American Indians.* Albuquerque: University of New Mexico Press, 1982.

Jacobs, Sue-Ellen. "Is the "North American Berdache" Merely a Phantom in the Imagination of Western Social Scientists?" In *Two-Spirit People: Native American Gender Identity, Sexuality, and Spirituality,* edited by Sue-Ellen Jacobs, Wesley Thomas, and Sabine Lang, 21–44. Chicago: University of Illinois Press, 1997.

Jacobson, Matthew Frye. *Whiteness of a Different Color: European Immigrants and the Alchemy of Race.* Cambridge MA: Harvard University Press, 1998.

James, C. L. R. *Beyond a Boundary.* London: Sportsman Book Club, 1964.

Jenkins, Sally. *The Real All Americans: The Team That Changed a Game, a People, a Nation.* New York: Doubleday, 2007.

Kaestle, Carl F. "Ideology and American Educational History." *History of Education Quarterly* 22, no. 2 (Summer 1982): 123–37.

———. "Social Change, Discipline, and the Common School in Early Nineteenth-Century America." *Journal of Interdisciplinary History* 9, no.1 (Summer 1978): 1–17.

Kerber, Linda. "The Republican Mother: Women and the Enlightenment–An American Perspective." *American Quarterly* 28, no. 2 (Summer 1976): 187–205.

Kimmel, Michael S. "Baseball and the Reconstitution of American Masculinity, 1880–1920." In *Sport, Men, and the Gender Order: Critical Feminist Perspec-*

tives, edited by Michael A. Messner and Donald F. Sabo, 55–65. Champaign IL: Human Kinetic Books, 1990.

———. *The Gendered Society*. New York: Oxford University Press, 2004.

———. *Manhood in America: A Cultural History*. 2nd ed. New York; Oxford: Oxford University Press, 2006.

———. "Men's Responses to Feminism at the Turn of the Century." *Gender and Society* 1, no. 3 (Sept 1987): 261–83.

Kyvig, David E. *Repealing National Prohibition*. Chicago: University of Chicago Press, 1979.

Landis, Barbara. "The Names." *Carlisle Indian Industrial School: Indigenous Histories, Memories, and Reclamations*, edited by Jacqueline Fear-Segal and Susan D. Rose, 186–97. Lincoln: University of Nebraska Press, 2016.

———. "NARA RG 75 FILE 13 Carlisle Indian School Student Names and Folder Number." http://home.epix.net/~landis/nararonan.html. Accessed April 11, 2012.

Laurie, Bruce. *Artisans into Workers: Labor in Nineteenth-Century America*. New York: Noonday Press, 1989.

Leahy, Todd, and Nathan Wilson. "My First Days at the Carlisle Indian School by Howard Gansworth: an Annotated Manuscript." *Pennsylvania History: A Journal of Mid-Atlantic Studies* 71, no. 4 (2004): 479–93.

Lears, T. J. Jackson. *No Place of Grace: Antimodernism and the Transformation of American Culture, 1880–1920*. New York: Random House, 1981.

"Lessons of the Carlisle Investigation." *The Quarterly Journal of the Society of American Indians* 2, no. 2 (April–June, 1914): 97–99.

Lomawaima, K. Tsianina. *They Called It Prairie Light: The Story of the Chilocco Indian School*. Lincoln: University of Nebraska Press, 1994.

Lomawaima, K. Tsianina, and Jeffrey Ostler. "Reconsidering Richard Henry Pratt: Cultural Genocide and Native Liberation in an Era of Racial Oppression." *Journal of American Indian Education* 57, no. 1 (2018), 79–100.

Lomawaima, K. Tsianina, and Teresa L. McCarty. *To Remain an Indian: Lessons in Democracy from a Century of Native American Education*. New York: Teachers College Press, 2006.

Lorde, Audre. "The Master's Tools Will Never Dismantle the Master's House." In *Sister Outsider: Essays and Speeches*, 100–103. New York: Penguin Press, 2020 (1984).

Lucas, John A., and Ronald A. Smith. *Saga of American Sport*. Philadelphia: Lea & Febiger, 1978.

Mac an Ghaill, Mairtin. *The Making of Men: Masculinities, Sexualities, and Schooling*. Buckingham: Open University Press, 1993.

Macleod, David. *Building Character in the American Boy: The Boy Scouts, YMCA and Their Forerunners*. Madison: University of Wisconsin Press, 1983.

Malsheimer, Lonna. "'Imitation White Man': Images of Transformation at the Carlisle Indian School." *Studies in Visual Communication* 2, no. 4 (Fall 1985): 54–74.

Mangan, J. A. *"Benefits Bestowed": Education and British Imperialism*. Manchester, UK: Manchester University Press, 1988.

————. *The Games Ethics and Imperialism: Aspects of the Diffusion of an Ideal*. Harmondsworth: Viking, 1986.

Mangan, J. A., and James Walvin. Introduction to *Manliness and Morality: Middle-Class Masculinity in Britain and America, 1800–1940*, edited by J. A. Mangan and James Walvin, 1–7. Manchester, UK: Manchester University Press, 1987.

McLoughlin, William. *Cherokee Renascence in the New Republic*. Princeton: Princeton University Press, 1989.

————. *Cherokees and Missionaries*. 2nd ed. Norman: University of Oklahoma Press, 1994.

Mead, Gary. *The Doughboys: America and the First World War*. London: Penguin, 2001.

Messner, Michael. "Boyhood, Organized Sports, and the Construction of Masculinities." *Journal of Contemporary Ethnography* 18, no. 4 (January 1990): 416–44.

————. *Power at Play: Sports and the Problem of Masculinity*. Boston MA: Beacon Press, 1992.

Miller, Neil. *Out of the Past: Gay and Lesbian History from 1860 to the Present*. Boston: Alyson Publications, 2005.

Mills, Billy, with Nicholas Sparks. *Lessons of a Lakota: A Young Man's Journey to Happiness and Self-Understanding*. Carlsbad CA: Hay House Press, 1990.

Morgan, Lewis Henry. *Ancient Society, or Researches in the Lines of Human Progress from Savagery through Barbarism to Civilization*. Chicago: Kerr, 1877.

Morgan, Thomas J. "A Plea for the Papoose." In *Americanizing the American Indian: Writings by the "Friends of the Indian,"* edited by Francis Paul Prucha, 239–51. Cambridge MA: Harvard University Press, 1973.

Morgensen, Scott L. "Cutting the Roots of Colonial Masculinity." In *Indigenous Men and Masculinities: Legacies, Identities, Regeneration*, edited by Robert Alexander Innes and Kim Anderson, 38–61. Winnipeg: University of Manitoba Press, 2015.

Moses, L. G. *Wild West Shows and the Images of American Indians, 1883–1933*. Albuquerque: University of New Mexico Press, 1996.

Mouffe, Chantal. "Hegemony and Ideology in Gramsci." In *Gramsci and Marxist Theory*, 168–206. London: Routledge and Kegan Paul, 1979.

Mrozek, Donald. "The Habit of Victory: the American Military and the Cult of Manliness." In *Manliness and Morality: Middle Class Masculinity in Britain and America, 1800–1940*, edited by J.A Mangan and James Walvin, 220–41. Manchester, UK: Manchester University Press, 1987.

————. *Sport and American Mentality, 1880–1910*. Knoxville: University of Tennessee Press, 1983.

Nandy, Ashis. *The Intimate Enemy: Loss and Recovery of Self under Colonialism*. Delhi: Oxford University Press, 1983.

Newcombe, Jack. *The Best of the Athletic Boys: The White Man's Impact on Jim Thorpe*. New York: Doubleday, 1975.

Nixon, Sean. "Exhibiting Masculinity." In *Representation: Cultural Representations and Signifying Practices*, edited by Stuart Hall, 294–329. London: Open University, 1997.

O'Brien, Greg. "Trying to Look Like Men: Changing Notions of Masculinity among Choctaw Elites in the Early Republic." In *Southern Manhood: Perspectives on Masculinity in the Old South*, edited by Craig Thompson Friend and Lorri Glover. Athens: University of Georgia Press, 2004.

Omi, Michael, and Howard Winant. *Racial Formation in the United States from the 1960's to the 1980's.* New York; London: Routledge Publishers, 1986.

Oriard, Michael. "Pigskin Pioneers: Slow Racial Progress and a Cloud of Dust." *Village Voice*, October 10, 2000. https://www.villagevoice.com/2000/10/10/pigskin-pioneers/.

———. *Reading Football: How the Popular Press Created an American Spectacle.* Chapel Hill; London: University of North Carolina Press, 1993.

———. *Sporting with the Gods.* Cambridge: Cambridge University Press, 1991.

Oxendine, Joseph. *American Indian Sports Heritage.* Champaign IL: Human Kinetics Books, 1988.

Paraschak, Victoria. "Doing Race, Doing Gender: First Nations, 'Sport,' and Gender Relations." In *Sport and Gender in Canada*, edited by Philip White and Kevin Young, 153–69. Toronto: Oxford University Press, 1999.

Park, Roberta J. "Muscles, Symmetry and Action: 'Do You Measure Up?' Defining Masculinity in Britain and America from the 1860s to the early 1900s." *International Journal of the History of Sport* 22, no. 3 (May 2005): 365–95.

Paxton, Katrina A. "Learning Gender: Female Students at the Sherman Institute, 1907–1925." In *Boarding School Blues: Revisiting American Indian Educational Experiences*, edited by Clifford E. Trafzer, Jean Keller, and Lorene Sisquoc, 174–86. Lincoln: University of Nebraska Press, 2006.

Pearce, Roy Harvey. *Savagism and Civilization: A Study of the Indian and the American Mind.* Berkeley: University of California Press, 1988.

Peavy, Linda, and Ursula Smith. *Full Court Quest: The Girls from Fort Shaw Indian School, Basketball Champions of the World.* Norman: University of Oklahoma Press, 2008.

———. "'Leav[ing] the White[s] . . . Far Behind Them': The Girls from Fort Shaw (Montana) Indian School, Basketball Champions of the 1904 World's Fair." In *The 1904 Anthropology Days and Olympic Games: Sport, Race, and American Imperialism*, edited by Susan Brownell, 243–77. Lincoln: University of Nebraska Press, 2008.

———. "World Champions: The 1904 Girls' Basketball Team from Fort Shaw Indian Boarding School." In *Native Athletes in Sport and Society: A Reader*, edited by C. Richard King, 40–78. Lincoln: University of Nebraska Press, 2005.

Pfister, Joel. *Individuality Incorporated: Indians and the Multicultural Modern.* Durham and London: Duke University Press, 2004.

Powers-Beck, Jeffrey. *The American Indian Integration of Baseball.* Lincoln: University of Nebraska Press, 2009.

Powers-Beck, Jeffrey. "'Chief': The American Indian Integration of Baseball, 1897–1945." *American Indian Quarterly* 25, no. 4 (Fall 2001): 508–38.

Pratt, Richard Henry. "The Advantages of Mingling Indians with Whites." In *Americanizing the American Indian: Writings by the "Friends of the Indian,"* edited by Francis Paul Prucha. Cambridge MA: Harvard University Press, 1973.

———. *Battlefield and Classroom: Four Decades with the American Indian, 1867–1904.* New Haven CT: Yale University Press, 1964.

Prucha, Francis Paul. *American Indian Policy in Crisis: Christian Reformers and the Indian, 1865–1900.* Norman: University of Oklahoma Press, 1976.

———. *The Great Father: The United States Government and the American Indians.* Lincoln; London: University of Nebraska Press, 1984.

Pugh, David. *Sons of Liberty: The Masculine Mind in the Nineteenth Century.* Westport CT: Greenwood Press, 1984.

Putney, Clifford. *Muscular Christianity: Manhood and Sports in Protestant America, 1880–1920.* Cambridge MA: Harvard University Press, 2001.

Rader, Benjamin G. *American Sports: From the Age of Folk Games to the Age of Spectators.* Englewood Cliffs NJ: Prentice-Hall, 1983.

———. *Baseball: A History of America's Game.* Urbana: University of Illinois Press, 1994.

Radin, Paul. *The Trickster: A Study in American Indian Mythology.* London: Routledge & Kegan Paul, 1956.

Reel, Estelle. *Course of Study for the Indian Schools of the United States, Industrial and Literary* Washington DC: Government Printing Office, 1901.

Riess, Steven A. "Sport and the Redefinition of American Middle-Class Masculinity." *International Journal of the History of Sport* 8, no. 1 (May 1991): 5–27.

Riney, Scott. *The Rapid City Indian School, 1898–1933.* Norman: University of Oklahoma Press, 1999.

Rivera, Pablo Navarro. "Acculturation under Duress: The Puerto Rican Experience at the Carlisle Indian Industrial School 1898–1918." *Centro Journal* 28, no. 1 (Spring 2006): 222–59.

Roediger, David R. *The Wages of Whiteness: Race and the Making of the American Working Class.* London and New York: Verso, 1991.

Rogin, Michael. "Make My Day! Spectacle as Amnesia in Imperial Politics." In *Cultures of United States Imperialism*, edited by Amy Kaplan and Donald E. Pease, 499–534. Durham NC: Duke University Press, 1993.

Rotundo, E. Anthony. *American Manhood: Transformations in Masculinity from the Revolution to the Modern Era.* New York: Basic Books, 1993.

———. "Learning about Manhood: Gender Ideals and the Middle-Class Family in Nineteenth Century America." In *Manliness and Morality: Middle Class Masculinity in Britain and America, 1800–1940*, edited by J. A Mangan and James Walvin, 35–51. Manchester, UK: Manchester University Press, 1987.

———. "Body and Soul: Changing Ideals of American Middle-Class Manhood." *Journal of Social History* 16, no. 4 (Summer 1983): 23–38.

Roubidoux, Michael. "Historical Interpretations of First Nations Masculinity and Its Influence on Canada's Sport Heritage." *International Journal of the History of Sport* 23, no. 2 (2006): 267–84.

Rubinfeld. Mark. "The Mythical Jim Thorpe: Re/presenting the Twentieth Century American Indian." *International Journal of the History of Sport* 23, no. 2 (2006): 167–89.

Russett, Cynthia Eagle. *Sexual Science: The Victorian Construction of Womanhood.* Cambridge MA: Harvard University Press, 1989.

Sabo, Donald, and Joe Panepinto. "Football Ritual and the Social Reproduction of Masculinity." In *Sport, Men, and the Gender Order: Critical Feminist Perspectives,* edited by Michael A. Messner and Donald F. Sabo, 115–26. Champaign IL: Human Kinetic Books, 1990.

Said, Edward. *Culture and Imperialism.* London: Vintage, 1994.

——. *Orientalism.* London: Penguin Books, 2003.

Scott, James C. *Domination and the Arts of Resistance: Hidden Transcripts.* New Haven CT: Yale University Press, 1990.

Segal, Lynne. *Slow Motion: Changing Masculinities, Changing Men.* Basingstoke, UK: Palgrave Macmillan, 2007.

Shopes, Linda. "Fells Point: Community and Conflict in a Working Class Neighborhood." In *The Baltimore Book: New Views of Local History,* edited by Elizabeth Fee, Linda Shopes, and Linda Zeidman, 126. Philadelphia: Temple University Press, 1991.

Slotkin, Richard. "Buffalo Bill's 'Wild West' and the Mythologization of the American Empire." In *Cultures of United States Imperialism,* edited by Amy Kaplan and Donald E. Pease, 164–81. Durham NC: Duke University Press, 1993.

——. *The Fatal Environment: The Myth of the Frontier in the Age of Industrialization, 1800–1890.* New York: HarperCollins, 1994.

——. *Gunfighter Nation: The Myth of the Frontier in Twentieth-Century America.* Norman: University of Oklahoma Press, 1998.

——. *Regeneration through Violence: The Mythology of the American Frontier, 1600–1860.* Middletown CT: Wesleyan University Press, 1973.

Smith, Phil. "Whiteness, Normal Theory, and Disability Studies." *Disability Studies Quarterly* 24, no. 2 (Spring 2004). http://www.dsq-sds.org/article/view/491/668.

Smith, Ronald A. *Sports and Freedom: The Rise of Big-Time College Athletics.* New York: Oxford University Press, 1988.

Smith, Timothy L. *Revivalism and Social Reform: American Protestantism on the Eve of the Civil War.* Baltimore MD: Johns Hopkins University Press, 1980.

Smits, David. "The 'Squaw Drudge': A Prime Index of Savagism." *Ethnohistory* 29, no. 4 (Autumn 1982): 281–306.

Spack, Ruth. *America's Second Tongue: American Indian Education and the Ownership of English, 1860–1900.* Lincoln: University of Nebraska Press, 2002.

Springwood, Charles Fruehling. "Playing Football, Playing Indian: A History of the Native Americans Who Were the NFL's Oorang Indians." In *Native Athletes in Sport and Society,* edited by C. Richard King, 123–42. Lincoln: University of Nebraska Press, 2005.

Standing Bear, Luther. *Land of the Spotted Eagle.* Lincoln: Bison Books, 2006.

——. *My People the Sioux.* Lincoln: University of Nebraska Press, 1975.

Stearns, Peter. *Be a Man! Males in Modern Society*. New York: Holmes & Meier Publications, 1990.

Steckbeck, John S. *The Fabulous Redmen: The Carlisle Indians and their Famous Football Teams*. Harrisburg PA: J. Horace McFarland, 1951.

Stefon, Frederick J. "Richard Henry Pratt and His Indians." *Journal of Ethnic Studies* 15, no. 2 (Summer 1987): 86–112.

Stoeltje, Beverly. "A Helpmate for Man Indeed: The Image of the Frontier Woman." *Journal of American Folklore* 88, no. 347 (January–March 1975): 25–41.

Strober, Myra, and Audri Gordon Lanford. "The Feminization of Public School Teaching: Cross-Sectional Analysis, 1850–1880." *Signs* 11, no. 2 (Winter 1986): 212–35.

Summers, Martin. *Manliness and Its Discontents: The Black Middle Class and the Transformation of Masculinity, 1900–1930*. Chapel Hill: University of North Carolina Press, 2004.

Swain, Jon. "Masculinities in Education." In *Handbook of Studies on Men & Masculinities*, edited by R. W. Connell, Jeff Hearn, and Michael Kimmel, 213–30. London: Sage Publications, 2005.

Szasz, Margaret Connell. *Education and the American Indian: The Road to Self-Determination since 1928*. 3rd ed. Albuquerque: University of New Mexico Press, 1999.

———. "Through a Wide-Angle Lens: Acquiring and Maintaining Power, Position, and Knowledge through Boarding Schools." In *Boarding School Blues: Revisiting American Indian Educational Experiences*, edited by Clifford E. Trafzer, Jean Keller, and Lorene Sisquoc, 187–201. Lincoln: University of Nebraska Press, 2006.

Tatonetti, Lisa. "Catholics, Carlisle, and Casting Stones: Richard Henry Pratt and the 1890 Ghost Dance." *Nineteenth-Century Contexts* 33, no. 3 (July 2011): 267–87.

Tengan, Ty P. *Native Men Remade: Gender and Nation in Contemporary Hawai'i*. Durham NC: Duke University Press, 2008.

Trennert, Robert. "Educating Indian Girls at Nonreservation Boarding Schools, 1878–1920." *Western Historical Quarterly* 13 (July 1982): 271–90.

———. "From Carlisle to Phoenix: The Rise and Fall of the Indian Outing System, 1878–1930." *Pacific Historical Review* 52 (August 1983): 267–91.

———. *The Phoenix Indian School: Forced Assimilation in Arizona, 1891–1935*. Norman: University of Oklahoma Press, 1988.

Turner, Frederick Jackson. *The Frontier in American History*. New York: Dover Publications, 1996.

Twain, Mark. *The Adventures of Huckleberry Finn*. London: Penguin Classics, 2003.

Tygiel, Jules. *Baseball's Great Experiment: Jackie Robinson and His Legacy*. New York: Oxford University Press, 1993.

"The Ugly, Fascinating History of the Word 'Racism.'" *Code Switch: Word Watch*. NPR, January 6, 2014. https://www.npr.org/sections/codeswitch/2014/01/05/260006815/the-ugly-fascinating-history-of-the-word-racism.

Waggoner, Linda. "On Trial: The Washington R*dskins' Wily Mascot: Coach William 'Lone Star' Dietz." *Montana: The Magazine of Western History*, Spring 2013, 24–47.

Warner, Glenn S. "The Indian Massacres." *Collier's Weekly,* October 17, 1931, 7–8, 61–63.

Warren, Allen. "Popular Manliness: Baden-Powell, Scouting, and the Development of Manly Character." In *Manliness and Morality: Middle-Class Masculinity in Britain and America, 1800–1940,* edited by J. A. Mangan and James Walvin, 199–219. Manchester, UK: Manchester University Press, 1987.

Watterson, John Sayle. *College Football: History, Spectacle, Controversy.* Baltimore MD: Johns Hopkins University Press, 2000.

Welter, Barbara. "The Cult of True Womanhood: 1820–1860." *American Quarterly* 18, no. 2, Part 1 (Summer 1966): 151–74.

Wheeler, Robert W. *Jim Thorpe: World's Greatest Athlete.* Norman: University of Oklahoma Press, 1975.

Whitson, David. "Sport in the Social Construction of Masculinity." In *Sport, Men, and the Gender Order: Critical Feminist Perspectives,* edited by Michael A. Messner and Donald F. Sabo, 19–30. Champaign IL: Human Kinetic Books, 1990.

INDEX

Page numbers in italics indicate illustrations.

CPSIA information can be obtained
at www.ICGtesting.com
Printed in the USA
LVHW111551011122
732099LV00002B/50